American Batsford Chess Library

Beating the King's Indian and Benoni

Anatoli Vaisser

An ICE Book
International Chess Enterprises, Seattle

International Chess Enterprises, Inc.
2005 Fifth Avenue, Suite 402
Seattle, Washington 98121-2850

P.O. Box 19457
Seattle, Washington 98109-1457

First published 1997

Typeset by First Rank Publishing, Brighton
and printed in Great Britain by
Redwood Books, Trowbridge, Wilts
for the publishers,
B. T. Batsford, 583 Fulham Road, London SW6 5BY
British Library Cataloging-in-Publication Data.
A catalog record for this book is
available from the British Library.

First published in the United States in 1997 by
International Chess Enterprises, Inc.
Originally published in Great Britain in 1997 by
B. T. Batsford.
Library of Congress Catalog Card Number: 97-071890
ISBN 1-879479-71-0

First American edition – 1997

Printed in the United Kingdom
All first editions are printed on acid-free paper

A BATSFORD CHESS BOOK

Contents

Part 2.
Systems specific to the King's Indian

(1 d4 ♘f6 2 c4 g6 3 ♘c3 ♗g7 4 e4 d6 5 f4)

Part 3.
Systems specific to the Modern Benoni

(1 d4 ♘f6 2 c4 c5 3 d5 e6 4 ♘c3 exd5 5 cxd5 d6 6 e4 g6 7 f4)

Symbols

⩲	White is slightly better	-+	Black is winning
±	White is clearly better	=	The position is equal
+-	White is winning	Ch.	Championship
⩱	Black is slightly better	corr.	Correspondence game
∓	Black is clearly better		

Preface

The King's Indian Defence currently enjoys a very high standing amongst queen's pawn openings: it figures in the repertoire of many of the world's leading grandmasters, with Garry Kasparov at their head. Black goes all out for complex play and will often launch an attack on the white king.

How is White to oppose this dynamic opening? The Four Pawns Attack offers a fitting answer: immediate and total occupation of the centre with pawns, seizure of the initiative, and sometimes a 'Romantic' attack against the king without shirking from sacrifices. At the same time it gives White a formidable weapon against the Modern Benoni, since the main lines of the Four Pawns Attack can also arise from the Benoni by transposition. It is worth noting, however, that most Modern Benoni specialists – such as Psakhis for example – no longer play that opening in its 'pure' form but only reach it via the move order 1 d4 ♘f6 2 c4 e6 3 ♘f3 c5. Among other things, this move order enables Black to avoid the dangerous Taimanov system (1 d4 ♘f6 2 c4 c5 3 d5 e6 4 ♘c3 exd5 5 cxd5 d6 6 e4 g6 7 f4 ♗g7 8 ♗b5+).

Often the name 'Four Pawns Attack' is reserved for systems arising after the King's Indian order of moves (1 d4 ♘f6 2 c4 g6 3 ♘c3 ♗g7 4 e4 d6 5 f4). Here, however, I have taken the more natural view that any system in which White plays d2-d4, c2-c4, e2-e4 and f2-f4, including the Taimanov and Mikenas systems in the Modern Benoni, is considered to belong to the Four Pawns Attack.

In the mid-1920s the Four Pawns Attack was employed by many of the 'greats' – such as Alekhine, Euwe and Bogolyubov – but it then went somewhat out of fashion. Over the past few decades, many grandmasters have played it; I can name Szabo, Sosonko, Knezevic, Kouatly, Nogueiras, Arencibia, Kozul, Glek, Piskov, Moskalenko, Komarov and Zsuzsa Polgar, recently joined by Cifuentes, Gabriel, Topalov and Lautier. However, its present level of popularity does scant justice to the variation's importance. It is significant that the Austrian Attack, which embodies ideas akin to the Four Pawns, is considered to be one of the most important replies to the Pirc Defence (1 e4 d6 2 d4 ♘f6 3 ♘c3 g6 4 f4).

It was exactly thirty years ago – in 1967 – that I started playing the Four Pawns Attack. I have remained true to it ever since, and it has repaid me handsomely: in the last 15 years (1982-1996) my score with it has been +31=10-2, for a rating of over 2700! I have now decided to draw up the balance sheet and publish my analyses, including prepared novelties – a rarity in any openings book. The format I have adopted is 'subjective', so it is natural that most of the principal games should be taken from my own practice. The book is basically designed to set out a White repertoire. Nonetheless, by examining all White's important moves, I have also provided King's Indian and Modern Benoni players – who have good reason to be afraid of the Four Pawns – with enough information to find their way quickly and effectively through the myriad complicated variations and to prepare against it. With a few exceptions this book is based on games played before 1 January 1997.

Before proceeding with my examination of the Four Pawns Attack, let me give King's Indian players a suggestion for a radical antidote to this attack: avoid it! This can be done as early as move one, with 1 d4 d6. Now 2 c4 is met by 2...e5, and 2 e4 by 2...♘f6, transposing to the Pirc. Black also has the following move order at his disposal: 1 d4 ♘f6 2 c4 d6 3 ♘c3 e5, or first 3...♘bd7, answering 4 e4 with 4...e5. Unfortunately, however, the knight on d7 and pawn on e5 do not always constitute the best set-up in the other King's Indian variations that may arise.

A word of advice to White: to play this opening successfully you must not only study the variations but also acquire a 'feel' for the resulting middlegame positions, for example those with a passed pawn on d5. Playing through the games in this book will help you to develop this 'feel'.

The author would be pleased to receive (c/o the publishers) any proposed analytical improvements that readers may have.

Anatoli Vaisser
Paris
August 1997

Note: Bold italic has been used throughout the book to denote the author's own novelties.

1 Main Line with 9...♖e8

Here we analyse the starting point of the main line of the Four Pawns Attack.

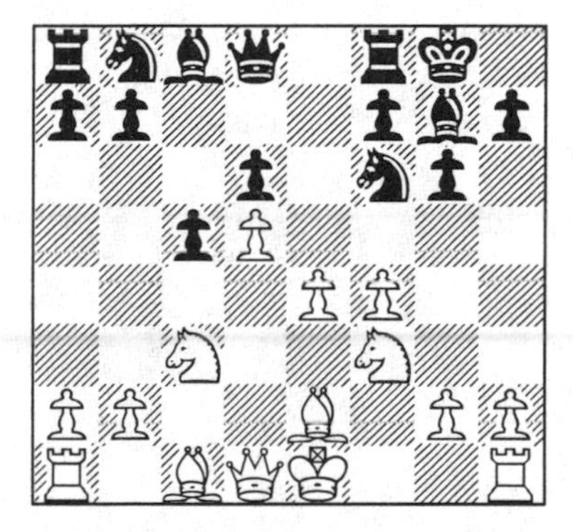

This position can be reached from the King's Indian Defence with the move order **1 d4 ♘f6 2 c4 g6 3 ♘c3 ♗g7 4 e4 d6 5 f4 0-0 6 ♘f3 c5 7 d5 e6 8 ♗e2 exd5 9 cxd5**, and from the Modern Benoni after **1 d4 ♘f6 2 c4 c5 3 d5 e6 4 ♘c3 exd5 5 cxd5 d6 6 e4 g6 7 f4 ♗g7 8 ♘f3 0-0 9 ♗e2**.

The material in this section is arranged as follows: this chapter deals with 9...♖e8, while 9...♗g4 is covered in Chapter 2 and 9...b5 and rare moves are dealt with in Chapter 3.

The common strategic goal for White in all this lines is the break e4-e5, either immediately or after due preparation; and sometimes involving the sacrifice of a pawn. As a result White gets a strong passed d-pawn and an initiative, which often results in a powerful attack. Black for his part needs to find a way of countering White's initiative. It is not uncommon for him to offer a counter-sacrifice of the exchange in order to stabilise the position. After **9...♖e8** we reach the following position:

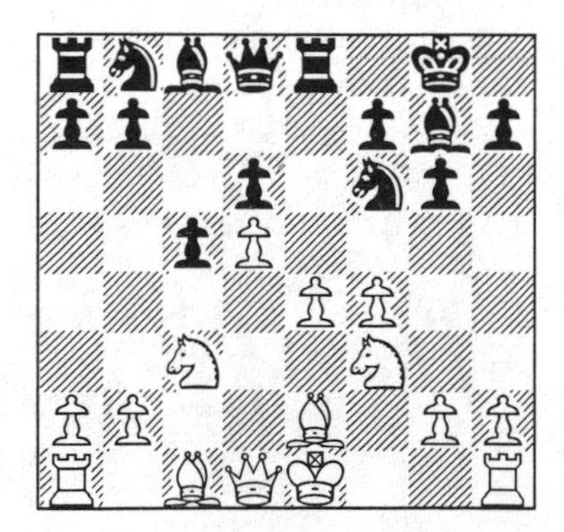

Now the main line 10 e5 dxe5 11 fxe5 ♘g4 12 ♗g5 ♕b6 13 0-0 ♘xe5 14 ♘xe5 is studied in Game 1 (Vaisser-Berthelot). The following deviations from the main line are also analysed: 14 d6 is considered in Game 2 (Vaisser-Degraeve) and 12...f6 in Game 3 (Cranbourne-Crespo). Less popular but interesting plans for White after 10 e5 dxe5 11 fxe5 ♘g4 are presented in Game 4 (Lagontrie-Boulard). Finally, the positional line 10 ♘d2 is covered in Game 5 (Vaisser-Ibragimov).

Game 1
Vaisser-Berthelot
French Team Championship 1992

1 d4 ♘f6 2 c4 g6 3 ♘c3 ♗g7 4 e4 d6 5 f4 0-0 6 ♘f3 c5 7 d5 e6 8 ♗e2 exd5 9 cxd5 ♖e8

10 e5

For the positional continuation 10 ♘d2 see Game 5, Vaisser-Ibragimov.

White's other possibilities are not well founded:

a) 10 ♕c2? is bad because of 10...♘xe4! 11 ♘xe4 ♗f5 12 ♗d3 ♗xe4 13 ♗xe4 ♕e7 14 ♘d2 f5 15 0-0 fxe4 16 ♖e1 e3 17 ♘f3 e2∓ Loeber-Hoerstmann, Soest 1996.

b) 10 0-0?! ♘xe4 11 ♘xe4 ♖xe4 12 ♗d3 ♖e8 13 f5 ♘d7 (13...c4!? 14 ♗c2!?) 14 ♘g5 ♘e5! (Not 14...♘f6?! 15 fxg6, followed by 16 ♕a4! with an initiative) 15 fxg6 (15 ♘xf7? is just losing after 15...♘xf7 16 fxg6 ♘e5 17 ♕h5 h6 18 ♖f7 ♘g4! 19 ♗xh6 ♗xh6 20 g7 ♕g5 21 ♗h7+ ♔xh7 22 ♕xg5 ♗xg5 23 ♖f8 ♗e6 0-1 Burkart-Schlosser, Tecklenburg 1988) 15...fxg6 16 ♗e4! (16 ♗c2 h6 17 ♘e6 ♗xe6 18 dxe6 d5∓ Bereolos-Oestrei, USA Team tournament 1993) 16...♖f8 17 ♖xf8+ ♕xf8 18 ♘e6 ♕e7 19 ♗g5 ♗f6 20 ♗h6 ♗d7 21 ♕b3 b6 22 ♖f1 ♘g4 and White's initiative does not compensate for the sacrificed pawn, Buck-Aldag, Niedersachsen 1995.

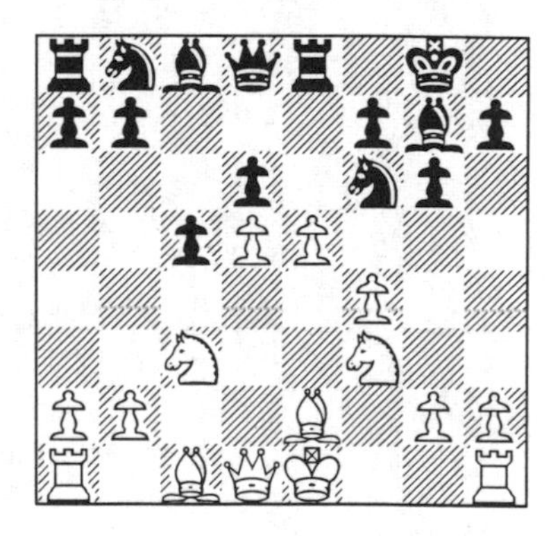

10 ... dxe5

The alternatives are all weaker:

a) 10...♘h5? 11 0-0 ♗g4 12 e6!?±.

b) 10...♘g4? 11 h3 (Also possible is 11 0-0!? dxe5 12 ♘g5 with an initiative) 11...♘h6 12 0-0 (12 g4!?) 12...♘f5 13 ♘e4! dxe5 14 fxe5 ♘d4 15 ♘xd4 ♖xe5 (15...cxd4 16 ♘d6±) 16

♘g5 ♖xd5 17 ♘xf7 ♕h4 18 ♕b3! with a big advantage for White, Capit-Llanes, Ibercaja 1995.

c) 10...♘fd7?! 11 exd6! (Of course, White can transpose to the classical line after 11 0-0 dxe5 12 fxe5 ♘xe5 13 ♗f4), when Black has tried a number of moves, but none have achieved equality:

c1) 11...a6 12 a4 ♘f6 (Or 12...♕b6 13 0-0 ♕xd6 14 ♘g5 ♘f6 15 ♗f3 ♘bd7 16 ♖e1 ♖xe1+ 17 ♕xe1± b6? 18 ♘xf7!± Rapoport-Widera, Katowice open 1995) 13 0-0 (White is also better after 13 ♘e5 ♕xd6?! 14 0-0 ♘bd7 15 ♘c4, Cockcroft-Planas, Spain 1983) 13...♗g4 14 ♘e5 ♗xe2 15 ♕xe2 ♕xd6 16 ♕f3 ♘bd7 17 ♘c4 ♕b8 with an edge for White, Lehmann-Toran, Munich 1954.

c2) 11...♘f6 12 ♘e5 (12 0-0) 12...♘bd7 13 0-0!? ♘b6 14 a4 ♕xd6 15 ♘b5 ♕d8 16 d6 ♘bd5 17 ♗c4 ♗e6 18 f5! gxf5 19 ♗g5 a6 20 d7! ♗xd7 21 ♘xf7! with a dangerous attack, Feldman-Shianovsky, Kiev 1986.

c3) 11...b5 12 ♘xb5! (This seems even stronger than 12 0-0!? a6 13 f5! ♘f6 14 fxg6 hxg6 15 ♗f4 as in the game Z. Szabo-Kecskes, Budapest 1995) 12...♕a5+ 13 ♔f2±.

c4) 11...♘b6 12 ♘b5 ♗g4 13 0-0 ♘a6 14 h3 ♗f5 15 ♘e5! ♗xe5 16 fxe5 ♖xe5, Bellinger-Shaw, corr. 1994, and now the simple 17 ♘c3 would have confirmed White's advantage.

11 fxe5 ♘g4

After 11...♘fd7, besides 12 ♗g5 and 12 ♗f4 White has the interesting additional alternative 12 e6!? fxe6 13 dxe6 ♘f6 14 ♕xd8 ♖xd8 15 ♗c4 with an initiative.

12 ♗g5

For the lines 12 0-0!? ♘xe5 13 ♗f4 (or 12 ♗f4 ♘xe5 13 0-0) and 12 e6 see Game 4, Lagontrie-Boulard.

12 ... ♕b6

The best move. The main alternative 12...f6 is examined in Game 3, Cranbourne-Crespo. Instead, after 12...♕a5 the black queen is less active than it is on b6, although having said that an eventual ♘d5 from White will not win a tempo, which is important in some variations.

12...♕a5 13 0-0 ♘xe5

13...♘d7? 14 e6! fxe6 15 dxe6 ♘de5 16 ♘xe5 ♘xe5 17 e7 c4 18 ♕d5+ ♕xd5 19 ♘xd5 gives White the advantage, Kluss-Zuelke, Nuremberg 1990.

14 d6

White can play also 14 ♘xe5 ♗xe5 (14...♖xe5 15 ♕d2 ♕b4 transposes into the game Krupkova-Repkova, note c2 to Black's 14th move in this game), when 15 ♗c4 practically forces Black to choose between 15...♕b4 (see line c, note to Black's 15th move in this game) and 15...♘d7 16 d6

♗d4+ 17 ♔h1 ♘e5 18 ♗d5 ♗e6, where apart from 19 ♘e4 (Nei-Westerinen, Helsinki 1966), White has the simple 19 ♗e7!? with an initiative. It is necessary to note that although 15 ♗b5?! ♗d7 16 ♕f3 is successful after 16...♗xb5? 17 ♕xf7+ ♔h8 18 ♗f6+ ♗xf6 19 ♕xf6+ ♔g8 20 ♕f7+ ♔h8 21 a4 ♗d7 22 ♖ae1± (Bronznik-Dzulganov, USSR 1990), it can be met by 16...f5 17 ♗c4 ♕b4! 18 ♕d3 ♕xb2 with good prospects for Black.

14...♗e6

Less precise is 14...♘bc6 15 ♘d5 ♗e6 16 ♘c7 ♘d7 17 ♔h1 h6 18 ♗h4 ♖ac8 19 ♘xe6 ♖xe6 20 ♗c4 ♖ce8 21 ♗xe6 ♖xe6± Petursson-Thorsteins, St John open 1988.

15 ♘d5 ♘bd7

15...c4 allows an unpleasant exchange of the important dark-squared bishop after 16 ♘f6+, while 15...♗xd5?! is not at all in the spirit of the position. After 16 ♕xd5 ♘bd7 17 ♘xe5 ♘xe5 18 ♖ad1 White is better, Bennett-De la Rosa, Geneva open 1994.

16 ♗d2!?

The immediate win of the exchange gives Black good compensation, as in the game Timmermanns-Aepfler, Germany 1994: 16 ♘c7 c4 17 ♘xa8 ♖xa8 18 ♕d2 ♘xf3+ 19 ♗xf3 ♕xd2 20 ♗xd2 ♗xb2 21 ♖ae1 ♗d4+ 22 ♗e3 ♗xe3+ 23 ♖xe3 ♖b8 24 ♖d1 ♘f6.

After 16 ♗d2!? Black has tried two possibilities and experienced problems in both:

a) 16...♘xf3+ 17 ♗xf3 ♕a6 18 ♗c3 ♗xc3 19 bxc3 ♗xd5, Neb. Ristic-Los, Belgrade GMA 1988, and now 20 ♗xd5! would have applied unpleasant pressure.

b) 16...♕d8 17 ♗c3 ♘xf3+ 18 ♗xf3 ♖b8 19 ♘c7 ♗xc3 20 bxc3 ♗c4 21 ♘xe8 ♗xf1 22 ♕xf1 ♕xe8 23 ♖e1 ♘e5 24 ♗d5 ♔g7 25 ♗xf7 ♕xf7 26 ♖xe5 with a slightly better ending, Cranbourne-Burijovich, Buenos Aires 1992.

13 0-0

After 13 ♘a4 ♕a5+ (The queen excursion 13...♕b4+?! 14 ♗d2 ♕e4 15 ♘c3 ♕f5 favours White. The game Kabiev-Podolny, corr. 1975, continued 16 0-0 ♗xe5 17 h3 ♘f6 [17...♗xc3! 18 hxg4 ♕e4] 18 ♘g5 ♗d4+ 19 ♔h1 ♕e5 20 ♗f4 ♕e7 21 d6 ♕f8 22 ♘b5 with a big advantage) 14 ♗d2 ♕d8 15 ♗g5 (What else?) Black has a pleasant choice between repeating the position with 15...♕a5+ and playing 15...f6, which is stronger here than after 12 ♗g5.

However, White does have a very interesting alternative to 13 0-0:

13 ♕d2!?

This move was invented by M. Blokh, a long-standing specialist in the Four Pawns Attack.

13...♘xe5

After 13...♘d7?! 14 d6?! is suspicious, e.g. 14...♘dxe5 15 ♘d5?! ♕xb2! 16 ♕xb2 ♘d3+! (Not 16...♘xf3+? 17 gxf3 ♗xb2 18 ♖b1+-) 17 ♔f1? (17 ♔d2!?) 17...♘xb2 18 ♗b5 ♗e6 19 ♘c7 ♖ed8 20 ♘xa8 ♖xa8 21 ♖e1 a6 22 ♖xe6! (22 ♗e2 b5∓) 22...fxe6 23 ♗d7 ♔f7 24 ♔e2 ♗f6 with a clear edge for Black, Komarov-Lamoureux, Cannes 1993. It is better to play 14 e6! fxe6 (14...♘de5 15 ♗b5!? needs further tests) 15 dxe6 ♕xe6 (15...♗xc3?! 16 bxc3 ♕xe6 17 0-0! ♘df6 18 ♖ae1 ♕c6 19 h3! ♘e4 20 ♕f4 h6 21 hxg4 hxg5 22 ♘xg5 ♘xg5 23 ♕xg5 ♔g7 24 ♗c4! ♖xe1 25 ♖xe1 ♕f6 26 ♖e7+ 1-0 Blokh-Feldman, USSR 1982) 16 ♘d5!? ♗e5 17 ♘xe5 ♕xe5 18 ♗f4 ♕e4 19 ♘c7, when White is clearly better (Blokh).

14 0-0-0

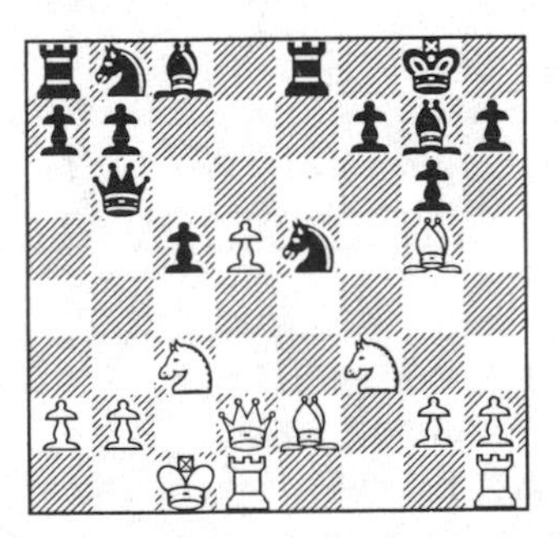

This is the point of Blokh's idea. The king moves out of immediate danger and the b2-pawn is protected at the same time.

14...♘a6

Black has also tried a number of other moves:

a) 14...c4?! 15 ♘xe5 ♗xe5 16 ♗xc4 ♕c5 17 ♗b3 ♘a6 18 ♖hf1! ♗g4 19 d6! ♖f8 20 d7! ♗xd1 21 ♖xd1± Blokh-Leluaschvili, corr. 1989/90.

b) 14...♗d7?! 15 ♘xe5 ♗xe5 16 ♖he1 ♘a6 17 d6! ♕a5?! 18 ♗c4 ♘b4, Bellinger-Ardin, corr. 1994, and now 19 ♕f2! gives White a clear advantage.

c) 14...♕a5, when instead of 15 ♖he1?! ♘bd7 16 d6 ♘b6! 17 ♗b5 ♗d7 18 ♘xe5 ♖xe5 19 ♖xe5 ♗xe5 20 ♗xd7 ♘xd7∓ Blokh-Mitenkov, USSR 1980, White should play first 15 ♘xe5!? (Blokh).

d) 14...♗f5 15 ♘xe5 ♗xe5 16 ♖he1! ♕b4! (otherwise 17 g4!) 17 a3! ♕b3 18 g4 ♗d7 19 ♗f3 and White's initiative is worth more than a pawn, Blokh-Schneider, corr. 1992.

15 ♘xe5 ♖xe5

It is too dangerous to play 15...♗xe5?!, e.g. 16 ♗b5! ♖f8 (16...♗xc3? fails to 17 ♕xc3 ♕xb5 18 ♗h6 f6 19 ♕xf6 ♕c4+ 20 ♔b1 ♕e4+ 21 ♔a1 ♕e7 22 ♖he1!) 17 ♖he1 (17 ♗e7!?) with strong pressure for White, for example 17...f6 18 d6! ♗g4 19 ♖xe5!±.

16 ♖he1

16 ♗f4?! is premature. After 16...♖e8 17 ♖he1?! ♗d7 18 d6 ♗e6 19 ♗xa6 ♕xa6 20 ♔b1 ♗d4 Black is clearly better, Blokh-Lukin, Russia 1992.

16...♘b4?!

In the event of 16...♗d7 17 d6 ♖ae8, the move 18 ♗f4 is much stronger than it was two moves ago. After 18...♖5e6 19 ♗c4 ♖xe1 20 ♖xe1 ♖xe1+ 21 ♕xe1 White keeps the initiative despite the exchange of rooks (21...♕b4? 22 ♗xf7+!).

17 ♗c4! ♖xe1 18 ♖xe1! ♗f5 19 d6!?

All White's pieces are well placed and his chances are preferable, Blokh-Sergeev, USSR 1983.

13 ... ♘xe5

Apart from 13...c4+, Black's alternatives are unattractive:

a) 13...♕xb2?! 14 ♘b5! ♘xe5 15 ♖b1 with advantage to White.

b) 13...♗f5?! 14 ♘a4! ♕a5 15 ♘h4! ♘xe5 (15...♗xe5? 16 ♗xg4 ♗xg4 17 ♕xg4 ♗d4+ 18 ♔h1 ♕xa4 19 ♘f5! gxf5 20 ♖xf5 h5 21 ♕g3+-, Semkov) 16 ♘xf5 gxf5 17 ♖xf5 ♘bd7 18 ♘c3± Semkov-Apicella, Bulgaria-France 1990.

c) 13...h6?! 14 ♘a4 (14 ♗f4!? g5 15 ♗c1) 14...♕c7 15 d6 ♕c6 16 ♗e7 ♗e6, Kakageldyev-Lerner, Riga 1972, and now 17 ♖c1! would have been in White's favour.

d) 13...♘d7 14 ♘a4!? ♕a5 15 ♗d2 ♕d8 16 e6! fxe6 17 ♘g5 ♗d4+ 18 ♔h1 ♘xh2 19 ♔xh2 exd5 with complicated play in which White's chances must be better, Dittmar-Krug, Wiesbaden open 1990.

e) 13...c4+!? 14 ♔h1

Now neither 14...♘f2+? 15 ♖xf2 ♕xf2 16 ♘e4 ♕b6 17 ♘d6 ♖f8 18 ♗e7 ♘d7 19 ♘xc4+- nor 14...h6?! 15 ♗f4!? (15 e6 fxe6 16 ♕c2 e5 17 d6 ♗f5 18 ♕a4 ♘c6 19 ♘d5 ♕xb2 20 d7 is unclear, Rojo-Sanz Alonso, Linares 1990) 15...g5 16 ♗c1± can be recommended, but instead

14...♘d7!?

is an interesting idea of Murey's which deserves close attention. Black opts for quick development instead of taking the pawn. White now has a choice of three moves:

e1) 15 d6?! is not very promising: 15...♘f2+! 16 ♖xf2 ♕xf2 17 ♘d5?! (17 ♗xc4?! ♘xe5 18 ♘e4 ♕b6 19 ♘xe5 ♖xe5 20 ♘f6+ ♗xf6 21 ♗xf6 ♖f5 22 ♗e7 ♗d7 and White has insufficient compensation for the exchange, Kouatly-Povah, Ramsgate 1979; 17 ♗h4!?) 17...♘xe5 18 ♘e7+ (It is too late to play 18 ♗h4? due to 18...♘g4! 19 ♘e7+ ♔f8 20 ♗xc4 ♕xh4!∓ Peev-Trapl, Decin 1978) 18...♔h8 19 ♘xe5 ♗xe5 20 ♘xc8 ♖exc8 21 ♗f3 ♖d8!∓ Pastor-Lybin, Frydek Mistek open 1996.

e2) 15 e6

Many of the following comments are based on Murey's previously unpublished analysis.

15...fxe6

15...♘de5? is just bad: 16

♘xe5 ♘xe5 17 ♕a4!±.

16 dxe6 ♘df6

16...♘de5? 17 ♘xe5 ♘xe5 18 ♘d5 ♕xb2 19 ♘f6+± and 16...♕xe6? 17 ♘d4! ♕d6 (17...♗xd4? 18 ♗xg4 ♕d6 19 ♘b5 ♕c5 20 ♘xd4 ♕xg5 21 ♘e6 ♕e5 22 ♕f3 ♔h8 23 ♕f7 ♖g8 24 ♖ae1 ♕xb2 25 ♘g5+-) 18 ♗xc4+ ♔h8 19 ♕xg4 ♘b6 (19...♕xd4 20 ♕xd4 ♗xd4 21 ♖ae1±) 20 ♘db5! ♕c6 21 ♕g3 ♘xc4 22 ♘c7± ♗e5? 23 ♘xe8.

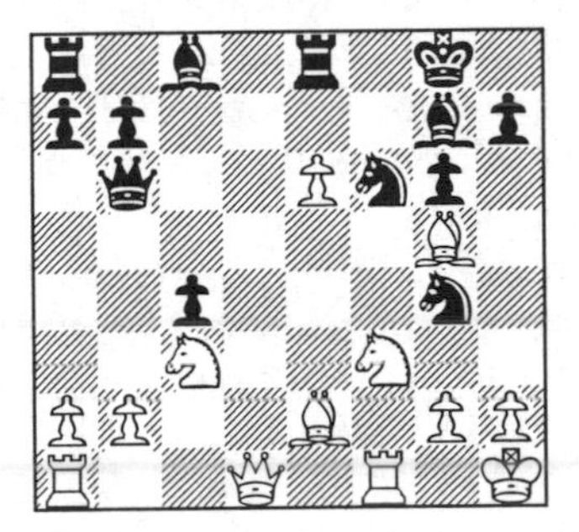

And now:

e21) 17 ♘d4? ♗xe6 18 h3 ♖ad8∓.

e22) 17 e7? ♖xe7 18 ♘d5 ♘xd5 19 ♕xd5+ ♗e6 20 ♕e4 ♖c7! 21 ♖ad1 ♖f8 22 h3 ♘f6 23 ♕h4 ♗d5∓ Jones-Povah, Chester 1979.

e23) 17 ♗xc4?! ♗xe6 18 ♗xe6+ ♖xe6 19 ♕d4 ♘e4 20 ♕xb6 axb6 21 ♘xe4 ♖xe4 22 h3 was approximately equal in Vaisser-Murey, Paris 1990.

e24) 17 h3! ♕xb2!

Both 17..♘f2+? 18 ♖xf2 ♕xf2 19 ♗xf6 ♗xf6 20 ♘e4+- and 17...♘e3? 18 ♗xe3 ♕xe3 19 ♗xc4 ♗xe6 20 ♖e1 ♕xe1+ 21 ♕xe1 ♗xc4 22 ♕h4± are bad for Black.

After 17...♕xb2 White has a choice:

e241) 18 ♖c1? ♘h5! 19 hxg4 (19 ♘d4? ♘g3+ 20 ♔g1 ♕xc3!-+; 19 ♘e4 ♘gf6 20 ♘xf6+ ♗xf6∓) 19...♘g3+ 20 ♔h2 ♘xf1+ 21 ♗xf1 ♗xc3∓.

e242) 18 ♘a4? meets with a fantastic refutation: 18...♘f2+!! 19 ♖xf2 ♘e4! 20 ♖f1 ♘g3+ 21 ♔g1 ♕xa1 22 ♕xa1 ♘xe2+ 23 ♔f2 ♗xa1 24 ♖xa1 ♗xe6! 25 ♖e1 ♖ac8 26 ♖xe2 c3-+ Kakageldiev-Murey, corr. 1972.

e243) Taimanov's proposition 18 ♕e1!? has never been tested.

e244) 18 ♕c1! ♕xc1 19 ♖axc1 h6

After Nunn's suggestion 19...♘h5 20 ♘e4 (Murey gives 20 hxg4 ♘g3+ 21 ♔g1! ♗xc3 22 ♗xc4! ♗xe6 [Not 22...♘e4? 23 ♖xc3!; 22...♗b2?! 23 ♖fe1!] 23 ♖xc3 ♘xf1 24 ♔xf1 ♗xc4 25 ♖xc4 ♖ac8, when the resulting ending is about equal) 20...♗xe6!? 21 hxg4 ♗xg4, White can continue with 22 ♗xc4+ ♔h8 23 ♘d6 ♘g3+ 24 ♔g1 with an advantage.

20 hxg4!

20 ♗d2?! favours Black after 20...♘h5 21 hxg4 ♘g3+ 22 ♔h2 ♘xf1+ 23 ♗xf1 ♗xe6 24 ♘b5 ♖ec8! 25 ♘d6 c3!

20...hxg5 21 ♘xg5

21 ♘b5? is poor: 21...♗xe6 22 ♘c7 ♘e4! 23 ♘xe8 ♖xe8 24 ♗xc4 ♘g3+ 25 ♔g1 ♗xc4 26

♖xc4 ♘xf1 27 ♖xf1 ♗f6∓.

21...♘h7! 22 ♘ce4

After 22 ♘xh7? ♔xh7 23 ♘b5! ♖xe6 (23...♗xe6?! 24 ♘c7 c3 25 ♗b5±) 24 ♗xc4 ♖e4 White is not better.

22...♘xg5 23 ♘xg5 ♗h6 24 ♖f6! ♔g7 25 ♖f7+ ♔g8 26 ♖f6

with a draw by repetition of moves (Murey).

e3) ***15 ♗xc4!*** The only move that promises anything for White, e.g. 15...♘dxe5 16 ♘xe5 ♘xe5 (16..♗xe5 17 d6!) 17 ♗b3± Vaisser-Murey, Evry (rapidplay) 1993.

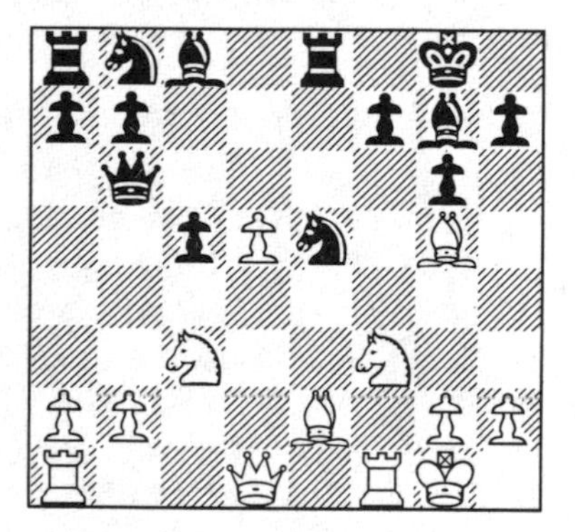

14 ♘xe5

14 ♕d2 is a little investigated alternative, while 14 d6 is considered in Game 2, Vaisser-Degraeve.

14 ... ♗xe5

14...♖xe5 is rather unpopular, but not so stupid after 15 ♕d2 ♗f5 and now:

a) 16 g4?! is too aggressive: 16...c4+ 17 ♖f2 ♗d3 18 ♗xd3 cxd3 19 ♕f4 f5 20 ♖d1 ♘d7 21 ♖xd3 ♖f8 with an initiative for Black, Krupkova-Grabics, Zanka 1995.

b) Interesting, but not sufficient for equality, is the immediate exchange sacrifice after 16 ♗f4 ♘d7?! 17 ♗xe5 ♘xe5 as in the game C. Hansen-Yurtaev, Gausdal 1990.

c) 16 ♗c4, after which Black has tried:

c1) 16...♘d7 17 d6 ♕b4? (17...♗e6! 18 ♘d5? ♖xd5! 19 ♗xd5 ♗d4+-+) 18 ♖f4! h6 19 ♗e7 ♕a5, Vaisser-Gufeld, Novosibirsk 1971, and now the simple development 20 ♖af1 would have assured White of an advantage.

c2) 16...♕b4 17 ♖f4 h6! 18 ♗d8 b6 was unclear in Krupkova-Repkova, Prague 1996.

15 ♗c4

15 ♕d2!? is not played often, but deserves further analysis. One recent example: 15...♘d7 16 ♖ad1 a6 17 ♔h1 ♗d4 18 ♕f4 f5, Thoma-Kahn, Budapest 1995, and now 19 d6! would have given White a strong attack.

15 ♗b5?! is an old and unsuccessful attempt to meet the Black set-up. After 15...♗d7 (This position also can arise after 15 ♗c4 ♗f5 16 ♗b5 ♗d7) 16 ♕f3 both 16...f5 17 ♗c4 ♕xb2 18 d6+ ♔h8 19 ♖ac1 ♗c6 20 ♕h3 ♘d7 21 ♘e2 ♗xd6 22 ♖cd1 ♗e5, Nei-Ciocaltea, Zinnowitz 1966, and 16...f6 17 a4 ♗xb5 18 ♘xb5 ♘d7 19 d6 ♕c6, Kakageldiev-

Zaid, USSR 1973, give Black an obvious advantage.

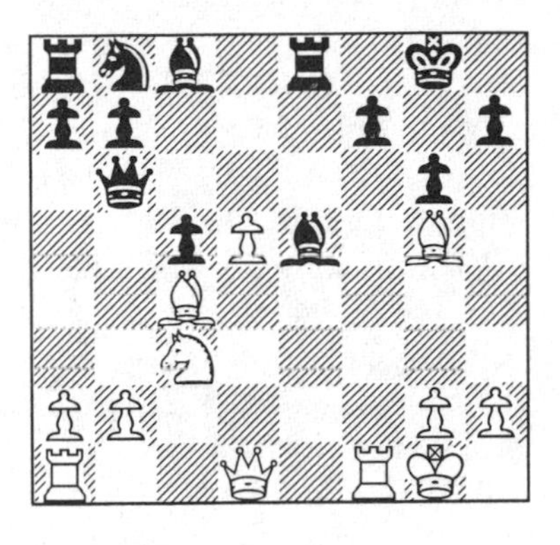

15 ... ♕xb2

This is one of the critical positions in the 9...♖e8 system. Apart from the text move, Black also has a choice between:

a) 15...♕d6? 16 ♘b5 ♗xh2+ 17 ♔h1 ♕g3 18 ♗f4 ♕h4 19 ♗xh2 ♕xc4 20 ♘d6 1-0 Serdt-Podgornik, Bled 1992.

b) 15...♘d7? 16 d6 ♗d4+ 17 ♔h1 ♘e5 18 ♘d5 ♕xd6 19 ♘f6+ ♔f8 20 ♗h6+ ♔e7 21 ♘d5+ ♔d7 22 ♕a4+ b5 23 ♗xb5+ 1-0 Dobos-Petersen, Aarhus 1991.

c) 15...♕b4

The theory of this line has an interesting history. Initially it was considered good for Black on the basis of the game Janosevic-Forintos, Vrnjacka Banja 1973: 16 ♕b3?! ♗f5 17 d6 ♕xb3 18 axb3 ♗xd6 19 ♘d5 ♘d7 20 ♖xf5! gxf5 21 ♗b5 ♗e5 22 ♗xd7 ♖ed8 23 ♗xd8 ♖xd8 24 ♘e7+ ♔f8 25 ♗xf5 ♔xe7 26 ♖xa7, although White succeeded in achieving a draw in the end. Then the error-filled game Szabo-Pietzsch, Salgotarjan 1967: 16 ♕f3 ♗f5 17 g4?? ♕xc4?? 18 gxf5 promised a clear advantage to White. Sometime later an evident improvement for Black was discovered: 17...♕xb2! 18 ♘e2 ♗d4+! 19 ♘xd4 ♕xd4+∓. Finally, 16 ♕f3 ♗f5 17 ♗b5 came into practice and again the evaluation of the line was changed, as we can see:

16 ♕f3 ♗f5

White's attack is too strong after 16...f5?! 17 ♕d3 ♔g7 (17...♕xb2 18 d6+ ♔g7 19 ♘b5 ♗d4+ 20 ♔h1 ♕xa1 21 ♖xa1 ♗xa1 22 ♕b1!±) 18 ♖ae1 ♗d7 19 ♗d2 ♕b6 20 ♖xe5!, Strating-De Bruijne, Leeuwarden 1995.

17 ♗b5

White has another try that is worth further analysis: 17 ♗b3 ♕g4 18 ♕xg4 ♗xg4 19 d6 ♗e6 20 ♘d5, Bellinger-Burd, corr. 1994.

17...♖f8 18 ♖ae1

Here White can also consider 18 ♗e7!? ♗g4! 19 ♕d3 ♕d4+ 20 ♕xd4 ♗xd4+ 21 ♔h1 ♖c8 22 h3 ♗d7 23 ♗c4 with good compensation for the pawn as in the game Vaisser-Degraeve, Cannes 1990.

18...f6

The knight move 18...♘d7? is bad: 19 ♗xd7 ♗d4+ 20 ♔h1 ♗xd7 21 ♖e7 ♗f5 22 g4 ♕xb2 23 ♘d1± Vegh-Pesztericz,

Hungarian Team Ch. 1994, while White has strong pressure after 18...♗xc3?! 19 ♕xc3 ♕xc3 (19...♕xb5? 20 ♗h6) 20 bxc3 a6 21 ♗e8! or 18...♗g4!? 19 ♕d3 ♕d4+ 20 ♔h1. Perhaps Black should consider the very sharp 18...♗d4+ 19 ♔h1 ♕xb2.

19 ♖xe5!

This is stronger than 19 a3?! ♗d4+ 20 ♔h1 ♕xb2 21 ♗h6 ♕xc3 22 ♗xf8 ♕xf3 23 ♖xf3 ♔xf8 24 ♖e8+ ♔f7 25 d6 a6 26 ♖e7+ ♔f8 27 ♗c4 ♘c6 28 ♖xh7, Matsula-Kharitonov, Kirov 1993, as now 28...♖d8! would have given Black an advantage.

19...fxe5 20 ♗h6 ♖f7 21 ♕g3 a6 22 ♗e8! ♖e7 23 ♗xg6! hxg6 24 ♖xf5

with a winning attack. This variation is not forced but it is rather convincing.

d) **15...♗f5!? 16 ♘b5!**

16 ♗b5?! ♗d7 transposes into the inferior line 15 ♗b5?! given above.

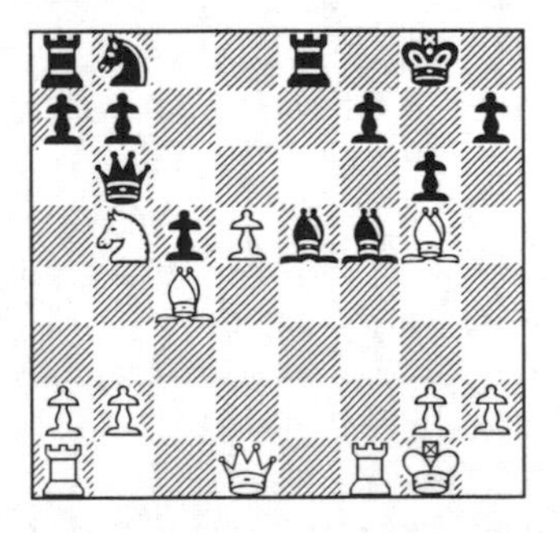

Here Black has a wide choice:

d1) 16...♖f8?! 17 a4 ♕a5 18 ♗e7 ♘d7, Sakovich-Didishko, USSR 1973, and now 19 d6!? would have promised an advantage.

d2) 16...h6 17 ♖xf5!? (If this is found not to work, White can follow the game Hausner-Tobyas, Czech Ch. 1992, with 17 ♗xh6 ♕f6 18 ♕d2 a6 19 ♘c3 b5 20 g4, where the position was not so clear) 17...gxf5 18 d6! hxg5 19 ♕h5 ♖f8 20 ♖f1 with a very strong attack.

d3) 16...♘d7 17 a4! (It is too early to play 17 d6? ♗e6! 18 ♕b3 ♗xd6 19 ♘xd6 ♕xd6∓) and now:

d31) 17...♕a5? 18 d6 ♗e6 19 ♗xe6 ♖xe6 20 ♕f3 f6 21 ♕xb7 ♘b6 22 ♗h6 f5 23 ♖ae1 1-0 Vaisser-Jojic, Paris 1990.

d32) 17...a5?! 18 ♖a3! ♗d4+ 19 ♔h1 ♘e5 20 ♖b3! ♗g4 21 ♕c1 ♕a6! 22 h3 is better for White, Vaisser-Podvrsnik, Ptuj 1989.

d33) Black has at his disposal an interesting queen sacrifice: ***17...a6!?*** 18 a5 axb5 19 axb6 bxc4 which awaits its first test.

d34) 17...f6 18 a5 ♕d8 19 ♗f4!? (The white bishop seems more safely placed on f4 than on h6. The game Vaisser-Akopian, USSR 1988, saw instead 19 ♗h6 ♔h8 20 d6 ♗xb2?! [It would have been better to play 20...a6! 21 ♘c7 ♗d4+ 22 ♔h1 ♘e5 with compensation] 21 ♖a2 ♘e5 22 ♗e2 ♗d4+ 23 ♘xd4 cxd4 24 ♕xd4 ♖e6, and now 25 ♖d2 would have promised an advantage to White, e.g. 25...♘c6 26 ♕b2! ♘xa5 27 g4 ♗e4 28 d7!) 19...♔h8 20 d6 a6 21 ♘c7 with complex play in which White's chances must be better, Strating-Nijboer, Amsterdam open 1995.

d4) **16...a6!**

This appears to give Black a forced draw.

17 d6 axb5

In the case of 17...♘d7 18 ♘c7 ♗d4+ 19 ♔h1 ♕xd6 20 ♘xa8 ♖xa8 21 ♕b3!? Black does not have enough compensation for the exchange.

18 ♗xf7+ ♔xf7

18...♔g7? 19 ♗xe8 ♗d4+ 20 ♔h1 ♕xd6 21 ♗xb5± Vaisser-Kozlov, USSR 1971.

19 ♖xf5+ gxf5

Again Black must accept the sacrifice. 19...♔g7? fails due to 20 d7 ♘xd7 21 ♕xd7+ ♔h8 (21...♔g8 22 ♕f7+ ♔h8 23 ♖xe5!±) 22 ♖f7 ♖f8, Van der Doef-Buisman, corr. 1974, and now White could have won with 23 ♖af1! ♗g7 24 ♖xf8+ ♖xf8 25 ♖xf8+ ♗xf8 26 ♕f7.

20 ♕h5+ ♔f8

Spasov, as Black against Wessman, Tunja 1989, went wrong here with 20...♔e6? 21 ♕xe8+ ♔xd6 22 ♖e1! c4+ 23 ♗e3 ♘c6 24 ♕xa8 ♗d4 25 ♖d1 ♔c7, and could have lost the game after 26 ♖xd4! ♘xd4 27 ♕f8.

After 20...♔g7 White has a perpetual check with 21 ♗h6+ ♔f6 22 ♗g5+. Since 21 ♗h6+ ♔f6 22 ♖f1? loses because of 22...♗d4+! (not 22...♗xh2+? 23 ♔h1 ♖e5 24 ♗g5+ ♔e6 25 ♕e8+ ♔d5 26 ♖d1+ mating, Strating-Bloemhard, Holland 1992) 23 ♔h1 ♖e5, the only try for a win is 21 ♕xe8; but this is less promising than in the game Wessman-Spasov.

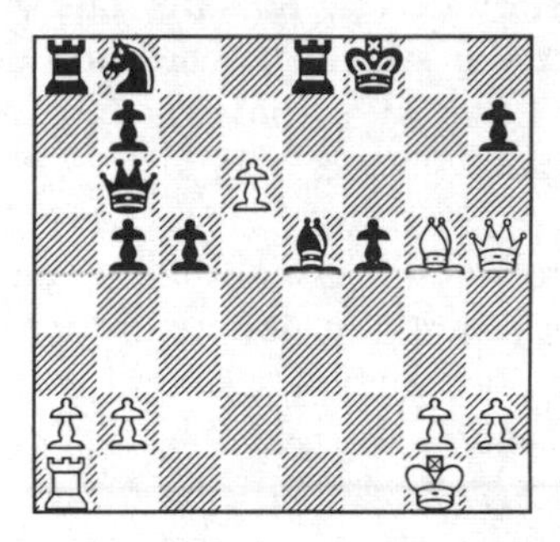

I analysed the critical position after 20...♔f8 in the local press in the annotations to my game against Kozlov, and concluded that White has nothing more than a draw by perpetual check: 21 ♗h6+ ♗g7 22 ♖f1 c4+ 23 ♔h1 ♕f2! 24 ♗xg7+ ♔xg7 25 ♕g5+ ♔f7 26 ♕h5+. When Yudovich then published this analysis in *Informator* this sharp position became the subject of much theoretical debate. Pukshansky claimed that White could win by 21 ♗h6+ ♗g7 22 ♗xg7+ ♔xg7 23 ♕xe8 c4+ 24 ♔h1 ♕xd6 (Or 24...♕f2? 25 d7 ♖xa2 26 ♖e1 ♘c6 27 d8♕ ♘xd8 28 ♖e7+ mating) 25 ♖e1 ♖a6(?) 26 ♖e7+ ♔h6 27 ♕f8+ ♔g5 28 ♕g8+! winning, and over a period of some fifteen years his analysis was passed from book to book. The power of White's attack was then confirmed by the game Reinemer-Hoerstmann, Wittlich 1990: 25...♔f6? (Instead of 25...♖a6?) 26 h4! ♖xa2 27 ♕h8+ ♔g6 28 ♕g8+ ♔f6 29 g4! f4? 30 ♕h8+ ♔g6 31 ♕e8+ ♔g7 32 ♖e7+±. I also believed all this analysis without sufficient checking until I played a little-known game against Bauer (French Team Cup 1992). My young and relatively inexperienced opponent knew nothing about this variation but found the only defence: 21 ♗h6+ ♗g7 22 ♗xg7+ ♔xg7 23 ♕xe8 c4+ 24 ♔h1 ♕xd6 25 ♖e1 *♕f8!* Now White has nothing more than a perpetual check after 26 ♕e5+ (26 ♕xb5 ♘a6) 26...♔g8 27 ♕d5+ ♔h8.

Other options do not give White more than a draw:

d41) 21 ♗h6+ ♗g7 22 ♕xf5+ ♔g8 23 ♖f1? (23 ♕d5+ ♔h8 24 ♗xg7+=) 23...♗d4+ (Thanks to this check Black can beat off the white attack and keep a great material advantage) 24 ♔h1 ♘a6 25 d7 ♖ed8.

d42) 21 ♖f1? c4+ (Not 21...♘d7? 22 ♕xh7 ♖e6? 23 ♖xf5+ ♗f6 24 ♗h6+ ♔e8 25 ♕g8+ ♘f8 26 ♕xf8+ ♔d7 27 ♕f7++-) 22 ♔h1 ♕xd6 23 ♕xh7 ♖e6 24 ♕xf5+ ♗f6 25 ♗xf6 ♖xf6 winning.

d43) 21 ♕xh7 ♕xd6 22 ♗h6+ ♕xh6 23 ♕xh6+ ♗g7 (Possible is 23...♔e7!?) 24 ♕d6+ ♔g8 25 ♕d5+ ♔h8 26 ♕xf5 ♘c6 27 ♕h5+ with perpetual check, as in Vaisser-Apicella, French Ch. 1996.

So we can conclude that at the moment the line 15...♗f5 16 ♘b5 leads to a more or less forced draw.

16 d6

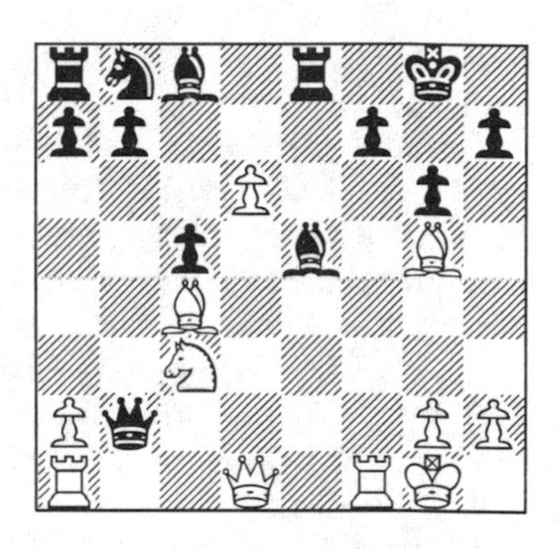

16 ... ♖f8!

This natural move was first played in the game Gorovaya-Kviatkowskaja, corr. 1970. During the course of the following 20 years, however, it was forgotten and only in 1990 did Marin bring it back into practice. Thanks to its re-emergence I was able to check my 1969(!) vintage analysis in the present game. Others are much weaker:

a) 16...♗f5? 17 ♖xf5! (In B. Vladimirov-Doda, Leningrad 1967, White inverted his moves, 17 ♗xf7+? ♔xf7 18 ♖xf5+, and could have been punished with 18...♔g7!) 17...gxf5 18 ♗xf7+! ♔f8 (After 18...♔xf7? 19 ♕h5+

♔f8 the quickest win was demonstrated in Vaisser-Jaikovsky, Moscow 1967, which up until now had followed Vladimirov-Doda: 20 ♗h6+! ♗g7 21 ♖f1!) 19 ♗xe8 ♕xc3 20 ♗e7+ ♔xe8 21 ♕h5+ ♔d7 22 ♕xf5+ ♔c6 23 ♕e4+ ♔d7. For a long time this position was considered to be drawn. In reality, instead of taking the perpetual check White can play ***24 ♖d1!*** and Black is helpless. For example: 24...♘c6 25 ♕f5+ ♔e8 26 ♕e6 or 24...♕b2 25 ♕a4+! b5 26 ♕g4+ winning.

b) 16...♗e6? 17 ♗xe6 fxe6 18 ♕f3 ♘d7 19 ♕f7+ ♔h8 20 ♕xd7 ♕xc3 21 ♖ad1 and the passed d-pawn assures White of a clear advantage.

c) 16...♗d4+?, after which I caused unnecessary problems for myself by playing for beauty in the game Vaisser-Zagorovsky, USSR 1976: 17 ♕xd4? cxd4 18 ♗xf7+ ♔g7 19 ♗xe8 dxc3! with an unclear position. Instead, the simple 17 ♔h1 gives White a clear advantage:

c1) 17...♗f5 18 ♖xf5! gxf5 19 ♗xf7+ ♔xf7 (19...♔f8 20 ♗xe8 ♕xc3 21 ♖c1+-) 20 ♕h5+ ♔f8 21 ♗h6+ ♗g7 22 ♕xf5+ ♔g8 23 ♖f1 1-0 Arencibia-Martin del Campo, Bayamo 1989.

c2) 17...♖f8 18 ♘b5! ♕xa1 19 ♕f3 ♕b2 20 ♘xd4 ♕xd4 21 ♗xf7+ ♔g7 22 ♗f6++-.

17 ♗xf7+

White's other choices are:

a) 17 ♖xf7? is just plain bad: 17...♖xf7 18 ♗xf7+ ♔g7-+.

b) The aforementioned game Gorovaya-Kviatkowskaja continued 17 ♘b5? ♕xa1 18 ♕f3 ♕b2 (We see a big difference here compared to note c2 on the previous move, where Black's bishop was placed on d4) 19 ♗xf7+ (19 ♗e7!?) and now the quickest way for Black to win was 19...♔h8! 20 ♗e7 ♗g4! 21 ♕xg4 ♕xb5 22 ♕e4 ♕xf1+.

c) 17 ♖c1!? seems less clear. At least the variation proposed by Konikowski can be improved: 17...♗xc3 18 ♗e7 ♗d4+ 19 ♔h1 ♘d7 20 ♗xf8 ♘xf8 and now instead of 21 ♖xf7 ♗e6 22 ♖xf8+ ♖xf8 23 ♗xe6+ ♔h8∓ (Konikowski) White should play ***21 ♖b1!*** ♕c3 22 ♗xf7+ ♔g7 23 ♖b3 ♕a5 24 ♕e2! with an advantage.

17 ... ♔g7

Black can also play 17...♖xf7 18 ♕d5 ♗d4+ 19 ♔h1 ♗f5 20 ♖ab1 ♗xc3! (Not 20...♕xc3? 21 ♖xb7 ♘d7 22 ♖xd7 ♖af8 23 ♖xf7 ♖xf7 24 d7+-) 21 ♖xb2 ♗xb2 22 g4 ♗e4+ 23 ♕xe4 ♖xf1+ 24 ♔g2 ♖f7 25 ♕e8+ ♖f8 26 ♕b5 ♗d4 27 ♕xb7 ♘d7 28 ♕xd7 ♖f2+ 29 ♔g3 ♖af8 30 ♕e6+ ♔h8! 31 ♕d5 with a probable draw.

18 ♗d5!

After 18 ♕d5? ♕xc3 19 ♖ad1 ♗f5 20 ♖f3 ♗d4+ 21 ♔h1 ♕xf3! 22 gxf3 ♖xf7 Black is clearly better, Semkov-Marin, Berga 1990.

18 ... ♕xc3

White has an advantage after both:

a) 18...♖xf1+?! 19 ♕xf1 ♗f5 20 ♖e1! ♕xc3 21 ♗xb7 ♗xd6 22 ♗xa8; and

b) 18...♗f5?! 19 ♕c1! ♕xc3 (19...♕xc1 20 ♖axc1 ♘c6 21 ♘b5±) 20 ♗h6+ ♔h8 21 ♕xc3 ♗xc3 22 ♗xf8 ♘d7 23 ♗e7 ♗xa1 24 ♖xa1; but

c) ***18...♘d7!*** could have posed some problems. White can probably hold a draw, but not more after 19 ♖xf8! ♘xf8 20 ♕c1! ♕xc3 21 ♗h6+ ♔h8 22 ♕xc3 ♗xc3 23 ♖f1 ♗d4+ 24 ♔h1 ♗f5 (24...♘e6 25 ♖f7) 25 g4 ♗xg4 26 ♗xf8.

19 ♖xf8 ♔xf8

Not 19...♕d4+? 20 ♖f2±.

20 ♕f1+ ♗f5

21 ♖d1!

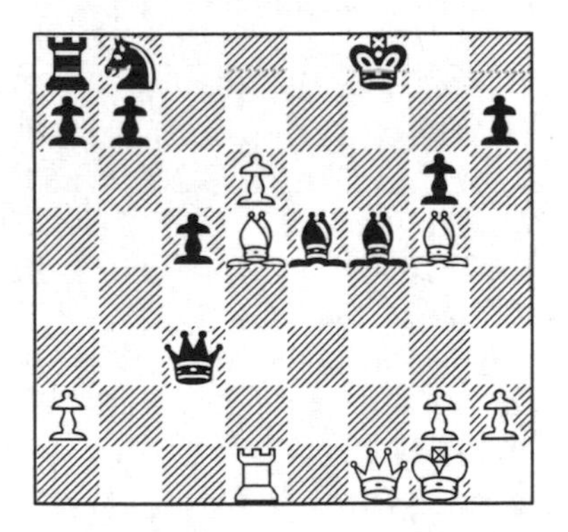

This is the point. Black has no comfortable defence to the twin threats of 22 ♗xb7 and 22 g4. If now 21...♕b4 then 22 a3!

21 ... ♘d7

22 g4 ♔g7

23 gxf5 ♕c2?

23...h6! was necessary (If 23...♖f8?! then 24 ♗e6!±). For example, 24 ♗e7!? (Or 24 ♗xb7 ♖b8 25 ♗d2 ♕d4+ 26 ♔h1 ♕h4 27 ♕g2 ♖xb7 28 ♕xg6+ ♔h8 with perpetual check, Kahn-Gladyszev, Budapest 1996) 24...♕c2 25 ♕f3 ♕xh2+ 26 ♔f1 gxf5 27 ♕xf5 ♕f4+ 28 ♕xf4 ♗xf4 29 ♗xb7 ♖b8 30 ♗c6 ♘e5 31 ♗e4 ♗g5 32 ♖d5 ♘f7 with equality, Elbilia-Berthelot, French Team Ch. 1993.

24 ♖d2 ♕xf5

25 ♕xf5 gxf5

26 ♗e7 ♗d4+

27 ♔f1 ♘e5

27...♗f6 doesn't work because of 28 ♖g2+ ♔h8 29 ♗e6 ♗xe7 30 dxe7 ♘f6 31 ♗f7 and Black is helpless.

28 ♖g2+ ♘g6

29 h4 ♔h8

29...♗f6 also loses: 30 h5 ♗xe7 31 dxe7 ♖e8 32 hxg6 hxg6 (32...♖xe7 33 gxh7+ ♔xh7 34 ♖g5+-) 33 ♖e2 ♔f6 34 ♖e6+ ♔f7 35 ♖b6+ ♔xe7 36 ♖xb7+ ♔d6 37 ♗f7. More resilient, however, was 29...♔h6! 30 ♗g5+ ♔g7 31 h5 ♘e5 32 ♖e2, although White still has a big advantage.

30 ♖xg6 hxg6

31 ♗xb7 ♖b8

32 d7 c4

33 d8♕+ ♖xd8

34 ♗xd8 ♔g7

35 ♗g5 c3

36 ♔e2 1-0

Game 2
Vaisser-Degraeve
Cappelle la Grande 1987

1 d4 ♘f6 2 c4 g6 3 ♘c3 ♗g7 4 e4 d6 5 f4 0-0 6 ♘f3 c5 7 d5 e6 8 ♗e2 exd5 9 cxd5 ♖e8 10 e5 dxe5 11 fxe5 ♘g4 12 ♗g5 ♕b6 13 0-0 ♘xe5

14 d6

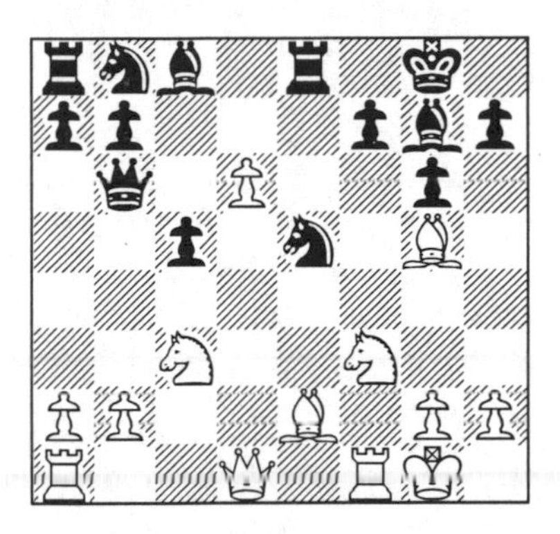

Over the years the position after 14 d6 has been of great importance to the theory of the Four Pawns Attack. Currently, however, it is perceived as less attractive for White than 14 ♘xe5 (see the previous game), because Black has a choice between a practically forced draw in the line 14...♕xb2 and complicated play with mutual chances after either 14...c4+ 15 ♔h1 ♕xb2 or 14...♗f5.

14 ... ♗f5!?

Black has a wide choice here:

a) 14...♗e6?! 15 ♘xe5! ♗xe5 (15...♕xb2?! 16 ♕a4! ♖f8 17 ♖fc1± Siegmund-Junge, corr. 1984; if now 17...♗xe5, 18 ♖ab1 traps Black's queen) 16 ♘d5 ♗d4+ (Black has nothing better: 16...♗xd5? 17 ♕xd5 ♗d4+ 18 ♔h1 ♖f8 19 ♖xf7!+- or 16...♕xb2?! 17 ♘f6+ ♗xf6 18 ♗xf6 ♕b4 19 ♗f3 ♘d7 20 ♖b1 ♕a5 21 ♗a1 and White's attack is worth much more then two pawns, Kaplun-Vicin, Odessa 1980) 17 ♕xd4 cxd4 18 ♘xb6 axb6 19 ♗b5 ♘c6, Peev-Vogt, Varna 1973, when White would have had a clearly better ending after 20 ♗f6!?

b) 14...♘bd7?! 15 ♗b5!? ♖e6 (Not 15...c4+? 16 ♔h1 ♘d3 17 ♗xc4 ♘f2+ 18 ♖xf2 ♕xf2 19 ♗h4! ♕xb2 20 ♗xf7+!, but 15...a6!? deserves attention) 16 ♗e7 ♘xf3+ 17 ♕xf3 ♗d4+ 18 ♔h1 ♘e5 19 ♕f4 ♗xc3 20 ♕h6 ♘d7? (20...♗d7 21 ♗xd7 ♘xd7 22 bxc3 f6 was necessary, although White still has a strong initiative) 21 ♖xf7! mating, Kouatly-Raupp, Berlin 1976.

c) 14...♘xf3+ 15 ♗xf3 ♗d4+?! (15...♕xb2 16 ♘d5 transposes to line d below and 15...c4+ 16 ♔h1 ♕xb2 to line e below) 16 ♔h1 ♕xd6? 17 ♗d5! (Also possible is 17 ♘b5 ♕b6 18 ♘xd4 cxd4 19 ♕d2 ♗f5 20 ♖ad1 ♘c6 21 ♗d5 with strong pressure, Arencibia-Gomez, Cuban Ch. 1988) 17...♗e6 18 ♗xb7 ♘d7 19 ♗xa8 ♖xa8 20 ♘b5. White is clearly better after both 20...♕d5 21 ♘xd4 cxd4 22 ♕f3!, as in the game Kouatly-Teichmann, London 1978, and 20...♕b6 21 ♘xd4 cxd4 22 b3 ♗f5 23 ♕f3!, Kouatly-Perdigo, Alès 1979.

d) **14...♕xb2 15 ♘d5 ♘xf3+**

Black has also tried 15...♘bc6?! (15...♘ec6?! is rather artificial, since 16 ♗c4 gives White good chances, while 15...♗f5 transposes to the main game) 16 ♖b1 (16 ♘f6+!?; 16 ♗f6!?) 16...♕xa2 (16...♘xf3+? 17 ♗xf3 is bad for Black. Now both 17...♕d4+ 18 ♔h1 ♖b8 19 ♘c7 ♗d7 20 ♘xe8 ♗xe8 21 ♗d5, Semkov-Spassov, Bulgarian Ch. 1988, and 17...♕e5 18 ♘f6+! ♗xf6 19 ♗xf6 ♕xf6 20 ♗xc6 ♗f5 21 ♗xe8 ♖xe8 22 ♖xb7, Fang-Van Wely, New York 1993, gave White a clear advantage) 17 ♘c7 ♗f5 18 ♘xe8 ♖xe8! (The only move. 18...♕xb1? 19 ♕xb1 ♗xb1 20 ♘c7 is just winning for White, who also has a big advantage after 18...♗xb1? 19 ♘xg7 ♗c2 20 ♕e1 ♕d5 21 ♘xe5 ♕xe5 22 ♗f6 ♕xd6 23 ♗c4, Vaisser-Belov, USSR 1983) 19 ♖xb7 ♘d4! 20 ♘xd4 cxd4 21 ♗f3!, when White's chances are slightly better, thanks to the d6-pawn.

16 ♗xf3 ♗d4+!

Or 16...♕d4+ with the same effect. This check is not only useful from a general point of view, driving the white king away, but, as we can see below, it is actually necessary for concrete tactical reasons.

17 ♔h1 ♕xa1 18 ♕xa1 ♗xa1 19 ♖xa1

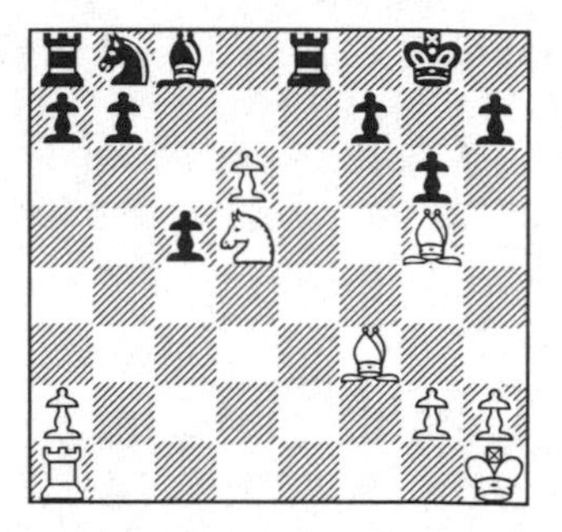

19...♖e5!

Probably Black can also achieve equality after 19...♘d7 with precise play, due to the position of White's king on h1. The game P. Garcia-Nunez, Ciego de Avila 1989, continued 20 ♗e7! (Not 20 ♘c7?! ♖e5!) 20...♖b8 21 ♘c7 ♖f8 22 ♖e1 b5! (This is better than Black's play in the game Vaisser-Khodos, Krasnodar 1978 [with the white king on g1]: 22...c4?! 23 ♗xf8 ♔xf8 [22...♘xf8 fails because of 24 ♖e8 c3 25 ♗e4 ♗f5? 26 ♖xb8 ♗xe4 27 ♘e6! fxe6 28 d7 c2 29 ♖xf8+ ♔g7 30 ♖f1+-] 24 ♖e8+ [Even stronger is 24 ♗d5! ♘f6 25 ♗xc4±] 24...♔g7 25 ♔f2 ♘f6 26 ♖d8 b5, and now 27 ♘e8+ would have been winning) 23 ♗xf8 (23 ♗d5? was proposed by Nunez as being advantageous for White, but the position turns in Black's favour after 23...♗b7! 24 ♗xb7 ♖xb7 25 ♗xf8 ♘xf8 26 ♖e8 ♔g7 27 ♖e7 ♖b8)

23...♔xf8 24 ♖e8+ ♔g7 25 ♗c6 b4! 26 h3 (If 26 ♗xd7? b3!∓. Note that this tactic doesn't work with the king on g1 instead of h1) 26...♘f6 and now instead of the losing 27 d7? ♗xd7! the game should have continued 27 ♖d8 c4! 28 ♘e8+! (Both 28 d7? ♘xd7 28 ♗xd7 b3 and 28 ♘a6? c3! are bad) 28...♘xe8 29 ♖xe8 b3 30 axb3 cxb3 31 ♔h2! b2! 32 d7 ♗xd7 33 ♖xb8 ♗xc6 with a drawn endgame.

20 ♗f4!

Here 20 ♘e7+? is bad: 20...♔g7 21 ♘xc8 (21 ♗f4 ♘d7 22 ♗xe5+ ♘xe5 23 ♘xc8 ♖xc8 24 ♗xb7 ♖d8∓ Scholseth-Nordahl, Gausdal 1993) 21...♘d7 22 ♗xb7 ♖b8 23 ♗c6 ♖xg5 24 ♗xd7 c4! 25 ♘xa7 (25 h4 c3! 26 ♗a4 ♖d5 27 ♘xa7 [or 27 d7 ♖xd7!-+] 27...♖b4 28 ♘b5 ♖xa4 29 ♘xc3 ♖xh4+ winning, Dobos-Schlosser, Balatonbereny 1989) 25...c3! 26 ♗a4, Tozer-Schlosser, Oakham 1988, and now the simplest way was 26...♖c5 27 ♗c2 (27 ♘b5 is met by 27...♖bxb5! 28 ♗xb5 c2!-+) 27...♖d5 28 ♖c1 ♖xd6 29 a4 ♖b2 30 h3 ♖d2 31 ♗e4 c2 32 ♔h2 f5 and Black wins.

If Black doesn't check on d4 (so that White's king stays on g1) our evaluation of this variation must be changed, as the game Pesztericz-Boros, Budapest 1995, demonstrated. To avoid the problems of move numbering we start from a deviation from line d analysed above: 14...♕xb2 15 ♘d5 ♘xf3+ 16 ♗xf3 ♕xa1? 17 ♕xa1 ♗xa1 18 ♖xa1 ♖e5 19 ♘e7+! ♔g7 20 ♘xc8 ♘d7 21 ♗xb7 ♖b8 22 ♗c6 ♖xg5 23 ♗xd7 c4 24 ♘xa7 c3 25 ♖c1! (Here this is possible) 25...♖b2 26 ♗c6 and White stands better.

There is one other nuance in this move order that is worth pointing out. After 16...♕xa1? White can try 17 ♘e7+?! ♔h8 18 ♕xa1 ♗xa1 19 ♖xa1, but in fact after the precise 19...♔g7! (but not 19...♘d7? 20 ♖e1 ♖f8 21 ♗h6 ♖d8 22 ♗d2! f6 23 ♗c3 ♖f8 24 ♘d5 ♖b8 25 ♗g4 b5 26 ♗xd7 ♗xd7 27 ♖e7+- Vaisser-Grigoriadis, Odessa 1977) 20 ♖e1 ♗e6! 21 ♗xb7 ♘d7 22 ♗xa8 ♖xa8 White does not have enough compensation for the pawn.

20...♖xd5!

The best plan is to return the exchange. White is much better after both 20...♘d7? 21 ♗xe5 ♘xe5 22 ♖e1 and 20...♖f5? 21 ♘e7+ ♔g7 22 ♘xf5+ gxf5 23 ♖e1 ♘d7 24 ♖e8! ♘b6 25 a4! with the idea of 25...♗d7 26 ♖xa8 ♘xa8 27 a5+-.

21 ♗xd5 ♘c6 22 ♗xc6 bxc6 23 ♖c1 ♗d7 24 ♖xc5 ♖b8 25 h3

with equality

e) 14...c4+ 15 ♔h1

By including the check and then playing 15...♘xf3 16 ♗xf3 ♕xb2 Black tries to obtain the same position as the last diagram, but with an extra tempo (…c5-c4). Two sidelines cannot be recommended:

e1) 15...♘d3?! 16 ♗xd3 cxd3 17 ♕xd3 ♗f5 (Or 17...♗e6 18 ♖ac1 ♕a6 19 ♕xa6 bxa6 20 ♖fd1 with a stable advantage in the ending, Peev-Vukic, Kapfenberg 1970) 18 ♕d2 ♘d7 19 ♖ad1 ♖b8, Gorelov-A. Shashin, Krasnodar 1980, and now 20 ♘d5! ♕xb2 21 ♘e7+ would have given White the better position.

e2) 15...♗e6?! 16 ♘xe5 ♗xe5 17 ♘d5 ♕xd6 18 ♘f6+ ♔f8 19 ♕xd6+ ♗xd6 20 ♖ad1 ♗c7 21 ♘xe8 ♔xe8 22 ♖c1 is clearly better for White, Konikowski-Molderer, Balatonbereny 1989.

e3) 15...♘xf3 16 ♗xf3 ♕xb2

When I analysed this position way back in 1979, I discovered what I believed to be a pleasing refutation of this move order. This line has not been in vogue since then, however, and to my regret no one has ever offered themselves as a victim.

In 1987 Konikowski published some analysis claiming that White wins easily after 17 ♗d5 ♗e6 18 ♗xe6 fxe6 19 ♕f3 ♘c6 20 ♕f7+ ♔h8 21 ♗f6 ♖g8 22 ♖b1 etc., and ever since then I have been hoping that somebody would find 19...♖f8! (instead of the suicidal 19...♘c6?) 20 ♕e4 ♘c6 21 ♕xe6+ ♔h8 22 ♘d5 ♖f5! with an advantage for Black, and would therefore try to trap me. But sadly this has not happened and I have therefore decided to publish my home preparation in this book.

17 ♗d5! ♗e6!

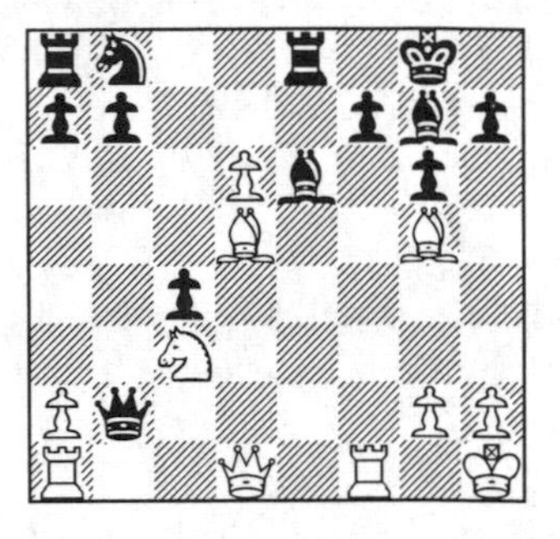

The only move. All the alternatives are losing: 17...♗f5? 18 ♗xf7+ ♔xf7 19 ♕d5+ ♔f8 20 ♗e7+ ♖xe7 21 dxe7+ ♔xe7 22 ♖ae1+; 17...♖f8? 18 ♗e7! (18 ♖xf7?! ♖xf7 19 ♗xf7+ ♔h8! is less clear) 18...♕xc3 19 ♖c1 ♕e5 20 ♗xf8; and 17...♕xc3? 18 ♗xf7+ ♔h8 19 ♗xe8 ♕xa1 20 ♖f8+!

18 ♖xf7!! ♔xf7

If 18...♕xc3?! 19 ♖e7! Black has two choices: 19...♖xe7?! 20 dxe7 ♘c6 21 ♗xe6+ ♔h8 22 ♖c1± and 19...♘c6! 20 ♖xe8+ ♖xe8 21 d7 ♖f8 22 ♗xe6+ ♔h8 23 ♖c1 ♕e5 24 ♕d5⩲, while if 18...♘c6 White can play 19 ♖xg7+ ♔xg7 20 ♗xc6 bxc6 21 ♖c1! with a strong initiative. Black could try one more alternative: 18...♗xf7 19 ♗xf7+ ♔h8 20 ♗xe8 ♕xc3 with complicated play.

19 d7!!

The only move!

19...♘c6!

19...♘xd7? is weaker: 20 ♗xe6+ ♖xe6 21 ♕xd7+ ♔g8 22 ♕xe6+ ♔h8 23 ♖c1 h6 24 ♕h3±.

20 dxe8♕+ ♖xe8 21 ♗xe6+

21 ♕f3+? doesn't work after 21...♔g8 22 ♗xe6+ ♖xe6 23 ♖f1 ♘e5 24 ♕d5 ♕b6.

21...♖xe6 22 ♕d7+ ♘e7 23 ♖f1+ ♗f6 24 ♗xf6

Black is the only one with chances to win the endgame after 24 ♘d5? (Or 24 ♕d4? ♘f5) 24...♕f2! 25 ♕xe6+ ♔xe6 26 ♖xf2 ♗xg5.

24...♖xf6

When I originally analysed this position, I believed that White was winning here, but I had missed Black's simple defence after 25 ♖e1? ♕b4 26 a3 ♕d6∓. What a pity! White has nothing better than a perpetual check after:

25 ♖xf6+ ♔xf6 26 ♘e4+ ♔f7 27 ♘g5+ ♔f6 28 ♘xh7+ ♔f7 29 ♘g5+ ♔f6.

e4) Black can avoid all these complications by a more precise move order:

15...♕xb2! 16 ♘d5

16 ♘xe5!? works well after 16...♕xc3? 17 ♗xc4 ♕xe5 18 ♗xf7+ ♔h8 19 ♗xe8 ♕xg5! 20 ♖c1 ♗d7 21 ♖c7 with the advantage, but 16...♖xe5! 17 ♗d2 poses some problems for White and needs to be tested. Another interesting possibility is 16 ♖c1!?, when one nice variation runs 16...♘xf3 17 ♗xf3 ♗xc3 18 ♖b1! ♕xa2! 19 ♗d5 ♗f5 20 ♖xf5! gxf5 (20...♖e1+? 21 ♕xe1 ♗xe1 22 ♖xf7±) 21 ♗xf7+ ♔xf7 22 ♕h5+ ♔f8 23 ♗h6+ ♗g7 24 ♕xf5+ ♔g8 25 ♕d5+ (25 ♖f1 doesn't win because of 25...c3!) 25...♔h8 26 ♗xg7+ with a perpetual check.

16...♘xf3 17 ♗xf3

Not 17 ♖b1? ♕xe2! 18 ♘e7+ ♕xe7!∓.

17...♕xa1 18 ♕xa1 ♗xa1 19 ♖xa1 ♘d7!

The alternative 19...♖e5 is similar to line d with one exception. After 20 ♗f4 ♖xd5! 21 ♗xd5 ♘c6 White can play 22 ♗xc4 with compensation for the pawn. 19...♘d7! is more ambitious.

20 ♗e7 ♖b8 21 ♘c7 ♖f8 22 ♖e1 b5

We have arrived at the position studied in line d above with an important extra tempo for Black (...c5-c4). The question is now whether White can even hold a draw. The game Mayer-Anageldiev, USSR 1977, (reached by another move order) continued 23 ♗c6 c3 (23...b4!?) 24 ♗xb5? (24 ♘d5!) 24...c2! 25 ♖c1 ♗a6 26 a4 ♗xb5 27 axb5 ♖fc8 with a clear advantage for Black.

15 ♘d5

Black can quickly gain an advantage after 15 ♗b5?! ♘bc6 16 ♘xe5 ♖xe5 17 ♗c4 (17 a4) 17...♕xb2 18 ♖c1 ♗e6 19 ♗xe6 ♖xe6 20 ♕f3 ♖f8, Kouatly-Jadoul, Ostend 1984.

15 ... ♕xb2

16 ♘e7+

Nowadays Black has found good antidotes to this move, so it is White's turn to propose something new. Perhaps the clever 16 ♖c1, waiting for the queen's knight to move? After 16...♘bd7 the check 17 ♘e7+! is increased in strength, while if 16...♘c6 White simply plays 17 ♘c7, keeping his pawn on d6. Another try was not successful in the game Fang-Minasian, Philadelphia open 1991: 16 ♘h4? ♗c2 17 ♕d2 ♕d4+ 18 ♕xd4 cxd4 19 ♘c7 ♘bc6 20 ♗b5 ♗f8 and Black is better.

16 ... ♖xe7

This is much stronger than 16...♔h8?! 17 ♘xf5 gxf5.

17 dxe7

Only once has White tried the unhappy 17 ♗xe7?! After the reply 17...♘bc6 18 ♖c1 ♘xe7 19 dxe7 ♘xf3+ 20 ♗xf3 ♖e8 21 ♔h1 ♗d4 Black's strong bishops assure him of an advantage, Safin-Akopian, Yurmala 1985.

17 ... ♘bc6

The knight is better placed here than on d7.

18 ♖c1?!

White needs an improvement here:

a) 18 ♕e1? was refuted in the game Rechlis-Badea, Haifa 1989: 19...h6 19 ♗h4 g5! 20 ♗g3 ♕xa1! 21 ♕xa1 ♘xf3+ 22 ♗xf3 ♗xa1 23 ♖xa1 ♘xe7 24 ♗xb7 ♖d8 with a clear advantage for Black.

b) 18 ♔h1!? seems the best here, posing a nice trap:

b1) 18...♘xf3?! 19 ♗xf3 ♕xa1? 20 ♗xc6! (Nunn) 20...♕xd1 21 ♖xd1+- Ilic-Sandic, Yugoslavia 1989.

b2) The ambitious 18...h6 19 ♗h4 ♘g4?! met with a precise answer in the game Barsov-Arsovic, Budapest 1991: 20 ♕d6! ♘e3 (Or 20...♖e8!? 21 ♖ae1! ♗c3 22 ♕xc5 ♗xe1 23 ♖xe1 and the knight on g4 is in danger) 21 ♖fe1 c4 22 ♗f2 ♘c2 23 ♗xc4! ♘xe1 24 ♖xe1 ♕xf2 25 e8♕+ ♖xe8 26 ♖xe8+ ♔h7 27 ♗xf7 ♕f1+ 28 ♘g1 ♗d4 29 ♗g8+ 1-0.

b3) After 18...♖e8 White can play 19 ♘xe5 (19 ♖c1?! transposes to 18 ♖c1?! ♖e8 19 ♔h1 considered below) and now Black has tried:

b31) 19...♕xe5 20 ♗c4 ♗e6?! (20...♘xe7!?) 21 ♗xe6 ♕xe6 22 ♖b1 f6 23 ♖e1 ♘e5 24 ♖xb7! fxg5 25 ♕d8 ♔f7 26 ♖f1+ ♗f6 27 ♖b8± Guidi-Mauro, corr. 1984.

b32) 19...♗xe5 20 ♖c1 ♗d4 21 ♖xf5 gxf5 22 ♗c4 ♘e5?! (Possible is 22...♘xe7!?) 23 ♖b1! ♕f2? (23...♕a3 24 ♗b5! ♘c6 [24...♘g4? 25 ♕xg4!+-] 25 ♗a4!±) 24 ♕a4! ♘c6 25 ♗d5+- Moutousis-Cela, Zouberi Zonal 1993.

All these variations need further tests.

18 ... ♖e8

19 ♘xe5

After 19 ♔h1, as well as 19...♘xe7 20 ♘xe5 ♕xe5 21 ♗c4 ♘c6 22 ♕b3, Peev-Makropoulos, Bulgaria-Greece 1973, 22...♕c7!? 23 ♖ce1! with compensation, Black has the unpleasant resource 19...h6! 20 ♗h4 ♘g4! (Or 20...♘xe7 21 ♘xe5! ♕xe5 22 ♗b5 ♘c6 23 ♖e1 ♗e4 24 ♕d7, Peev-Sykora, Moscow 1977, and now the move 24...♖e6 would have been approximately equal) 21 ♖e1?! (21 ♕d2 ♕xd2 22 ♘xd2 ♘xe7 23 ♖xc5∓) 21...♖xe7! 22 ♖xc5 ♗f6 23 ♗xf6 ♕xf6 24 ♔g1 ♗e4!∓ 25 h3? ♕f4 26 ♕c1 ♕g3 0-1 Schoen-Safin, Germany 1995.

19 ... ♕xc5

20 ♗b5 ♗e6?!

My idea of 20...♗e4! was successfully tested by Marin against Barsov (Budapest open 1990). That game continued 21 ♗h4 (21 ♕d7 ♕d4+; 21 ♕b3!? ♗d5∓, Marin) 21...♕b2 22 ♕g4 ♗d4+ 23 ♔h1 f5 24 ♗c4+ ♔g7 25 ♕g3 ♘xe7 with a clear advantage for Black.

21 ♗xc6 ♕d4+!

A necessary intermediate check. 21...bxc6? loses after 22 ♕d8 ♕d4+ 23 ♔h1 ♕d7 24 ♖cd1 ♗d4 25 ♗f6! h6 26 ♖fe1! ♔h7! 27 ♖xe6 ♕xe6 28 ♗xd4 ♕xe7 29 ♕xe7 ♖xe7 30 ♗xc5.

22 ♔h1 bxc6

23 ♗e3 ♕xd1?!

23...♕xe3? 24 ♕d8 was bad, so the only move was 23...♕h4! with an unclear position.

24 ♖fxd1 ♗d4?

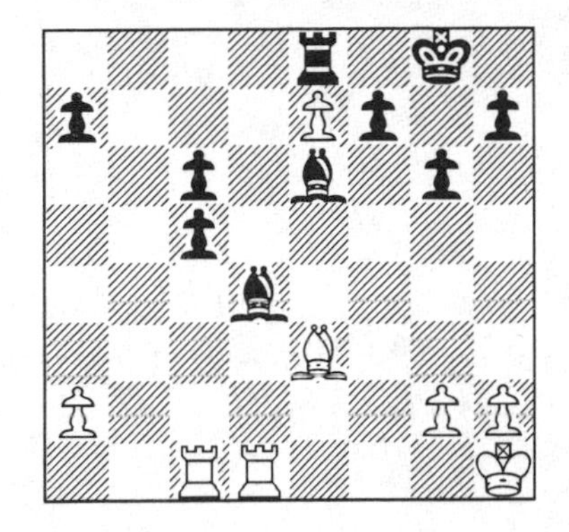

After 24...♗d5 25 ♗xc5 ♗f6 26 ♖e1 ♗e6 White has a slight plus but one which will be very difficult to convert into a win

25 ♖xc5! ♗xe3

Black loses quickly after 25...♗xc5? 26 ♖d8 ♗d7 27 ♗xc5, and more slowly after 25...♗f6 26 ♖d8! ♖xd8 27 exd8♕+ ♗xd8 28 ♖xc6.

26 ♖d8 ♗xc5

27 ♖xe8+ ♔g7

28 ♖g8+ ♔xg8

29 e8♕+ ♗f8

29...♔g7 would not have helped to save the a7-pawn after 30 ♕xc6 ♗b6 31 ♕c3+! ♔g8 32 a4.

30 a4 ♗b3?

Only active counterplay would have given Black any chances to save the game: 30...c5! 31 ♕a8 c4 32 ♕xa7 c3 33 ♕c7 ♗g7 34 a5 ♗f5 35 a6 c2 36 a7 ♗e4 37 ♕c8+ ♗f8.

31 a5! ♗c4

32 ♕xc6 ♗e2

33 a6 1-0

At last the a7-pawn falls (33...h5 34 ♕b7 ♗c5 35 ♕b8+ ♔h7 36 ♕e5 wins a bishop).

Game 3
Cranbourne-Crespo
corr. 1988-89

1 d4 ♘f6 2 c4 g6 3 ♘c3 ♗g7 4 e4 d6 5 f4 0-0 6 ♘f3 c5 7 d5 e6 8 ♗e2 exd5 9 cxd5 ♖e8 10 e5 dxe5 11 fxe5 ♘g4 12 ♗g5

12 ... f6?!

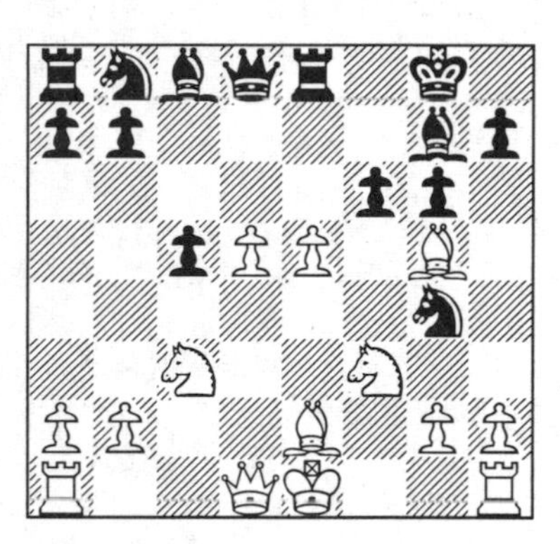

This move is certainly worse than 12...♕b6. Instead of trying to ride the storm of White's initiative with an extra pawn, Black will suffer for nothing.

13 exf6 ♗xf6
14 ♕d2!

Also possible are 14 ♗xf6 ♕xf6 15 0-0 ♘e3 16 ♕d2 ♘xf1 17 ♖xf1 ♗f5 and 14 ♗f4 c4 15 ♕d2 ♗f5 16 ♘d4 ♗xd4 17 ♕xd4 ♘c6 18 ♕c5 ♘ce5 19 0-0, Grivas-Fernandez, Sharjah 1985, with complicated play in both cases.

14 ... ♗f5

Black's problems are not resolved by other moves:

a) 14...b5 transposes to Game 11, Blokh-Kitchev.

b) 14...♘d7?! 15 0-0 ♘de5 16 ♗xf6 ♘xf6 (Or 16...♕xf6 17 ♘g5! ♕b6 18 ♘ge4 c4+ 19 ♔h1 ♗f5 20 d6! ♘d3, Peev-Donner, Cienfuegos 1973, and now according to Peev White could have won after 21 d7! ♖e5 22 ♗xg4 ♗xe4 23 ♖ae1! ♕d4 24 ♖xe4 ♖xe4 25 ♘xe4 ♕xe4 26 ♕g5! ♕d4 27 ♕e7!) 17 ♗b5! ♘xf3+ 18 ♖xf3 ♖f8 19 d6 ♗f5 20 ♖e1! with a large advantage, Arencibia-Salcedo, Bogota 1990.

c) 14...♘e5?! 15 0-0-0! ♘xf3 16 ♗xf6 ♘xd2 17 ♗xd8 ♖xd8 18 ♖xd2 with a clear advantage.

d) 14...♗xg5 15 ♕xg5 and now:

d1) 15...♕b6?! 16 0-0-0! ♘f2 17 d6 ♕d8 18 ♗c4+ ♔g7 19 ♕xc5 ♘xd1 20 ♖xd1 ♗f5 21 ♘d5 ♘c6 22 ♘c7 with a clear edge for White, Kuempers-Eitel, Bayern 1991.

d2) 15...♘e5 16 ♕xd8 (Even stronger is the move 16 0-0-0!?) 16...♘xf3+ 17 ♔f2 ♖xd8 18 ♗xf3 ♘d7 19 ♖he1 with a small but stable advantage for White, Vaisser-Levic, Vrnjacka Banja 1986.

d3) 15...♘e3 16 ♕xd8 ♖xd8 17 ♔f2 ♘g4+!? 18 ♔g3 ♘e3 19 ♖ae1 ♘f5+ 20 ♔f2 ♘d7 21 ♘e4 ♖f8 22 d6 with an unpleasant position for Black,

Forintos-Enklaar, Wijk aan Zee 1974.

d4) 15...♘a6 16 ♕xd8 ♖xd8 17 h3 ♘e3 18 ♔f2 ♘f5 19 ♗xa6!? bxa6 20 ♖ad1 ♖b8 21 b3 ♘d6 22 ♘e5 ♖f8+ 23 ♔g3 ♗f5 24 ♖he1± Forintos-Ghitescu, Wijk aan Zee 1974.

d5) 15...♗f5 16 ♕xd8 (Or 16 h3 ♘e5 17 ♕xd8 ♘xf3+ 18 ♔f2 ♖xd8 19 ♗xf3 ♘a6, and now instead of 20 g4?! ♗d3! 21 ♖he1 ♖d7 22 ♖e3 c4 23 ♖ae1 ♘c5 with equality, Gnichtel-Dobos, Budapest 1996, White should try 20 ♖ad1! with the idea of 20...c4 21 ♖d4! which promises an advantage for White) 16...♖xd8 17 h3 ♘f6 18 g4! ♗e4 19 g5 ♗xf3 20 ♗xf3 ♘e8 21 0-0 with a clear advantage, Krupkova-Peng, Kishinev Women's Interzonal 1995.

d6) 15...♕xg5 16 ♘xg5 and:

d61) 16...♘e3 17 ♔f2 (17 ♔d2!?) and now:

d611) 17...♘f5?! 18 ♗b5 (18 ♘e6!?) 18...♗d7 19 ♘e6 ♖c8 20 ♖ad1 a6 21 ♗e2± Kniest-Heck, Giessen open 1993.

d612) 17...♗f5?! 18 ♘e6!? (18 h3 h6?! 19 ♘f3 a6?! 20 g4 ♗d7 21 ♗d3 ♔g7 22 ♖ae1 1-0 was Vaisser-Khalafian, Yerevan 1996) 18...♗xe6 19 dxe6 ♖xe6? (19...♘c2±) 20 ♖ae1 ♘c6 21 ♗f3 ♖ae8 22 ♘e4+- Reinemer-Maniocha, Porz open 1993.

d613) 17...♘c2! 18 ♖ac1 (18 ♖ad1!? ♖f8+ 19 ♘f3) 18...♖f8+ 19 ♗f3 ♘d4!? (19...♘b4?! 20 ♖hd1 ♗f5 21 ♘e6 ♘d3+ 22 ♖xd3 ♗xd3 23 ♘xf8 ♔xf8 24 d6! ♘d7 25 ♖e1 ♖e8 26 ♖xe8+ ♔xe8 27 ♗xb7± Kahn-Balogh, Budapest 1993) 20 ♖he1 ♘a6 21 a3 ♗g4 22 ♔g3 ♗xf3 23 ♘xf3 ♖ad8 24 ♖e5± Dobos-Balogh, Budapest 1995.

d62) 16...♗f5 17 h3 (It would be interesting to try out 17 ♘e6!?) and now:

d621) 17...♘e3? 18 g4! h6! (Not 18...♗d7? 19 ♔d2! ♘g2 [19...♖e5 20 ♘ge4+- Vaisser-Arizanov, Pula open 1988] 20 ♖hf1 h6 21 ♘ge4 ♔g7 22 ♖f2 ♘h4 23 ♖af1 ♖e7 24 d6 1-0 Petursson-Blumberg, San Bernardino 1989) 19 ♘f3 ♗e4 20 ♘xe4 ♖xe4 21 ♔f2 ♘xd5 22 ♖hd1 ♘b6 23 ♖d6 ♔f7 24 ♗d3 ♖e6 25 ♗xg6+± Vegh-Metaxas, Iraklion 1992.

d622) 17...♘e5!? was played in Kakageldyev-Kapengut, Leningrad 1969. Here 18 0-0-0!? c4 19 ♘ge4 or 18 ♘ge4 would have kept a small plus for White.

15 0-0! ♗xg5

White was preparing 16 ♗f4, followed by h2-h3 and g2-g4, so this exchange seems logical. What happens if Black waits?

a) The old game Vaisser-Kaminnik, Rostov 1970, saw 15...♘a6?! 16 ♗f4! ♘b4 and now instead of 17 ♗b5?! c4! with counterplay, White should have continued 17 h3 ♘e5 18 ♘xe5 ♗xe5 19 ♗xe5 ♖xe5 20 g4 ♗d7 21 a3 ♘a6 22 ♕f4 with a clear edge.

b) 15...♘d7 16 ♗f4!, a move I proposed as an improvement to my game against Thipsay, Delhi 1987, where after 16 h3?! ♗xg5 17 ♘xg5 ♘e3 18 ♖xf5 ♘xf5 19 ♗b5! Black could have continued 19...♘d6!, when White can equalise only with precise play: 20 ♘e6 ♕e7 21 ♘c7 ♖ac8 22 ♘xe8 ♖xe8 23 a4! a6 24 ♗xd7 ♕xd7 25 ♕f2! My suggestion was checked in the game Arencibia-Paneque, Holguin (match) 1988, where after (16 ♗f4) 16...♘ge5 Arencibia has suggested 17 d6! ♘xf3+ 18 ♗xf3 ♗d4+ 19 ♔h1 ♘e5 20 ♗d5+ ♔h8 21 ♘b5 with a clear edge for White. Another good option for White is 16 ♗b5!? instead of 16 ♗f4.

16 ♕xg5?!

Here I want to bring to your attention some old analysis of mine, which I have kept under wraps for more than a quarter of a century:

16 ♘xg5! *♘e3 17 ♗b5!*

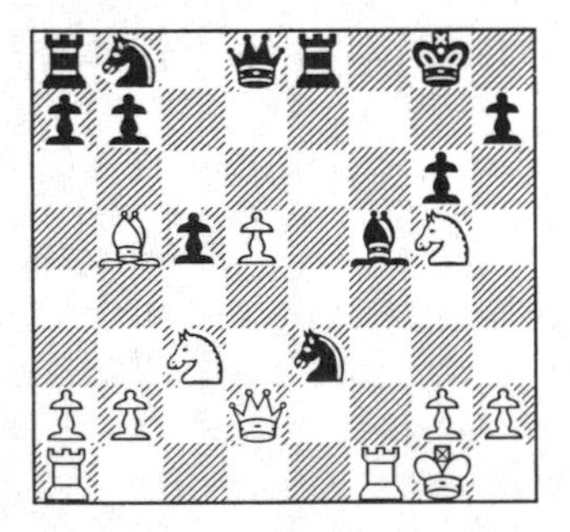

Also possible is 17 ♖xf5!? gxf5 18 ♘ce4! f4, as in Kret-Findlay, Toronto 1995, and now 19 ♕c3! would have assured a strong initiative.

17...♘xf1

White is better in the case of 17...♘d7 18 ♖xf5! ♘xf5 19 ♘e6 or 17...♖e5!? 18 ♘f3 ♘xf1 19 ♖xf1 ♖e7 20 d6.

18 ♖xf1

In return for the sacrificed exchange White has a strong attack.

18...♖f8

Other moves give White an advantage which is somewhere between clear and decisive:

a) 18...♘d7 19 d6!

b) 18...♗d7 19 d6!

c) 18...♘c6 19 g4! h6 (19...♗xg4 20 ♕f4) 20 gxf5 hxg5 21 f6 ♔f7 22 ♕xg5 a6 23 ♕h6.

d) 18...♖e5 19 ♕f4! ♕e7 20 ♘f3 ♖e4 21 ♘xe4 ♕xe4 22 ♕d6!

19 ♗c4!

White must be precise. 19 d6? spoils all the previous efforts: 19...♘c6! 20 ♕d5+ (Or 20 ♗c4+ ♔h8 21 ♘ce4 ♕a5! with enough play) 20...♔g7! 21 ♖xf5 ♖xf5 22 ♘e6+ ♔h8! 23 ♘xd8 ♖xd5 24 ♘xb7 ♘a5! 25 ♘xa5 ♖xd6 with an unclear position.

19...h6!

19...♘d7? 20 d6+ ♔h8 21 ♖e1! ♘f6 22 ♖e7 is desperate for Black, while White is also much better after 19...♕f6 20 d6+ ♔h8 21 ♘d5.

20 d6+ ♔g7 21 ♖xf5 hxg5 22 ♖xc5 ♘c6 23 ♘e4

With one (and soon a second) pawn for the exchange and a powerful attack White is clearly better.

16 ... ♕xg5?!

Black has two alternatives:

a) 16...♘e3? is not good: 17 ♕h6! ♕e7 (If 17...♘xf1 18 ♘g5 ♕e7 19 ♖xf1 ♕g7 20 ♕xg7+ ♔xg7 21 g4 and, even without queens, the attack continues) 18 ♗b5! ♗d7? (better is 18...♘d7, but still not good enough) 19 ♖ae1 ♗xb5 20 ♘xb5 ♘a6 21 ♘g5 and White won, Peev-Janosevic, Nis 1972.

b) The best option is 16...♘d7 17 h3 (17 ♗b5!?) 17...♘e3 18 ♕h6 ♘xf1 19 ♘g5 ♕e7 20 d6 and Black now has a choice between perpetual check with 20...♕g7 21 ♗c4+ ♔h8 22 ♘f7+ and a complicated and risky continuation 20...♕e3+ 21 ♔xf1 ♘f8 22 ♖d1 ♖ad8!, Schrammel-Zsu. Polgar, Fonyod 1983.

17 ♘xg5 ♘e3
18 ♗b5! ♖d8?

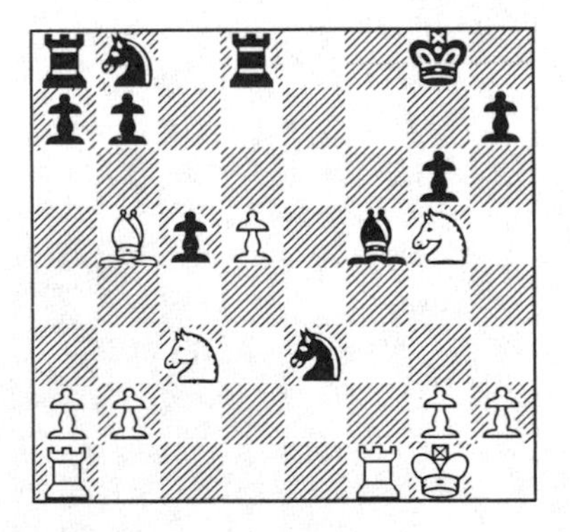

18...♖f8!? 19 ♖f2 a6 was necessary in order to minimise White's advantage. Now White sacrifices a whole rook and starts a terrible attack. The end of the game is a splendid and thematic illustration of the enormous strength of White's pieces in harmony with the passed d-pawn.

19 ♖fe1!! ♘c2
20 ♖e7! a6

Nothing can save Black:

a) 20...♘xa1 21 g4! ♗c2 22 ♗c4 ♖d7 23 d6+ ♔h8 24 ♖e8+ ♔g7 25 ♘e6+.

b) 20...h6 21 ♖f1 hxg5 22 g4 a6 23 ♗a4!

c) 20...♘d7 21 ♖f1 ♘f6 22 ♗c4.

White has a decisive advantage in all three cases.

21 ♗c4 b5
22 ♖f1 bxc4
23 g4! ♘e3

Otherwise:

a) 23...♗xg4 24 ♖ff7 ♗f5 25 ♖g7+ ♔h8 26 ♖xh7+ ♔g8 27 ♘ce4 ♘d7 28 ♘e6 winning.

b) 23...h6 24 ♘h7! ♗xg4 25 ♖ff7 ♘d7 26 ♘e4 mating.

c) 23...♘d4 24 gxf5 gxf5 25 ♘xh7 winning.

24 gxf5! ♘xf5

Or 24...♘xf1 25 f6 ♖f8 26 ♖g7+ ♔h8 27 ♖xh7+ ♔g8 28 f7+ ♖xf7 29 ♖xf7 ♘e3 30 h3! and wins.

25 ♖c7! ♘d7
26 ♘ce4! ♘f8
27 ♘f6+ ♔h8
28 ♖xf5! gxf5

29 ♘e6 ♖d6?

This accelerates the inevitable end.

30 ♖g7 1-0

Game 4
Lagontrie-Boulard
French Corr. Ch. 1987

1 d4 ♘f6 2 c4 g6 3 ♘c3 ♗g7 4 e4 d6 5 f4 0-0 6 ♘f3 c5 7 d5 e6 8 ♗e2 exd5 9 cxd5 ♖e8 10 e5 dxe5 11 fxe5 ♘g4

12 0-0

12 ♗f4 ♘xe5 13 0-0 reaches thc game continuation via a transposition of moves.

Another interesting and little explored idea for White is

12 e6 fxe6 13 d6!?

13 0-0 has proved to be less promising: 13...exd5! 14 ♘xd5 (Or 14 ♗g5 ♕d6! 15 h3 ♘f6 16 ♗xf6 ♗xf6 17 ♘xd5 ♔h8 18 ♘xf6 ♕xf6 19 ♗b5 ♘c6 20 ♕c2 ♗f5 with pleasant equality for Black, Klompus-Waagmeester, corr. 1990) 14...♗e6 15 ♘f4 (White's show of aggression 15 ♗c4 ♘c6 16 ♗g5 ♘f6 17 ♘e5, as in Kotov-Burechell, Stockholm 1959, fails to 17...♘xe5! 18 ♗xf6 ♘xc4 19 ♗xd8 ♖axd8 20 ♘e7+ ♔h8 21 ♘xg6+ hxg6 and Black's three pieces are stronger than the queen) 15...♕xd1 16 ♖xd1 ♗f7 17 ♘g5 ♘e5, Khodos-Portisch, Lipetsk 1968, and now instead of 18 ♗e3? ♗c4! White could have achieved some compensation for the pawn with 18 ♘xf7 ♘xf7 19 ♗c4.

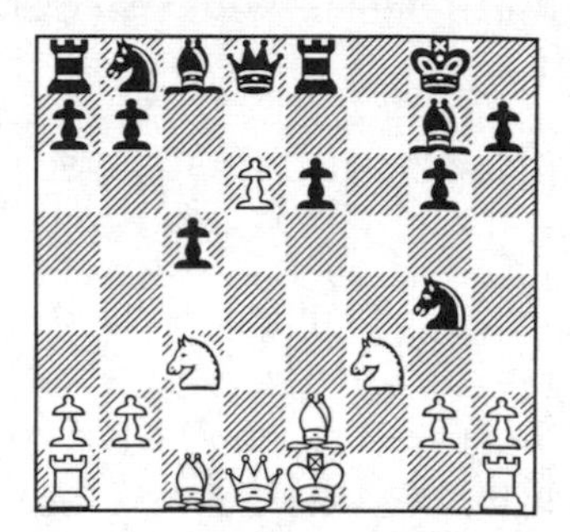

13...♗d7

Several other moves have also been tried here:

a) 13...♘e5 (13...a6 14 a4!?; 13...♖f8!?) 14 0-0 (14 ♘e4!?) 14...♘xf3+ 15 ♗xf3 ♗d4+ 16 ♔h1 ♕xd6 17 ♘b5 ♕d7 18 ♘xd4 cxd4 19 ♗h6 ♘c6 20 ♖c1 ♕d6 21 ♕b3 ♗d7 22 ♕xb7 ♖ac8 23 ♕a6 e5 24 ♗e4 with rich play for only one pawn, Berkovich-A. Kuzmin, Moscow 1981.

b) Two examples after the move 13...♘c6:

b1) 14 ♘g5 ♘h6 15 0-0 ♘f5 16 ♘ge4 h6 17 ♘b5 ♖f8 18 ♘c7 ♖b8 19 ♗c4 ♘cd4 20 ♘xc5 ♕xd6 21 ♘5xe6 ♗xe6 22 ♘xe6 ♕c6! 23 ♘xg7+! ♔xg7 24 ♗d3± Vasilchenko-Kovalev, Katowice 1990.

b2) 14 0-0 ♗d7 15 ♘e4 ♕b6 16 ♘fg5 c4+ 17 ♔h1 ♘e3 18 ♗xe3 ♕xe3 19 ♖f3 ♕d4 20 ♕e1 ♖f8 (If 20...h6?! 21 ♖d1 ♕e5 22 ♕h4! ♘d4 23 ♖xd4! ♕xd4 24 ♘f7 with a strong attack) 21 ♖d1 ♕e5 22 ♗xc4 h6

23 ♖xf8+ ♖xf8 24 ♘f3± Michaelsen-Uhlmann, German Bundesliga 1995.

c) 13...♕b6 14 ♘g5 ♘e5 15 0-0 ♘bc6 16 ♘ge4 (16 ♕e1!? ♘d4 17 ♕h4 h6 18 ♘ge4 ♘f5 19 ♕h3 looks reasonable for White) 16...♘d4 17 ♘a4?! ♕c6 18 ♘axc5 b6 19 ♕xd4! (Probably not quite correct, but amusing) 19...♘f3+ 20 ♗xf3 ♗xd4+ 21 ♔h1 ♕b5 22 ♗e3 ♗g7? (22...♗xe3!?) 23 a4! ♕xb2 24 d7 ♗xd7 25 ♘xd7 ♖ed8 26 ♖ab1 ♕a3 27 ♘ef6+ ♔h8 28 ♗xa8 ♖xa8 29 ♗d4 ♕xa4 30 ♖f4 ♖d8 31 ♗e5 ♕a5 32 ♖bf1 ♕d2 33 ♘e8 ♔g8 34 ♖f8+ 1-0 Bach-Watzke, Dresden 1996.

14 ♘g5 ♘e5 15 0-0 ♗c6 16 ♗f4 ♘bd7 17 ♕e1 h6

Black tried another plan in the game Bach-Schoene, RLNN 1990: 17...c4!? 18 ♔h1 b5 19 ♕g3 b4 20 ♕h3 (A typical manoeuvre of the white queen) 20...♘f8 21 ♘ce4 ♗xe4 22 ♘xe4 ♕a5 23 ♘g5! h6 24 ♘e4 ♕d5 25 ♕e3 ♘fd7 26 ♖ad1 with complicated play not unfavourable to White.

18 ♘ge4 a6 19 a4

Now instead of 19...♖b8?! 20 ♕g3 b5?! 21 axb5 axb5 22 ♗xe5! ♘xe5 23 ♖a7 ♗d7 24 ♗xb5! c4 25 ♖c7 with a big advantage for White, Michaelsen-Holzer, Oberwart open 1992, it was better to give back a pawn immediately: 19...b5!? 20 axb5 axb5 21 ♖xa8 ♕xa8 22 ♗xe5! ♗xe5 23 ♗xb5, when equality is not far off.

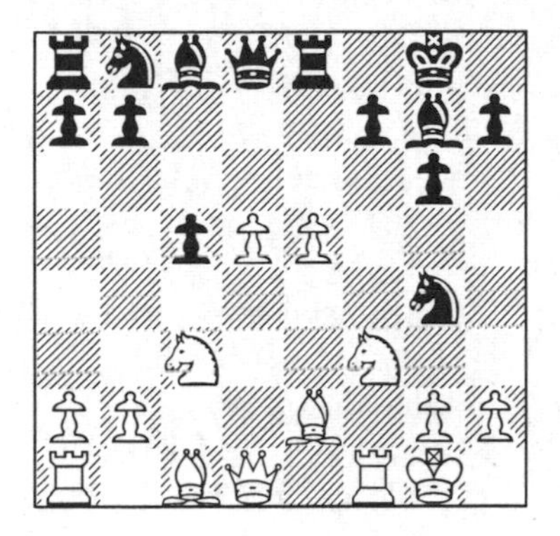

12 ... ♘xe5

12...♗f5?! allows a transposition to the game Semkov-Apicella in the line 12 ♗g5 ♕b6 13 0-0 ♗f5 after 13 ♗g5! (13 ♗b5!?) 13...♕b6 14 ♘h4, with an advantage for White.

13 ♗f4 ♘bd7

Instead of this solid move, Black can play:

a) 13...a6?! is original, but looks suspicious, e.g. 14 ♕d2 ♘bd7 15 d6 b5 16 ♘d5 ♖a7, Ellenbroek-Legemaat, Enschede 1995.

b) 13...♘xf3+ 14 ♗xf3 may transpose to 13...♘bd7 after 14...♘d7. Less well founded is 14...♕f6?! 15 ♗g3! ♘d7 16 d6 ♖b8 17 ♔h1 and Black's queen is obliged to go home: 17...♕d8 with a good position for White.

c) 13...♕b6 may also transpose to 13...♘bd7 after 14 d6 ♘bd7. A difference arises if Black takes the b2-pawn as in the main line 14 d6 (Game 2).

The position of White's bishop on f4 instead of g5 is in White's favour in the variation 14...♕xb2 15 ♘d5 ♘xf3+ 16 ♗xf3 ♕d4+ 17 ♔h1 ♕xa1 18 ♕xa1 ♗xa1 19 ♖xa1, as Black has no good defence to the twin threats of 20 ♘c7 and 20 ♘f6+.

d) 13...♗f5!?

This move seems to be the best here. It is natural to develop the bishop first.

14 ♘xe5 ♗xe5 15 ♕d2

The old game Chacet-Murey, Moscow 1960, saw instead 15 ♗xe5!? ♖xe5 16 ♕d2 ♘d7 17 ♖ad1 (If 17 g4 ♗xg4! 18 ♗xg4 ♖g5 19 h3 f5 winning the second pawn). Now instead of 17...♕b6? 18 g4 ♗e4 19 ♗b5! c4+ 20 ♖f2 ♗f3 21 ♗xd7 ♗xd1 22 ♕xd1 with a clear advantage for White, Black should have played 17...h5!, preventing 18 g4, with the better chances.

15...♘d7 16 ♖ad1

Perhaps it was time to exchange bishops with 16 ♗xe5!?

16...a6

16...♗d4+!? 17 ♔h1 a6 18 g4 ♗xc3 19 bxc3 ♗e4+ looks satisfactory for Black

17 ♗xe5 ♘xe5 18 ♕f4 c4 19 g4!

The game Vaisser-Renet, Brussels Zonal 1993, continued 19...♕b6+ 20 ♔h1 (20 ♖f2!?) 20...♗d3? (20...♕xb2!?) 21 ♗xd3 ♘xd3 22 ♕xf7+ ♔h8 23 ♖d2 with an advantage for White, thanks to the strong passed d-pawn.

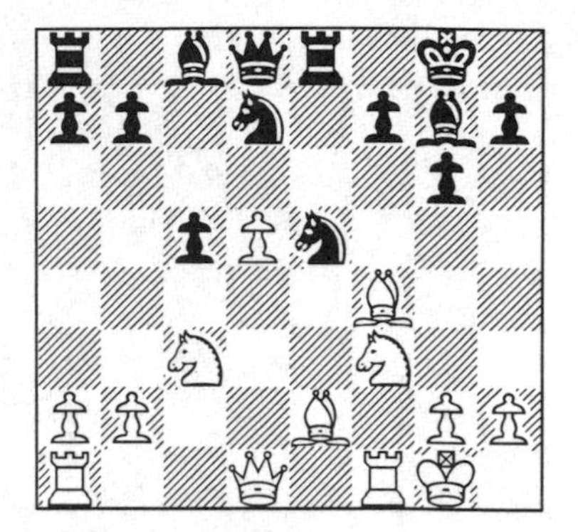

14 d6

Taking into account the problems that White met in the game S. Ivanov-Shulman (see commentary to the next move), Belov has proposed 14 ♗b5!? ♕b6 (stronger is 14...a6!) 15 ♘xe5 ♗xe5 16 ♗xe5 ♖xe5 17 ♕f3 ♖f5 18 ♕e2 with a draw by repetition of moves.

14 ... ♘xf3+

Let us see what happens if Black tries to vary:

a) 14...♖b8 15 ♘d5 b5 16 ♘c7! ♖f8 17 ♘xe5 ♘xe5 18 ♕d5 is slightly better for White.

b) 14...a6?! 15 ♘d5 ♖f8 16 ♘g5 ♘c6?! 17 ♗c4 b5?

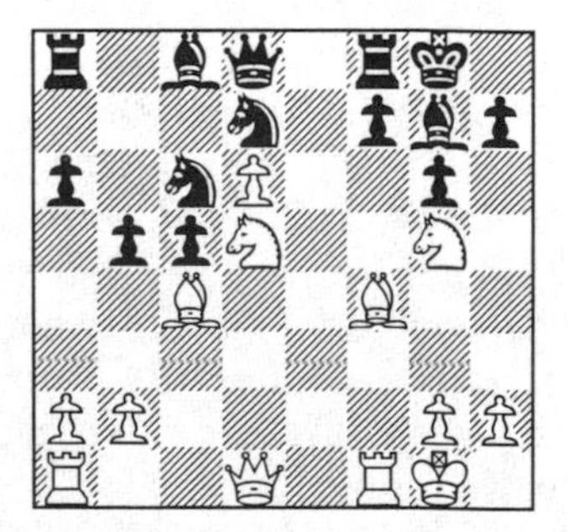

runs into 18 ♘xf7! ♖xf7 19 ♘e7+ ♘xe7 20 ♗xf7+ ♔xf7 21 dxe7 ♗d4+ 22 ♕xd4! ♕xe7 23 ♗g5+ 1-0 Alcock-Fayne, corr. 1990.

c) 14...♕b6!?

This move, which was considered for a long time to be incorrect, was rehabilitated in the game S. Ivanov-Shulman, Minsk 1995, which continued: 15 ♘xe5? ♘xe5! 16 ♗xe5?! (Belov suggested as an improvement now or one move earlier 16 ♘d5!? ♕xd6 17 ♗g5 ♕c6 18 ♘e7+ ♖xe7 19 ♗xe7 ♗f5 with an unclear position. In fact I prefer Black here) 16...♖xe5 17 d7 ♗xd7 18 ♕xd7 ♕xb2. The point! White cannot keep his extra piece and finds himself in a difficult position. Now instead of 19 ♖ac1? ♖f5! with a winning position for Black, it would have been better to play 19 ♕xf7+ ♔h8 20 ♗f3 ♕xc3 21 ♕xb7 ♖ae8, although Black keeps an edge because the a7-pawn is untouchable (22 ♕xa7?? ♕d4+ 23 ♕xa1!-+).

An answer, from White's viewpoint, to the Shulman challenge was given in the game Vaisser-Nataf, French Team Ch. 1997 (added as this book was going to press):

15 ♗b5!

(see following diagram)

Here Black again has a choice:

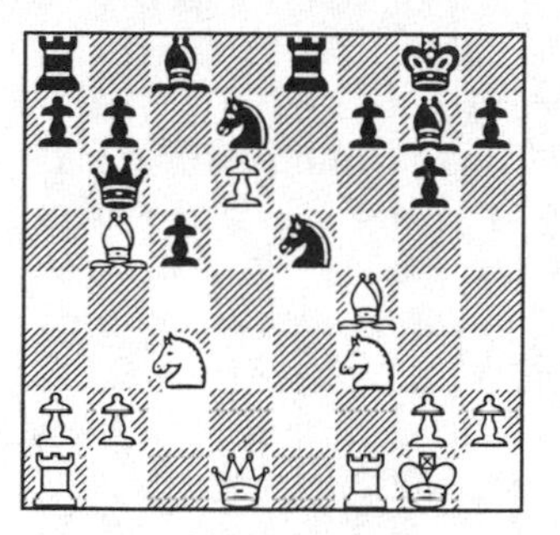

c1) Accepting the sacrifice 15...♘xf3+? 16 ♕xf3 ♗d4+ (or immediately 16...♗xc3) 17 ♔h1 ♗xc3 18 ♕xc3 ♕xb5 gives White a decisive attack: 19 ♖fe1! ♖f8 (No help is offered by 19...♖xe1+ 20 ♖xe1 ♘f8 21 ♗h6 ♘e6 22 ♕f6 ♕d3 23 ♕d8+! mating) 20 ♗h6 f6 21 ♗xf8 ♔xf8 22 ♕h3! h5 23 ♕e6 ♔g7 24 ♕e8 ♕xb2 25 ♖e7+ ♔h6 26 h4! winning.

c2) White is also clearly better after 15...♖f8?! 16 a4! c4+ 17 ♔h1 ♘d3 18 ♗g3 ♘xb2 19 ♕c2 ♕a5 20 ♘d5 a6 21 ♗e1 c3 22 ♗xc3 ♗xc3 23 ♘xc3 axb5 24 ♕xb2 b4 25 ♘e4.

c3) Black again runs into problems after 15...a6?! 16 ♗xe5 ♗xe5 (16...axb5? 17 ♘d5) 17 ♗xd7 ♗xd7 18 ♘d5.

c4) 15...c4+! 16 ♔h1 ♘d3 17 ♗xc4! ♘xf4 18 ♘g5

18 ♗xf7+ was a very interesting alternative: 18...♔xf7 19 ♘g5+ ♔g8 20 ♖xf4 ♘f6! (The only defence, but one which allows Black to hold a draw. Others are weaker: 20...h6? 21 ♘d5! ♕c5 [21...♕xd6 22 ♕b3!]

22 ♖c1 ♖e1+ 23 ♕xe1 ♕xd5 24 ♕e8+ ♘f8 25 ♖xf8+ ♗xf8 26 ♕xg6+ ♗g7 27 ♕h7+ ♔f8 28 ♖f1+ winning; 20...♘c5?! 21 ♘a4! ♘xa4 22 ♕d5+ ♗e6 23 ♘xe6 ♕c6 [23...♗xb2? 24 ♘g5+ ♔h8 25 ♕f7 ♗g7 26 ♖h4+-] 24 ♕xc6 bxc6 25 ♘xg7 with an advantage in the endgame; and 20...♘f8?! 21 ♕d5+! ♗e6 22 ♖xf8+ ♖xf8 23 ♕xe6+ ♔h8 24 ♘f7+ ♖xf7 25 ♕xf7 with a slight plus for White, for example 25...♕xb2 26 ♖d1! ♖f8 27 ♕e7 ♕b4 28 h3 and the pawn on d6 is very annoying) 21 ♘d5! (21 ♖xf6? doesn't work due to 21...♗xf6 22 ♕d5+ ♗e6! 23 ♘xe6 ♕xb2! 24 ♖f1 ♕xc3 and White's initiative doesn't compensate for the material losses) 21...♕xb2 22 ♘e7+ (In the case of 22 ♖b1 ♘xd5!? 23 ♖xb2 ♘xf4 24 ♕b3+ ♗e6 25 ♘xe6 ♔h8! 26 ♖f2 ♖xe6 Black has more than enough compensation for a queen) 22...♖xe7 23 dxe7 ♗d7 24 ♖b1 (Black is better after 24 ♖d4? ♗c6! 25 ♖d2 ♕b5 26 ♖d8+ ♘e8) 24...♕e5! 25 ♖d4! ♕xe7 (25...♕xg5? 26 ♖xd7 ♖e8 27 ♕b3+ ♔h8 28 ♕f7 ♕f5 29 ♖bd1 ♕b5 30 ♖d8 is winning for White) 26 ♕b3+ ♔h8 (26...♔f8?! is dangerous for Black: 27 ♖xd7! ♕xd7 28 ♘e6+ ♔e7 29 ♘xg7 ♖c8 30 ♖d1 ♘d5! 31 ♕f3! with an attack) 27 ♘f7+ ♔g8 28 ♘g5+ with a draw by a perpetual check.

18...♘e5!

White has a strong attack after either 18...♘e6?! 19 ♖xf7 ♘xg5 20 ♖e7+ ♔f8 21 ♕d5 or 18...♕xb2 19 ♖xf4! ♕xc3 20 ♗xf7+ ♔h8 21 ♖h4.

19 ♖xf4 ♘xc4

A very complicated position arises after 19...♕xb2 20 ♖xf7! ♔h8!

20 ♖xc4 h6!

Now the best was 21 ♘d5! ♕xd6 22 ♘c7 ♕xd1+ 23 ♖xd1 hxg5 24 ♘xe8 ♗e6 25 ♘c7 ♖c8 26 ♘xe6 ♖xc4 27 ♖d8+ ♔h7 28 ♘xg5+ ♔h6 29 ♘xf7+ with an ending which is slightly more pleasant for White.

15 ♗xf3 ♘e5

15...♗d4+?! 16 ♔h1 ♘e5 is less precise because of 17 ♘b5! (17 ♗d5!?) 17...♘xf3 18 ♕xf3 ♗f5 (18...♗d7 19 ♘xd4 cxd4 20 ♗g5!±) 19 ♘c7 ♗xb2 20 ♘xe8 ♗xa1 21 ♘c7 with the advantage.

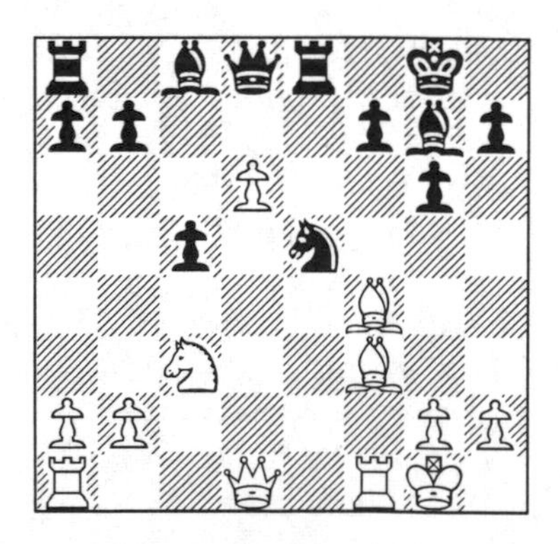

16 ♘b5!?

This is stronger than 16 ♗d5?! ♗e6 17 ♘e4 c4! with

good counterplay.

16 ... ♖f8

The alternatives are unpleasant for Black:

a) 16...♘xf3+?! 17 ♕xf3 ♖f8 18 ♘c7 ♖b8 19 ♖ae1, Destrebecq-Garabedjan, St Etienne 1980, transposes to the position considered below with a rook on f1 instead of a1, a difference that favours White.

b) White is better after 16...c4?! 17 ♘c7 ♘d3 18 ♘xe8 ♕xe8 19 ♗g3.

c) Black cannot be satisfied with 16...♗f5?! 17 ♘c7 ♘xf3+ (17...♘d3!?) 18 ♕xf3 ♗xb2 19 ♘xe8 ♗xa1 20 ♘c7 ♗d4+ 21 ♗e3 ♖c8 22 ♗xd4 cxd4 (22...♕xd6 23 ♘b5 ♕b6 24 ♗a1 ♕xb5 25 ♕c3+-) 23 ♕f4 and White has a large advantage, Szabo-Zuckermann, Las Vegas 1973.

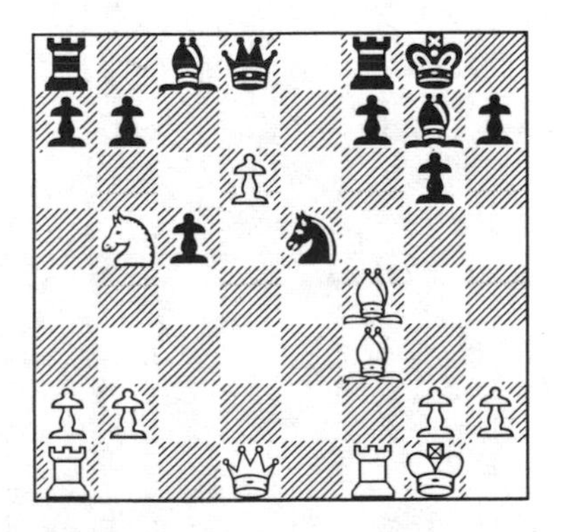

17 ♘c7 ♖b8
18 ♖e1 ♘c6!

The most accurate move. Black can also try:

a) 18...♘xf3+?! 19 ♕xf3 ♕f6 20 ♘e8! ♕d4+ 21 ♗e3 ♕xb2 22 ♖ab1 ♕c3 23 ♘xg7 ♕xg7, Balogh-Ribli, Budapest 1972, when despite Black's extra pawn, White is slightly better.

b) A very unusual and unclear position arises after

18...♘c4!? 19 b3!? ♗d4+ 20 ♕xd4 cxd4 21 bxc4

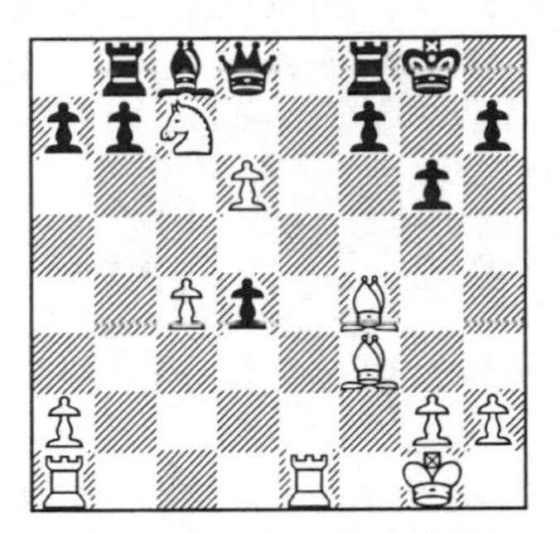

Who is better? A very good question! Now let us return to 18...♘c6!

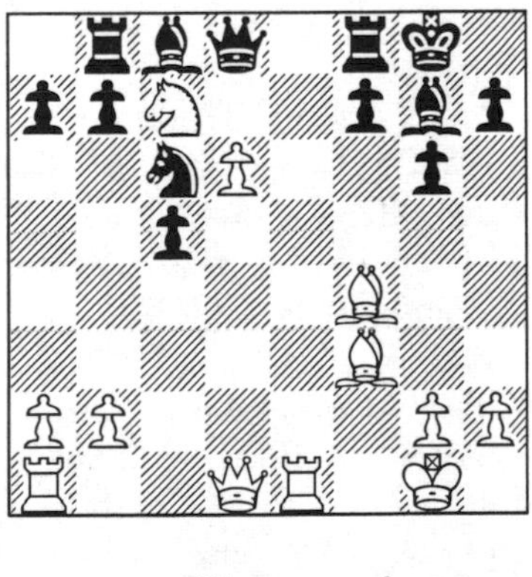

19 ♖e7! ♗xb2
20 ♗xc6 bxc6
21 ♕e1 ♗f5?!

This is the critical moment of the game:

a) After 21...♗xa1? White

wins, e.g. 22 ♕xa1 f6 (22...♗f5 23 ♕f6!+-) 23 a3! ♗f5 24 ♕a2+ ♔h8 25 ♗h6 ♖g8 26 ♕f7 ♖b1+ 27 ♔f2 ♖b2+ 28 ♔f3 ♖b3+ 29 ♗e3.

b) After 21...♗d4+ 22 ♔f1! (22 ♔h1? ♗xa1 23 ♕xa1 ♗f5-+) 22...♖b2 23 ♖d1 ♖f2+ 24 ♕xf2 ♗xf2 25 ♔xf2 White keeps the initiative in a complicated position.

c) 21...♖b4!

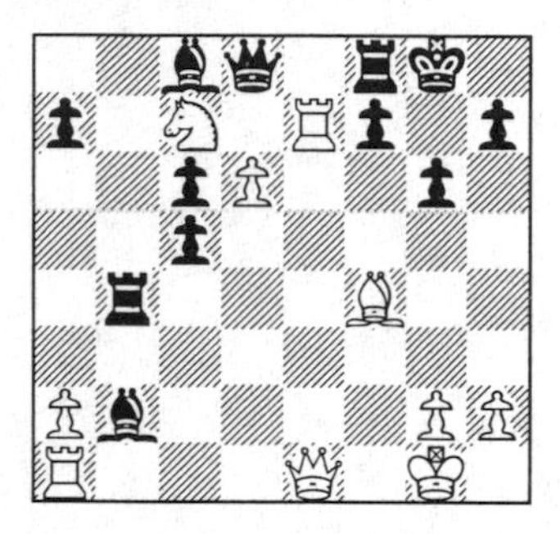

According to Boulard this move allows Black to draw.

22 ♗e5

Not 22 ♗h6? ♕xd6 23 ♗xf8 ♔xf8 24 ♖e8+ ♔g7 25 ♖xc8 ♕d4+ 26 ♔h1 ♗xa1 27 ♘e8+ ♔h6 28 ♕c1+ ♕f4 29 ♕xa1 ♖c4 and Black wins.

22...♗xa1 23 ♕xa1

The same result follows 23 ♗xa1 ♕xd6 24 ♘e8 ♕xe7! 25 ♕xe7 ♖b1+ 26 ♔f2 ♖xa1 27 ♘f6+ ♔g7 28 ♘h5+.

23...♗f5 24 ♕c3

This is more precise than 23 ♔f2.

24...♖e4 25 ♗h8 f6 26 ♗xf6 ♕xd6 27 ♖g7+ ♔h8 28 ♖f7+

with a perpetual check. The endgame after 28 ♖xg6+?! ♖xf6 29 ♕xf6+ ♕xf6 30 ♖xf6 is certainly not better for White.

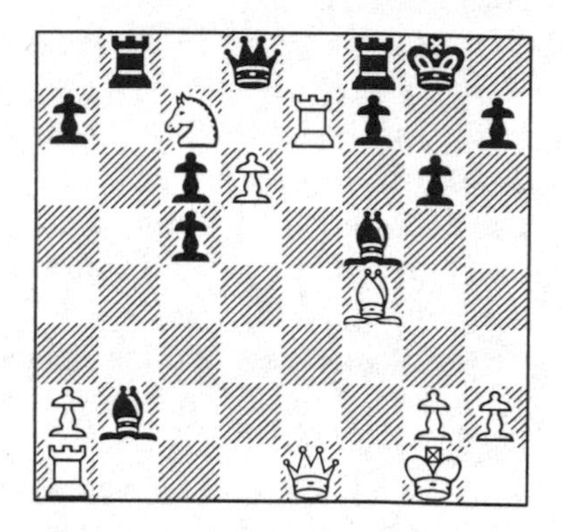

22	**♖d1**	**♗d4+**
23	**♔h1**	**♖b2**
24	**♗e5**	**♗f2**

24...♕b8? 25 ♘e8! winning.

25	**♕a5**	

25 ♕c3? ♖c2 26 ♕f3 ♗h4 turns the game in Black's favour.

25	**...**	**♗g4**
26	**♗xb2**	**♗xd1**
27	**♗e5**	**♗g4**
28	**♕d2**	**♗d4**
29	**♕f4**	**♕c8**

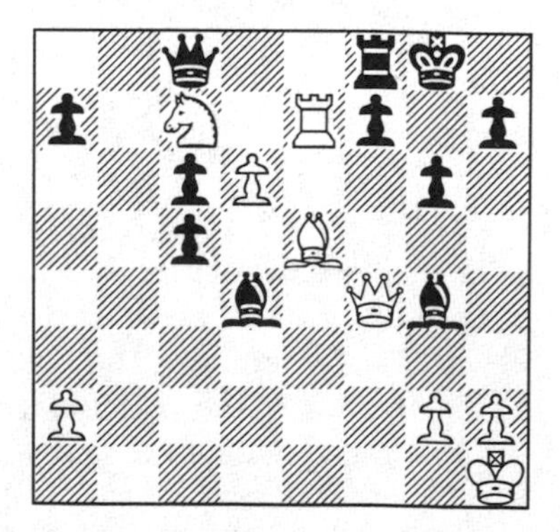

30 ♘e8?

This allows Black to achieve a theoretical draw by sacrificing his queen. 30 ♗xd4! cxd4 31 h3 would have retained some winning chances.

30...♕xe8 31 ♖xe8 ♖xe8 32 ♗xd4 cxd4 33 h3 ♗e6 34 ♕xd4 ♗xa2 35 ♕xa7 ♗e6 36 ♕c7 g5 37 d7 ♗xd7 38 ♕xd7 ♖e1+ 39 ♔h2 h6 40 ♕xc6 ♖e6 41 ♕d5 ♔g7 42 ♔g3 ♖g6 43 ♔g4 ♖e6 44 ♕d4+ ½-½

Game 5
Vaisser-Ibragimov
Bern 1992

1 d4 ♘f6 2 c4 g6 3 ♘c3 ♗g7 4 e4 d6 5 f4 0-0 6 ♘f3 c5 7 d5 e6 8 ♗e2 exd5 9 cxd5 ♖e8

10 ♘d2

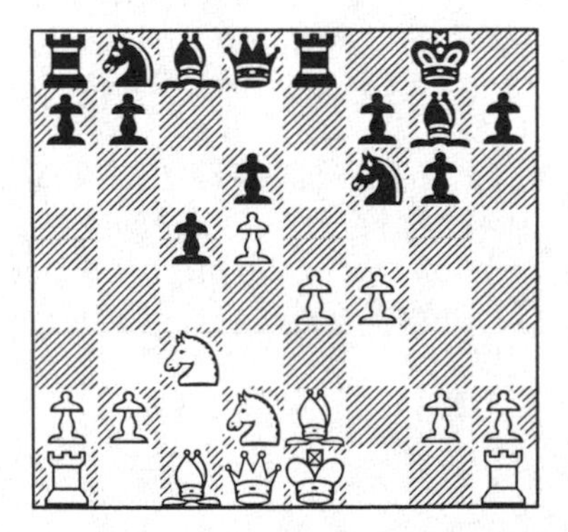

If White is not ready for the enormous complications that arise after 10 e5 then he can opt for the quieter but no less dangerous 10 ♘d2. White's overall plan is first to finish his development and then to prepare e4-e5.

10 ... ♘a6

Black has no less than five plausible alternatives:

a) The rare 10...♘g4?! does not seem good enough for equality after 11 ♗xg4 and now:

a1) 11...♗xc3?! 12 bxc3 ♕h4+ 13 g3 ♕xg4 14 ♕xg4 ♗xg4 15 ♔f2

Not 15 ♖b1?! ♘d7!

15...f5 16 ♖e1 ♘d7 17 c4 ♖e7

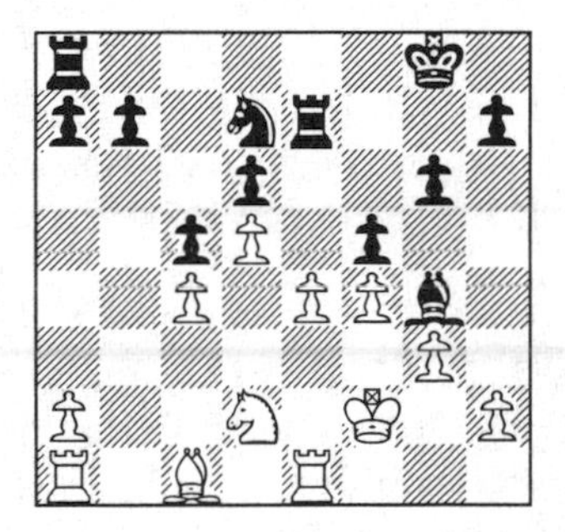

and now instead of 18 ♖b1?! ♖ae8 19 ♖xb7 fxe4 20 ♖e3 (20 ♘f1 ♘e5!) 20...♗f5 with equality, Christiansen-Ghitescu, Thessaloniki Olympiad 1984, it would have been better to play ***18 ♗b2!*** ♖ae8 19 ♖e3 fxe4 20 ♖ae1 ♗f5 (White is winning after 20...♘b6? 21 ♘xe4 ♘xc4 22 ♘f6+ ♔f7 23 ♘xe8 ♖xe3 24 ♘xd6+ ♘xd6 25 ♖xe3) 21 g4! ♗xg4 22 ♘xe4 ♔f8 23 ♘xd6 ♖xe3 24 ♖xe3 ♖xe3 25 ♔xe3 and White has an advantage in the ending.

a2) 11...♕h4+ 12 g3 ♕xg4

13 ♕xg4 ♗xg4 14 ♘b5 (14 ♔f2!?) 14...♘a6! 15 ♘xd6 (After 15 h3?! ♖xe4+! 16 ♘xe4 ♗f3 17 0-0 ♗xe4 18 ♘c3 ♗d3 19 ♖f3 ♘b4 20 ♗d2 ♗d4+ 21 ♔h2 ♗c4 Black has more than enough compensation, Panchius-Liberzon, Israel 1983) 15...♘b4 and in this position White has tried:

a21) 16 ♘xe8?! ♘c2+ 17 ♔f1 ♗h3+ 18 ♔e2 ♖xe8 19 ♖b1 and Black has an initiative that guarantees at least a perpetual, e.g. 19...♗g4+ 20 ♔f1 ♗h3+ 21 ♔e2 ♗g4+ 22 ♔d3 ♘b4+ 23 ♔c4 ♗e2+ 24 ♔b3 ♗d3 25 ♖a1 ♗c2+ (25...♘c2!? 26 ♖b1 ♘d4+ 27 ♔c3 ♗xb1 28 ♘xb1 ♖xe4∓) 26 ♔c4 ♗d3+.

a22) 16 0-0?! ♘c2 17 ♘xe8 ♗d4+ 18 ♔h1 ♖xe8 19 ♖b1 ♗e2 20 e5, Peicheva Juergens-Nickl, Dortmund 1993, and now Black could have obtained a good position with 20...♗xf1 21 ♘xf1 ♖d8 22 d6 f6.

a23) I recommend the improvement ***16 h3!***, which gives an advantage to White.

b) The inclusion of the moves

10...a6?! 11 a4

weakens the important b6-square and cannot be recommended for Black. If Black forces the sequence …a7-a6, a2-a4 early in the Classical lines of the Modern Benoni then the best solution for White is to transpose to this line of Four Pawns Attack. Take a look at the way I was trapped by Yrjola, Sochi 1994: 1 d4 ♘f6 2 c4 e6 3 ♘f3 c5 4 d5 exd5 5 cxd5 d6 6 ♘c3 a6?! 7 a4 g6 8 ♘d2! ♘bd7 9 e4 ♗g7 10 ♗e2 0-0 11 0-0 ♖e8 12 f4! and we arrived at the position of variation b2.

b1) 11...♘g4 12 ♘c4! (This is better than 12 ♗xg4?! ♕h4+ 13 g3 ♕xg4 14 ♕xg4 ♗xg4 15 ♔f2 ♗d4+ 16 ♔g2 ♘d7 17 h3 ♗xc3 18 bxc3 ♗e2 19 ♖e1 ♗d3 20 ♖e3 c4 21 ♗a3 ♘b6! 22 ♗xd6 ♘xd5 23 ♖xd3 cxd3 24 c4. Boleslavsky considered this position as unclear, but the game Otero-Miguel, La Coruna 1993, proved that only White has any problems: 24...♘c3!? 25 ♔f3 b5! 26 axb5 axb5 27 ♖xa8 ♖xa8∓) 12...f5! (It is too dangerous to play 12...♗xc3+? 13 bxc3 ♖xe4 14 0-0 f5 15 a5 ♘f6 16 ♘b6 ♖a7 17 ♗f3 ♖e8 18 c4 ♘bd7 19 ♖b1± Fridstein-Landgraf, corr. 1967) 13 ♗xg4 fxg4 14 e5 dxe5 15 0-0 exf4 (Or 15...e4 16 ♗e3 b6 17 a5 b5 18 d6 ♗e6 19 ♘b6 ♖a7 20 ♗xc5±) 16 ♗xf4 ♗d4+ 17 ♔h1 and White is slightly better, Schmidt-Aepfler, Germany 1994.

b2) 11...♘bd7 12 0-0

and now:

b21) After the slow 12...♖b8?! 13 ♔h1 ♕c7 (13...c4 doesn't help: 14 e5! dxe5 15 ♘xc4 b5!? 16 axb5 axb5, Larsen-Ljubojevic, Milan 1975, and now 17 ♘d6! b4 18 ♘xe8 ♕xe8 19 ♘b5 would have assured White of an advantage)

14 ♖a2 b6 (Even worse is 14...c4?! 15 e5! dxe5 16 ♘xc4 e4 17 f5! ♖a8 18 ♗f4± Toth-Nunn, Reggio Emilia 1983) 15 b3 ♘f8 (15...♘g4? 16 ♘db1), Izeta-Fernandez, Spanish Ch. 1987, White could have obtained a clear advantage by playing 16 ♗d3.

b22) 12...c4! 13 ♔h1! ♘c5 14 e5 dxe5 15 fxe5

15 ♘xc4!? is not a bad move either.

15...♖xe5

Or 15...♘fd7 16 e6! fxe6 17 ♘xc4 with better chances for White.

16 ♘xc4

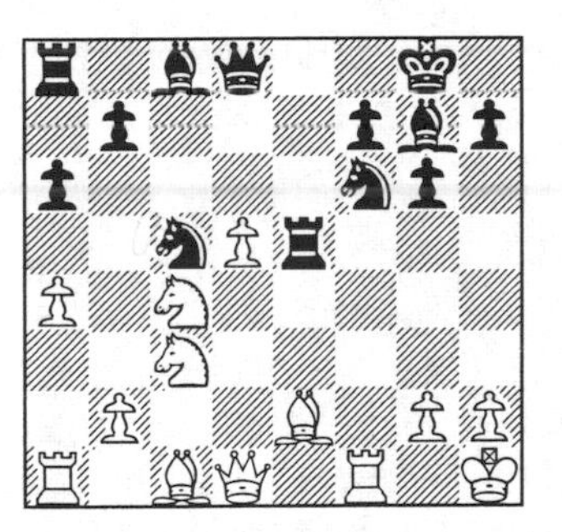

16...♖e8

If 16...♖f5 17 ♗f4! is to White's profit, e.g. 17...♘fe4 18 ♘xe4 ♘xe4 19 ♕c2 ♘g5 20 a5 ♖xd5 21 ♘b6± Farago-Bistric, Sarajevo 1983; 17...♗d7 18 ♘e3 ♖xf4 19 ♖xf4 ♕e8 20 ♘c4 ♘xa4 21 ♘xa4 ♗xa4 22 ♖xa4 b5, Csonkics-Chelushkina, Subotica Interzonal 1991, and now the simplest was 23 ♘d6! ♕b8 24 ♘xb5 winning; and 17...g5 18 ♗e3 ♖xf1+ 19 ♕xf1 ♘fe4 20 ♘xe4 ♘xe4 21 ♗d3 ♘d6 22 ♗b6± Lukacs-Karlsson, Helsinki 1983.

In Glek-Tseshkovsky, Budapest 1989, Black tried to resolve the problems of this difficult position with an exchange sacrifice: 16...♖xe2!? 17 ♘xe2 ♗g4 18 ♘e5 ♘ce4, and now instead of 19 ♗f4 White could have played 19 ♘xg4 ♘xg4 ***20 ♕b3!*** with the better chances, e.g. 20...♕h4 21 ♗f4 g5 22 ♗g3 ♘xg3+ 23 ♕xg3 ♕xg3 24 ♘xg3±.

17 ♗g5 h6 18 ♗h4 ♘ce4

Now White has a pleasant choice between 19 ♘xe4 ♖xe4 20 ♗g3 ♘xd5? (20...h5!? Yrjola) 21 ♖xf7! ♗e6 22 ♖xb7 ♔h8 23 ♕c2, Yrjola-Vaisser, Sochi 1984, and 19 d6 g5 (19...♘xc3!? 20 bxc3 ♗e6) 20 ♗e1 ♗e6 21 ♘xe4 ♘xe4 22 ♗a5 as in the game Beliavsky-Velimirovic, Moscow Interzonal 1982, in both cases with a clear advantage.

c) 10...b6?! 11 0-0 ♗a6 12 a4! ♗xe2 13 ♕xe2

This rare line is similar to 11 ♘d2 in the system 9...♗g4. The difference is that here Black cannot meet the White move ♘c4 with ...♘b6 and after, for example, 13...a6 14 ♘c4 ♖a7 15 ♕f3 ♖d7! 16 ♗d2 b5 17 axb5 axb5 18 ♘xb5 ♘xe4 19 ♗a5 ♕e7 20 f5 White is better, A. Zaitsev-Zhuravlev, USSR 1965.

d) 10...♘bd7 11 0-0 c4

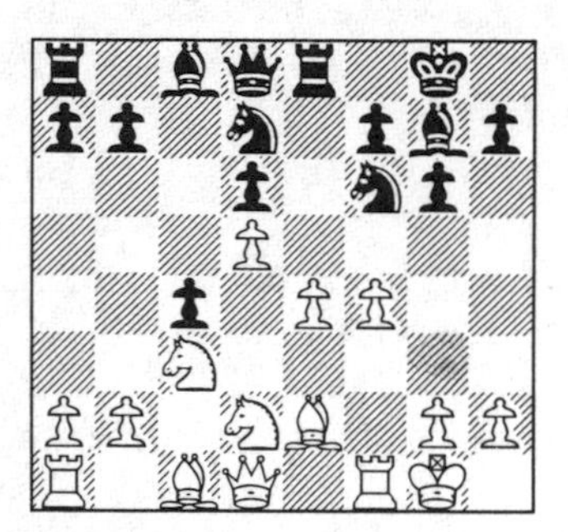

and now:

d1) Black has easy play after 12 ♗xc4?! ♘c5 13 e5 dxe5 14 fxe5 ♖xe5 15 ♘f3 ♖e8 16 ♔h1 a6 (The immediate 16...♘fe4!? 17 ♘xe4 ♘xe4 deserves attention) 17 a4 ♘ce4 18 ♘xe4 ♘xe4 19 ♕b3 ♘d6, Toth-Velimirovic, Budva 1981.

d2) 12 e5?! is premature due to 12...dxe5 13 ♘xc4 ♘b6!, when Black has more than comfortable equality after 14 fxe5 ♘fxd5 15 ♘xd5 (15 ♘d6 ♘xc3 16 bxc3 is slightly better for Black because of 16...♖f8! 17 ♘xf7 ♕xd1 18 ♗xd1 ♗e6 19 ♘h6+ ♔h8 20 ♖e1 ♖ae8, as in Kurtenkov-Ghinda, Primorsko 1985) 15...♕xd5 16 ♕xd5 (16 ♘d6 ♕c5+ 17 ♔h1 ♖e7 is no better) 16...♘xd5 17 ♗f3, Sines-Ljuboevic, Yugoslav Ch. 1982, and now 17...♘b6!?

d3) **12 ♔h1 ♘c5 13 e5 dxe5 14 fxe5**

After 14 ♘xc4 Black's best is 14...exf4! 15 ♗xf4 ♘ce4 16 ♗f3 ♘xc3 17 bxc3 ♘e4 18 ♕b3 b6! 19 ♗xe4 (Not 19 d6?! ♗a6 20 ♗xe4 ♖xe4 21 ♘d2 ♖e8 22 ♖fe1 ♕d7 23 ♘f3 ♗b7∓ Dlugy-Vaisser, Havana 1985) 19...♖xe4 20 ♘d2 ♖e8 21 ♖ae1 ♗f5 22 c4 ♕d7 23 ♘f3 ♖xe1 24 ♖xe1 ♖e8 25 ♗e5 ♗g4 26 ♗xg7 ♗xf3 27 ♗e5 ♕f5 with equality, Meduna-Poloch, Ceske Budejovice open 1995.

14...♖xe5 15 ♘xc4 ♖e8

15...♖f5?! 16 ♗f4! (16 ♗f3 b6! 17 d6, Haba-Renet, Thessaloniki Olympiad 1988, and now 17...♖b8 would have given Black enough play) 16...♘h5 (16...♘xd5?! 17 ♘e3!±; 16...g5 17 ♗e5! ♘fe4 [Not 17...b5?! 18 ♘xb5 ♘ce4 19 ♕d4 ♕xd5 20 ♗f3 ♗e6 21 b3± Pigusov-Chekhov, Irkutsk 1983] 18 ♗xg7 ♖xf1+ 19 ♕xf1 ♔xg7 20 ♘xe4 ♘xe4 21 ♖d1±) 17 ♗e3 ♖xf1+ (17...b6!?) 18 ♕xf1 b6 (Or 18...♗xc3 19 bxc3 ♘e4 20 ♗xh5 ♕h4 21 ♕f3 gxh5 22 ♗d4± Kindermann-Danner, Zurich 1994) 19 ♖d1, Pekarek-Suba, Warsaw 1987, and now after the best move 19...♕f6 White gets an advantage, for example, by playing 20 ♗xc5 bxc5 21 ♗xh5.

16 ♗g5 h6 17 ♗h4 ♘ce4 18 ♘xe4

18 d6 is also interesting.

18...♖xe4 19 ♗g3 ♕xd5!

Not 19...♘xd5? 20 ♖xf7! ♗e6 21 ♖xb7± Tasic-Murey, Cannes 1992.

20 ♕xd5 ♘xd5 21 ♗f3 ♖d4 22 ♖ad1 ♘b6

It is worse for Black to play

22...♘e7? 23 ♖xd4 ♗xd4 24 ♖d1 ♘f5 25 ♗e5 ♗xe5 26 ♖d8+ ♔g7 27 ♘xe5 ♔f6 28 ♖e8, when the pin of the c8-bishop assures an advantage for White, Vaisser-Andres, Bayamo 1985.

23 ♖xd4 ♗xd4 24 ♖d1 ♗f6 25 b3 ♘xc4 26 bxc4 a5

White has more than enough pressure for a pawn, but the players agreed a draw in Chandler-Sax, Sarajevo 1985.

If White is not satisfied with this variation he can try:

d4) 12 a4 ♘c5

This line is particularly important because Black can practically force this position with another move order, namely 10...c4 11 a4 ♘a6 12 0-0 ♘c5. Now White has two possibilities:

d41) 13 ♗f3 b6

13...♗h6?! is suspicious. White can play 14 e5 dxe5 15 fxe5 ♖xe5 16 ♘xc4 ♗xc1 17 ♖xc1 ♖e8, Zakharevich-Petrushin, Azov 1993, and now 18 b4 with an advantage. The quiet 14 ♕c2 may be even stronger. The game Padevsky-Ciocaltea, Havana Olympiad 1966, continued 14...♘d3 15 ♘xc4 ♘xc1 16 ♕xc1 ♗d7 (If 16...♗g4 White has a strong reply: 17 ♕d1! ♖c8 18 b3 ♗xf3 19 ♕xf3 with a great advantage to White, Uhmann-Felix, Karvina 1989) 17 b3 and White is clearly better.

The game Gutman-Petkevich, USSR 1967, saw instead 13...♗d7 14 e5 dxe5 15 fxe5 ♖xe5 16 ♘xc4 ♖e8, and now 17 ♗f4 ♘fe4 (17...♗f5?! 18 ♘d6) 18 ♘xe4 ♘xe4 19 ♖c1 would have been slightly better for White.

14 e5 dxe5 15 fxe5 ♖xe5 16 ♘xc4 ♖e8

This is safer than 16...♖f5 17 d6 ♖b8 18 ♘b5! ♗e6 19 ♘e3 (19 ♕c2!? is not bad) 19...♗b3, Zaharevich-Gleizerov, USSR 1987, and now following analysis by Gleizerov, 20 ♘xf5! ♗xd1 21 ♘e7+ ♔h8 22 ♖xd1 (22 ♘c6?! ♗xf3 23 ♘xd8 ♗d5!∓) with good compensation for the queen.

17 d6

17 ♗g5 is not dangerous for Black. After 17...♗f5! 18 b4?! ♗d3 the game turns in his favour.

17...♗e6!

Worse is 17...♗a6?! because of 18 ♘b5!

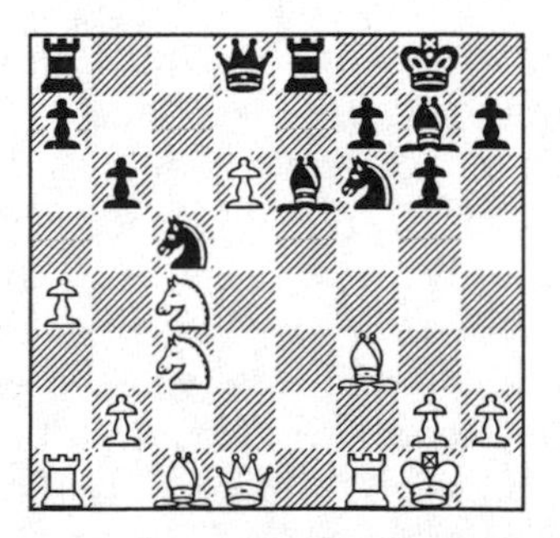

In this critical position 18 ♗xa8? does not work due to 18...♗xc4 19 ♗c6 ♖e6! with good chances for Black.

Against Granda Zuniga, Buenos Aires 1992, Chernin continued 18 ♗e2 and now, as he noted, Black could have obtained sufficient counterplay with 18...♘h5!? 19 g4 ♕h4, threatening 20...♘g3.

Perhaps White should try 18 ♘d5!? with some hopes for an advantage.

d42) 13 e5!? dxe5 14 ♘xc4 e4 (14...exf4 15 ♗xf4 ♘ce4 is also playable) 15 ♗e3 ♘d3 16 ♗xd3 exd3 17 ♕xd3 ♗f5 18 ♕d2 ♖c8 19 b3 ♘g4! (Only the nice combination that starts with this move gives Black hopes of equality. In the case of 19...♘e4?! 20 ♘xe4 ♗xa1 21 ♘ed6 ♗c3, Balashov-Dvoretsky, Moscow 1967, 22 ♕c1! would have given White the better chances) 20 ♗d4 ♗xd4+ 21 ♕xd4 ♖xc4! 22 bxc4 ♖e3 23 h3 ♖d3 24 ♕xa7 ♕h4 25 ♖a2 ♘e3 26 ♕b8+ ♔g7 27 ♕e5+, Pomar-Toran, Palma de Mallorca 1966, and now instead of 27...f6? 28 ♕e7+ ♔h6 29 ♘e4 with a large advantage for White, Black should have played 27...♔h6! 28 ♘e4 (Or 28 ♖c1?! ♘xg2! with a strong attack) 28...♘xf1 29 ♘f6 ♘e3 30 ♘g8+ with a perpetual check (Dvoretsky). I would not be surprised if White can improve his play in this line.

e) 10...c4!? After 11 a4 (11 0-0 b5!) 11...♘a6 12 0-0 ♘c5 play transposes to variation d4.

11 0-0 ♖b8!?

A clever, flexible move. At the moment the black knight on a6 keeps its options open of hopping to either b4 or c7. It is less precise to play 11...c4?!, because of 12 e5 dxe5 13 ♘xc4 and White has saved an important tempo when compared to line d2 above, by missing out ♔h1. The game Hvenekilde-T. Horvath, Copenhagen 1983, continued 13...e4 14 ♗e3 ♘b4! 15 d6 ♗e6 16 ♘b5! ♘d3 17 ♗xd3 exd3, and now White should have simply played 18 ♕xd3 and if 18...a6 then 19 ♘c7! ♘xc7 20 ♗b6 with an advantage.

Another reasonable line is

11...♘c7 12 a4

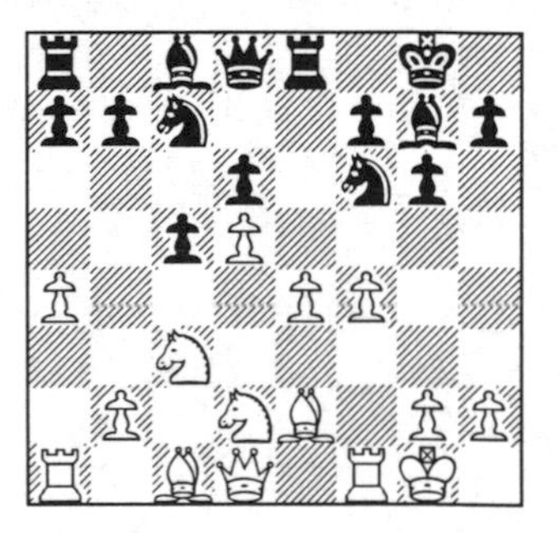

After 12 ♗f3 ♖b8 13 ♘c4 b5 14 ♘xd6 (14 ♘a5?! ♗d7 15 e5 dxe5 16 fxe5 ♖xe5 17 ♗f4 ♖f5 18 ♗g3 b4∓) 14...♕xd6 15 e5 ♕d8! 16 d6 ♘e6 17 exf6 ♗xf6 18 ♗c6 ♗d7 19 ♗xd7 ♗d4+! 20 ♔h1 ♕xd7 21 f5 gxf5 22 ♘d5 ♔h8 23 ♘e7 ♕xd6 24 ♘xf5, Zilberman-Rechlis, Israeli Ch. 1994, White has a certain initiative for the pawn, but not more.

12...b6

12...a6 13 ♗f3 ♖b8 (13...b5?! doesn't work without preparation: 14 axb5 axb5 15 ♖xa8 ♘xa8 16 ♘xb5 ♗a6, Bronznik-Gazik, Bratislava 1992, and now White should have played 17 ♕a4! ♕b6 18 ♘xd6 ♕xd6 19 e5 ♕b6 20 exf6 ♗b5 21 ♘c4 with a clear advantage) 14 a5! (14 ♘c4 allows the possibility of an interesting sacrifice: 14...b5 15 axb5 axb5 16 ♘a5 ♗d7 17 e5 dxe5 18 d6 [18 fxe5 ♖xe5 19 ♘b7!? ♖xb7 20 d6, suggested by Giffard, needs further analysis] 18...e4! 19 dxc7 ♕xc7 20 ♗e2 c4 with full compensation for the piece, Kolbaek-Andersen, Vejle 1967) 14...♗d7 15 ♖e1 ♗b5, Paramos-Marin, Ibercaja open 1994, and now 16 ♘db1 would have been slightly better for White.

13 ♗f3 ♖b8 14 ♖e1 ♗a6

After 14...a6?! 15 ♘c4 b5 16 ♘xd6 ♕xd6 17 e5 ♕d8 18 d6 ♘e6 19 axb5 axb5 20 exf6 ♗xf6 we obtain the position from the game Zilberman-Rechlis above with some important differences: the white rook is on e1 and the a-file is open. This changes the evaluation to White's profit. The game Kozul-Marovic, Toronto 1990, continued 21 ♘d5 ♗d4+?! (After the best move 21...♗b7!? 22 f5!? ♗xd5 23 ♕xd5 ♘d4! 24 ♗f4 White also keeps an edge, according to Kozul) 22 ♗e3! ♗b7 23 ♗xd4 ♗xd5 24 ♗e5 ♗xf3 25 ♕xf3 with a clear advantage for White.

An interesting alternative is the active 14...h5!?, as played in the game Rogers-Kristiansen, Thessaloniki Olympiad 1984, which continued 15 ♘c4 (15 h3 ♘g4 is not as dangerous for White as some commentators have claimed. After ***16 e5!*** ♘h6 17 ♘c4 ♘f5 with complicated play, I prefer White). Now instead of 15...♗a6?! 16 ♘a3 ♗b7 17 ♗e3 ♕d7 18 h3 a6 19 ♘c4 b5 20 ♘xd6!±, Rogers proposed 15...♘g4!? 16 ♗xg4 ♗xg4 17 ♕d3 ♗c8! with an unclear position.

15 ♘db1

This is better than 15 ♘f1 ♗xf1 16 ♖xf1 a6 17 ♔h1 ♘d7, Begovac-Wojtkiewicz, Bern 1991, when Black was without problems.

15...♘d7 16 ♘a3 c4 17 ♘cb5! ♗xb5 18 axb5 c3 19 ♖b1 cxb2 20 ♗xb2 ♗xb2 21 ♖xb2 ♕f6

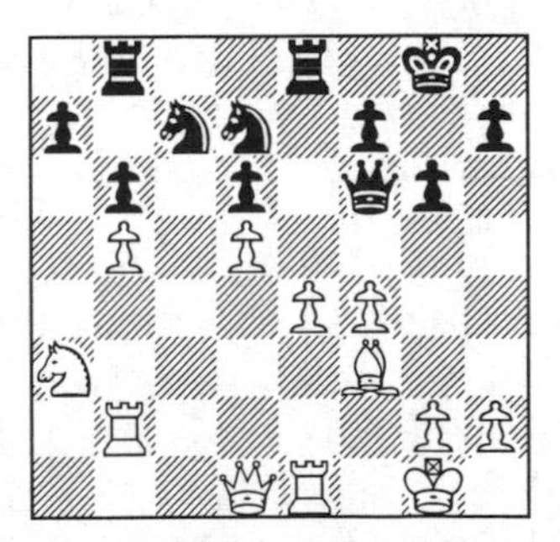

The game Malich-Tringov, Sarajevo 1965, arrived at this position. Now White should have played ***22 ♕d2***, followed by ♘c4 and eventually e4-e5, with the better chances. Note that the capture 22...♘xd5? fails to 23 e5!

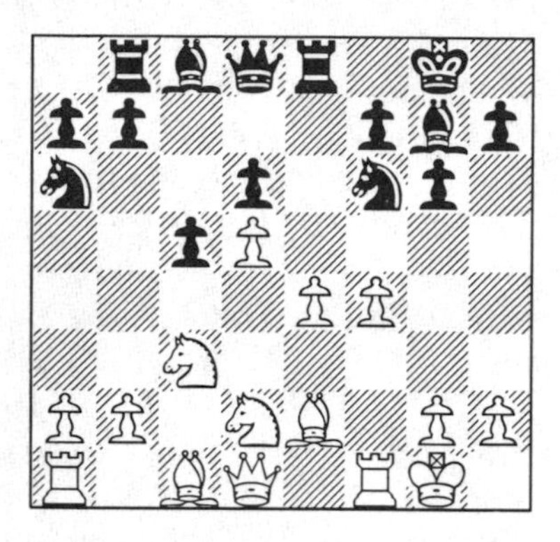

12 ♔h1?

Suddenly this lost tempo turns the game in Black's favour. Instead, 12 ♖e1 is a more useful waiting move. The game might continue in the spirit of the previous line 11...♘c7, when the line recommended in *ECO* needs more tests: 12 ♖b1 ♗d7 (If 12...♘c7?!, then 12 b4 or 12 a3 b5 13 b4, blocking the queenside) 13 e5 dxe5 14 fxe5 ♖xe5 15 ♘c4, followed by 16 ♗f4 with good compensation for a pawn.

12 ... ♘c7

13 a4 a6

Mikhail Gurevich demonstrated an interesting idea after Smirin's suspicious 13...h5?! (USSR Ch. 1988): 14 f5! a6 15 a5 gxf5 15 ♗xh5 ♘b5 17 exf5 ♖e5 18 ♗f3 ♖xf5 19 ♘c4 ♕c7 20 ♗d2 and White stood better.

14 a5 ♗d7

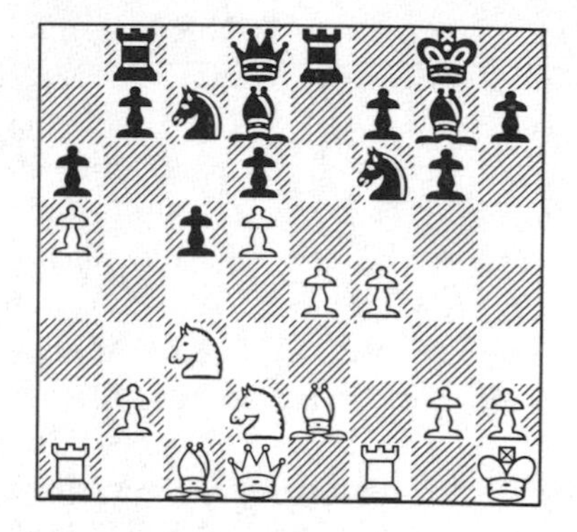

15 e5

The quiet 15 ♗f3 is also insufficient for equality: 15...♘b5 (15...♗b5?! 16 ♖e1 ♗d3 17 ♕b3 ♕d7 18 ♘c4 ♗xc4 19 ♕xc4 ♘b5 20 ♗e3 ♘d4 21 ♗xd4 cxd4 22 ♘a4 ♕d8 23 ♕b4 with an equal position, Arakelian-Ibragimov, Podolsk 1993) 16 e5 (After 16 ♖e1 ♘d4 17 ♘c4 ♗b5 18 ♘b6 ♘d7! the position of Black's knight in the centre is very annoying, while 16 ♘xb5 ♗xb5 17 ♖e1 c4 18 ♖a3 ♖c8 19 ♘f1 ♘d7, Toth-De Firmian, Biel 1986, is no better. Things would turn out quite differently if White had played 12 ♖e1 instead of 12 ♔h1. Then he could play 16 ♘c4 here with an advantage) 16...dxe5 17 fxe5 ♖xe5 18 ♘c4 ♖f5! 19 ♘e3 ♖f4 20 ♘e2 ♖h4 21 g3 ♖e4! 22 ♗xe4 ♘xe4 with a strong initiative for Black, Ufimtsev-Tal, USSR 1967.

15 ... dxe5

16 ♘c4 ♗b5!

16...e4?! 17 ♗e3 is worse.

17	**d6**	**♘e6**
18	**fxe5**	**♘d7**
19	**♗f4**	**♘xf4**
20	**♖xf4**	**♘xe5**

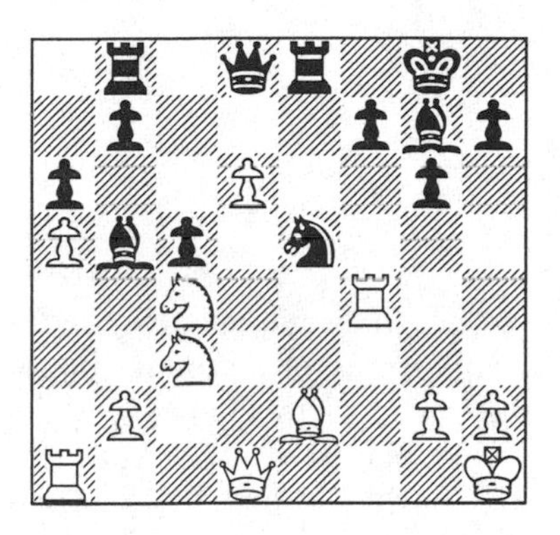

20...♗xc4 looks good, when 21 ♗xc4 ♘xe5 gives Black a plus.

21	**♘xb5**	**axb5**
22	**♘b6**	**c4?!**

It would have been better to play 22...♖e6 23 d7 ♕c7!, threatening 24...♘xd7. 24 ♗xb5 does not avoid the threat: 24...♘xd7! 25 ♘d5 ♕e5! and Black exchanges the dangerous d6-pawn while keeping his extra pawn.

23	**♕d5**	**♖e6**
24	**♖d1**	**♘d3**
25	**♗xd3**	**cxd3?**

A decisive mistake. Why not 25...♖xd6 instead? After the queen sacrifice 26 ♗xc4!? ♖xd5 27 ♗xd5 ♔h8 28 ♖xf7 the position is unclear.

26 d7

Black has nothing with which to oppose the terrible passed d-pawn.

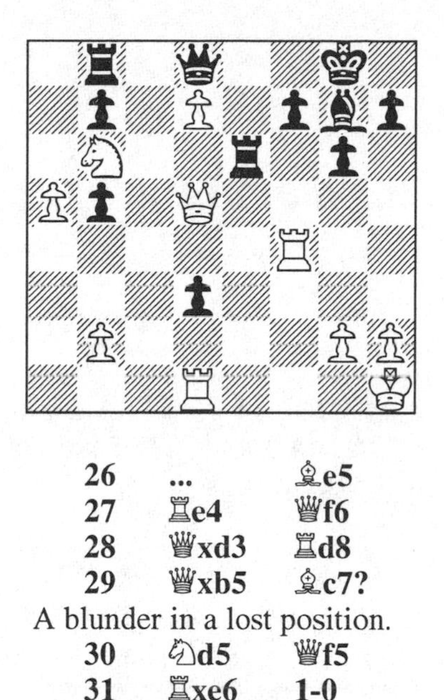

26	**...**	**♗e5**
27	**♖e4**	**♕f6**
28	**♕xd3**	**♖d8**
29	**♕xb5**	**♗c7?**

A blunder in a lost position.

30	**♘d5**	**♕f5**
31	**♖xe6**	**1-0**

This game illustrates a situation where White made a mistake in the opening and found himself in an inferior version of the typical Four Pawns Attack middlegame. As you can see, if you have a good feel for this type of position and your opponent does not, you still have chances, even if the opening goes slightly awry.

At the present time the main line 9...♖e8 10 e5 dxe5 11 fxe5 ♘g4 12 ♗g5 ♕b6 13 0-0 leads logically to a more or less forced draw. White players hoping for more should consider 10 ♘d2 (Game 5), 12 0-0 ♘xe5 13 ♗f4 (Game 4), 12 e6 (Game 4, pages 32-33) and 13 ♕d2 (Game 1, pages 10-12).

2 Main Line with 9...♗g4

1 d4 ♘f6 2 c4 g6 3 ♘c3 ♗g7 4 e4 d6 5 f4 0-0 6 ♘f3 c5 7 d5 e6 8 ♗e2 exd5 9 cxd5 ♗g4

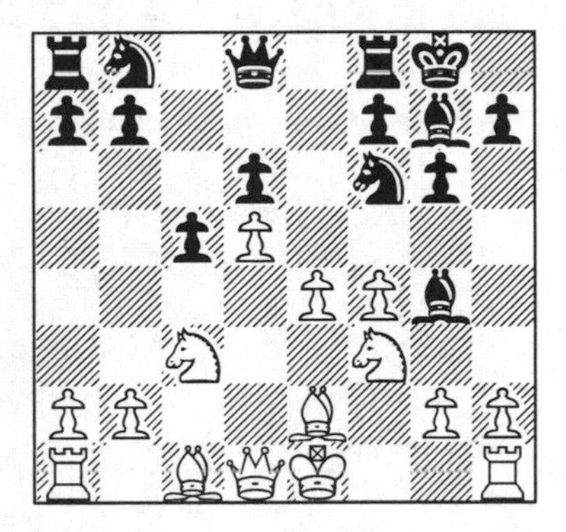

9...♗g4 is Black's most solid continuation in the Four Pawns Attack. Once again, White's main idea will be to prepare e4-e5; and Black, whilst trying to hold up this advance, must also try to develop counterplay on the queenside. After an eventual exchange of Black's light-squared bishop on f3, White will also often use his strong centre as the basis for a direct pawn storm on the kingside with, for example g2-g4, h2-h4, and g4-g5.

The first two games in this chapter present the main line of this system. In Game 6, Vaisser-Yrjola, Black plays for ...b7-b5, while game Vaisser-Berelovich (Game 7) is concerned with various plans involving ...c5-c4. Sidelines for Black are examined in Game 8, Vaisser-Smirin, while White's sidelines are seen in Game 9, Monin-Shchekachev.

Game 6
Vaisser-Yrjola
Helsinki 1991

1 d4 ♘f6 2 c4 g6 3 ♘c3 ♗g7 4 e4 d6 5 f4 0-0 6 ♘f3 c5 7 d5 e6 8 ♗e2 exd5 9 cxd5 ♗g4

10	**0-0**	**♘bd7**
11	**♖e1**	**♖e8**
12	**h3**	**♗xf3**
13	**♗xf3**	

(see following diagram)

This is the critical position of the 9...♗g4 variation.

13	**...**	**♕a5!**

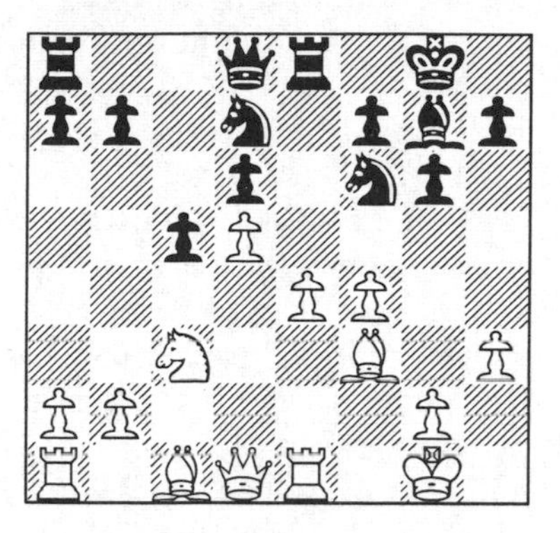

The point of this move is that White now has no time to play 14 a4?!, preventing 14...b5, because of 14...c4! 15 ♗e3 (15 ♘b5 a6) 15...♘c5 16 ♗xc5 ♕xc5+ 17 ♔h1 ♘d7 with a comfortable position for Black.

13...c4 and 13...♖c8, preparing ...c5-c4, are considered in the next game. Here we discuss Black's other plans without ...c5-c4:

a) 13...♖b8!? 14 a4 h5 (14...h6!?) 15 ♖e2 (15 g4!? hxg4 16 hxg4 ♘h7 17 g5 is well justified here. White gains a tempo compared to variation b2) 15...a6 16 a5 b5 17 axb6 ♖xb6 18 ♕d3 ♕c8 19 ♖a4 ♕b7 20 ♕c4 ♕c8?! 21 ♕a2 ♘h7 22 ♗e3 ♗h6 23 ♘b1 ♕b7 24 ♘a3 g5 25 fxg5 ♗xg5 26 ♘c4± Vaisser-Brito, Las Palmas 1995.

b) 13...a6 14 a4 (Note that this move is not automatic: 14 g4!? h6 15 h4 b5 16 g5 hxg5 17 hxg5 ♘h7 also deserves attention) and now:

b1) Black's attempt to attack on the queenside using piece play, without moving pawns, is suspicious: 14...♕a5 15 ♗e3 ♕b4 16 ♕c2 ♘b6?! 17 ♗f2 ♘fd7? 18 a5 ♘c4 19 ♘a2! ♕b5 20 ♗e2+-.

b2) A typical pawn sacrifice occurred in the game Yrjola-Pedzich, Cappelle la Grande 1992: 14...♖b8 15 g4 (15 a5!?) 15...h6 16 h4 ♘h7 17 g5 c4 18 ♗e3 ♖c8?! 19 ♗g4 ♖c7 20 e5! dxe5 21 f5 with a strong initiative.

b3) Passive play does not promise much: 14...♖c8 15 ♔h1 ♕c7 16 ♖e2 ♕b8 17 a5 ♖e7 18 ♗e3 ♖ce8 19 ♗f2 ♗h6 20 ♕c1! b5 (20...♘e5 21 fxe5!) 21 axb6 ♕xb6 22 ♗h4 ♖b8 23 g4 ♗g7 24 ♕e1 ♖be8 25 ♗g3 h6 26 e5! dxe5 27 fxe5 ♘h7 28 e6 fxe6 29 d6 ♖f7 30 ♘d5 ♕b3 31 ♖a3 ♕c4 32 ♘e7+ ♖fxe7 33 dxe7± Banikas-Arakhamia, Ikaros open 1995.

b4) 14...c4 is discussed in the next game.

14 ♗e3

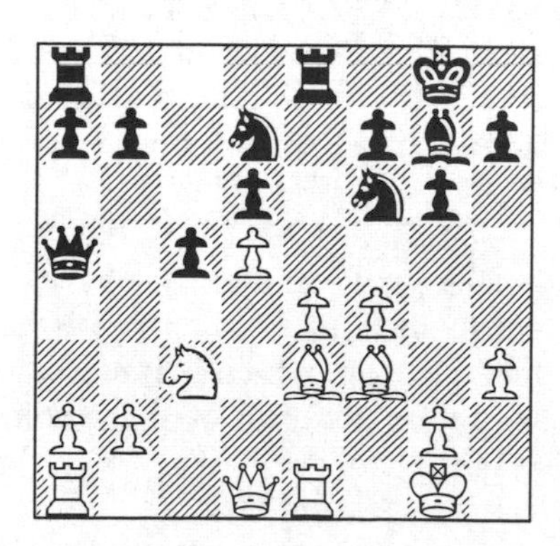

If White wishes to avoid a theoretical battle, he may choose to pay more attention to 14 g4 or to the game Bulthaupt-Lindemann, German Bundesliga 1996: 14 ♖e2 b5 15 ♕e1 b4 16 ♘d1 c4 17 ♗d2 ♕b6+ 18 ♔h1 ♘c5 19 e5 ♘d3 20 ♕g3 ♘d7? (20...dxe5) 21 e6 ♘f6 22 f5 with an initiative.

14 ... b5

The game Vaisser-Kindermann, Biel 1991, saw instead 14...♖ac8?! (Black mixes two different plans) 15 g4! h6 16 h4 b5? (16...g5? is also bad: 17 hxg5 hxg5 18 e5! dxe5 19 fxg5 ♘h7 20 ♘e4 with a clear edge, but 16...♘b6!?, liberating the d7-square for the king's knight, deserved attention) 17 g5 hxg5 18 hxg5 ♘h7 19 ♗g4 ♖cd8 20 e5! dxe5 21 f5 e4! 22 fxg6 (22 f6? ♘hxf6 23 gxf6 ♘xf6 is in Black's favour) 22...fxg6 23 ♗e6+ ♖xe6? (23...♔h8 would have been more resilient, but White still has good attacking chances after 24 ♕g4) 24 dxe6 ♘e5 25 e7! ♖e8 26 ♕d5+ ♔h8 27 ♔g2 ♖xe7 28 ♖h1 ♖f7 29 ♖af1! ♖xf1 (29...♕c7 30 ♕a8+ ♗f8 31 ♘d5+-) 30 ♔xf1 1-0.

15 a3 ♘b6

Black players have also experimented with other moves in this position, which is important for the evaluation of the whole system:

a) 15...♖ac8!? 16 g4?! (This move is effective only if Black cannot comfortably free the d7-square for the knight on f6; and here that is not the case) 16...♘b6 17 e5 ♘c4 18 exf6 ♘xe3 19 ♖xe3 ♖xe3 20 fxg7 ♖ce8 (One might think that, in comparison with the main line, White has an extra tempo, g2-g4, but in reality he has one tempo less, because the f3-bishop is not protected) 21 ♔f2 b4! 22 axb4 ♕xb4 23 ♘e2 ♕xb2 24 ♖xa7 c4! 25 ♖a6 ♖d3 26 ♕e1 ♖ee3 0-1 Elbilia-Loeffler, Cannes open 1993. Three years later Elbilia improved upon his previous play with 16 ♗f2! a6?! 17 ♗g3 ♘b6 18 e5 dxe5 19 fxe5 ♘fd7, and now the simple 20 e6 would have fixed White's advantage, Elbilia-Grivas, Yerevan Olympiad 1996.

b) 15...♖ab8!? 16 ♗f2 h6 and now, instead of the logical plan 17 ♖e2!? preparing ♕e1 and e4-e5 with good chances, in the game Vaisser-Hernandez, Las Palmas 1995, White missed a tactical nuance: 17 e5? dxe5 18 fxe5 ♖xe5! 19 ♖xe5 ♘xe5 20 ♗e2 (The intended 20 ♗xc5? runs into 20...♘xf3+ 21 gxf3 [or 21 ♕xf3?? b4 winning a piece] 21...♕c7 with a strong initiative) 20...c4 and White did not have enough compensation for the pawn.

c) 15...b4 16 axb4 ♕xb4 17 ♕c2 ♘b6 18 ♗f2 ♘fd7 19 ♖e2 ♗d4 20 ♔h1 ♗xf2 21 ♖xf2 c4 22 ♖e2 a5 23 ♗g4 ♘f6 24 ♕d2

♘xg4 25 hxg4 ♘d7, Lautier-Smirin, Cap d'Agde 1996, and now after 26 ♖a4! (Forcing Black's queen to the c5-square) 26...♕c5 27 g5 White is better.

16 e5

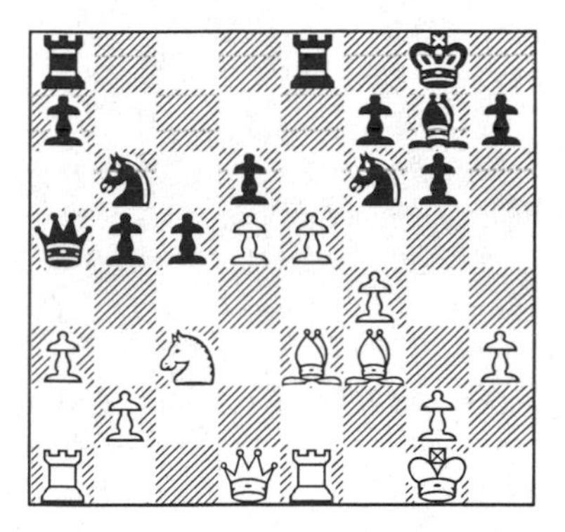

The result of the spectacular game Kozul-Nunn, Wijk an Zee 1991, (negative for White) practically closed discussion about the move 16 ♗f2; but in reality matters are not so clear. That game continued 16....♘c4 17 ♕c2 ♘d7 18 ♗e2 (18 a4? b4 19 ♘b5 a6!) 18...♖ab8 19 a4 b4, and now instead of 20 ♗xc4? bxc3 21 b3 a6! 22 ♖ec1 ♘b6 23 ♗f1 c4 24 ♗xc4 ♘xc4 25 bxc4 ♖b2 26 ♕d3 ♖d2 27 ♕f3 f5! with a decisive advantage for Black, White should have played 20 ♘b5! At the very least, the line proposed by Nunn: 20...♘xb2 21 ♘xd6 b3 22 ♕b1 ♘xa4 23 ♘xe8? ♗xa1 24 ♕xa1 b2 25 ♕a2 ♕xe1+! 26 ♗xe1 b1♕ 'and Black wins' can be improved by 23 ♖a3! ♕b4 24 ♖xb3 ♕xb3 25 ♕xb3 ♖xb3 26 ♘xe8 with an unclear position.

16 ... ♘c4

16...dxe5?! 17 fxe5 ♖xe5 18 ♗xc5 ♖xe1+ 19 ♕xe1 ♘bd7 20 ♗d4 is promising for White.

17 exf6 ♘xe3

17...♗xf6? does not work: 18 ♗d2 ♘xb2 19 ♘e4! ♗d4+ 20 ♔h2 ♕d8 (Or 20...♘xd1 21 ♗xa5 ♗xa1 22 ♖xd1 ♗g7 23 ♘xd6+-) 21 ♕c2 ♘c4 22 ♗c3 f5 23 ♘g5 ♖xe1 24 ♖xe1 ♘xa3 25 ♕e2! and White is winning.

18 ♖xe3 ♖xe3

19 fxg7 ♖ae8

20 f5!

The alternative 20 ♕d2!? (Hoping to provoke 20...f5?! 21 ♔f2! ♖3e7 22 g4) worked out well in the game Elbilia-San Marco, Cannes open 1995: 20...♕b6?! (Better is 20...c4!?) 21 f5 c4 22 ♔h1 gxf5 23 ♖f1 ♖8e5 24 ♕f2 b4 25 axb4 ♕xb4 26 ♗e4! ♖3xe4 27 ♘xe4 ♖xe4 28 ♕xf5 ♖e7 29 ♕f6 with a large advantage for White.

20 ... gxf5

In the game Dearing-Moss, Hastings 1996, Black tried 20...b4 21 axb4 ♕xb4 22 ♕d2 ♕f4?! (22...♕h4!?) 23 ♖f1 ♕xf5? and now 24 ♗e4! ♕g5 25 ♖f3 wins for White.

In my game with Kruger (San Bernardino 1989) Black played the unfortunate 20...♕d8 21 ♕d2 ♕h4? (21...a6!) which led to a clear advantage for White after 22 ♘xb5 ♕g3 23 ♖f1.

21 ♕d2

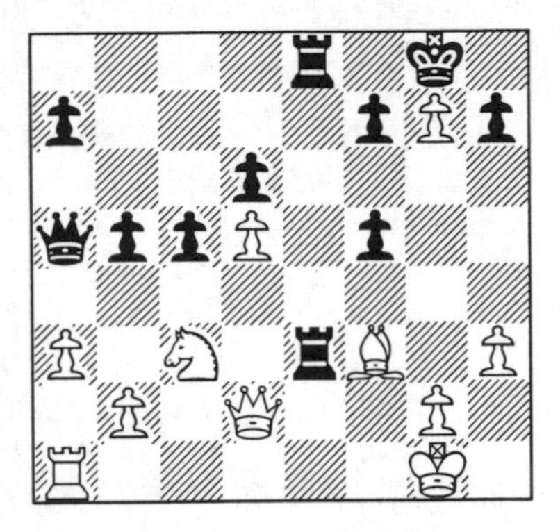

21 ... b4?!

Black's overly-aggressive pawn move gives White a clear advantage. The critical position for this line arises after 21...a6!? 22 ♖f1 ♕d8 (22...c4 23 ♕d4) 23 ♘d1!? (23 ♗d1 ♕g5 24 ♕f2 ♖8e5 25 ♗c2? b4) 23...♖3e5 24 ♕h6. I believe that White's chances are better here.

22	**♘e2**	**c4**
23	**♘g3**	**c3**
24	**bxc3**	**bxc3**
25	**♕c2**	**♕b6**
26	**♔h2**	**♕b2**
27	**♖a2!**	**♕b6?**

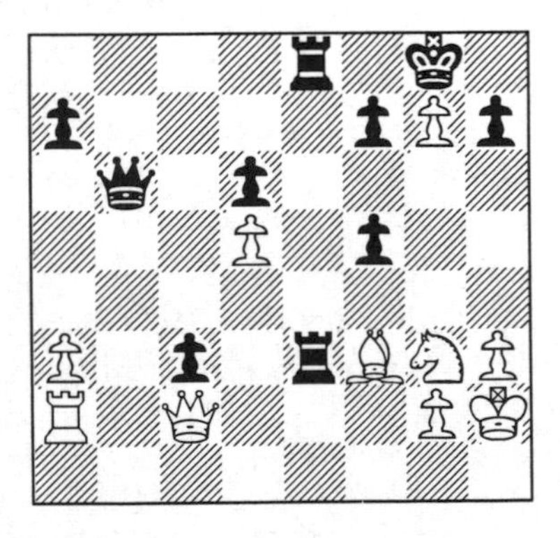

The endgame after 27...♕xc2 is not exactly a dream for Black, but it was still better than the text move.

28	**♘xf5**	**♖3e5**
29	**♘h6+**	**♔xg7**
30	**♘g4**	**♕d4**
31	**♘xe5**	**♕xe5+**
32	**g3**	**♖c8**
33	**♕d3**	**f5**
34	**♖e2**	**♕f6**
35	**♖f2**	**♖b8**
36	**♗d1**	**♕e5**
	1-0	

We now look at Black's plans involving ...c5-c4 in the main line.

Game 7
Vaisser-Berelovich
Groningen 1993

1 d4 ♘f6 2 c4 g6 3 ♘c3 ♗g7 4 e4 d6 5 f4 0-0 6 ♘f3 c5 7 d5 e6 8 ♗e2 exd5 9 cxd5 ♗g4 10 0-0 ♘bd7 11 ♖e1 ♖e8 12 h3 ♗xf3 13 ♗xf3

13 ... ♖c8

Instead:

a) First we consider Black's play without 13...a6 14 a4. This gives White some additional possibilities and so cannot be recommended.

13...c4?! 14 ♗e3 ♕a5

14...a6? is too slow because of 15 ♗d4! and the immediate 16 e5!

15 ♗d4!

After 15 ♔h1 ♘c5 16 ♗xc5

♕xc5 17 e5 the resulting positions are similar to those in which the moves 13...a6 14 a4 are inserted. Nevertheless, we should note one particularity to this move order: instead of 15...♘c5 Black can play 15...♖e7!?, and after 16 ♗d4 ♘c5 (Or 16...♖ae8 17 ♖e2! b5 18 a3 a6 19 ♕g1 ♕c7 20 ♖ae1 with a pleasant position for White in Komarov-Niermann, Cattolica open 1993) 17 b4! cxb3 18 axb3 ♕b4 19 ♘a2 ♕b5 20 e5 (20 ♗e2!?) and now not 20...♘e8? 21 ♖e3± Glek-Korolev, corr. 1988, but the more resilient 20...dxe5! 21 fxe5 ♘fd7. There is no direct refutation: 22 b4 ♘d3 23 ♗e2 ♗xe5 (23...♖xe5) is not good for White.

15...♘c5

If 15...♖e7 16 b4! is still possible.

16 b4!

The most energetic way to refute Black's set-up.

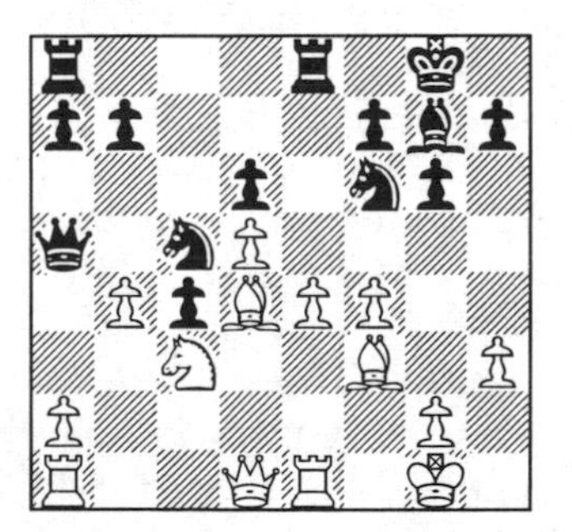

Neither of the responses considered below promise Black an easy life:

a1) 16...♕xb4?! 17 ♖b1 ♕a5 18 ♖b5 ♕a6 19 ♗xc5 ♘xe4! (Much better than 19...dxc5? 20 e5 ♘d7 21 d6 ♖ab8 22 a4 b6 23 ♘d5 and Black is suffocating, Komarov-Strovsky, Belfort 1992) 20 ♘xe4 ♕xb5 21 ♗f2! (21 ♗xd6? ♖xe4 22 ♖xe4 ♕b6+=) 21...♕a6 22 ♖e2 and White still has the better chances.

a2) 16...cxb3 17 axb3 ♕b4 18 ♘a2 ♕b5

Or 18...♕xb3 19 ♗xc5 ♕xd1 20 ♖exd1 dxc5 21 d6 ♖ab8 22 ♘c3 a6 23 ♖db1±.

19 ♗e2!

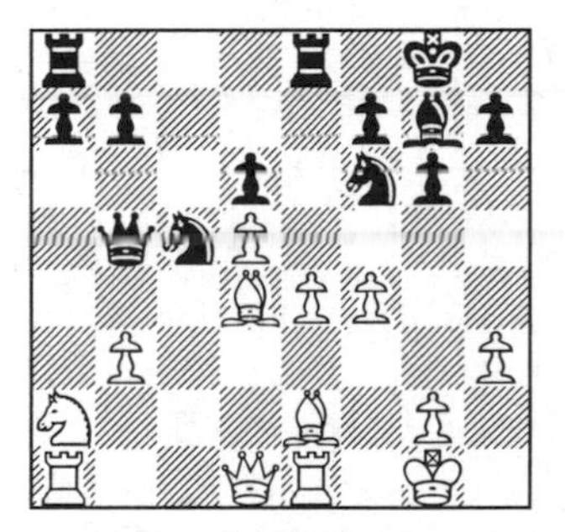

Instead, after the repetition of moves 19 ♘c3 ♕b4 20 ♘a2 ♕b5, Kouatly and A. Kuzmin agreed a draw (Doha 1993). Let us try to continue the analysis.

19...♕xb3

After 19...♕d7!? 20 ♗xc5 dxc5 21 ♗f3 ♘h5 22 ♗xh5 ♗xa1 23 ♕xa1 gxh5 24 ♘c3 White's attack is going to be very dangerous.

20 ♗xc5 ♕g3

Or 20...♕xd1 21 ♖axd1 dxc5 22 e5 ♘d7 23 ♗b5 ♖ed8 24 e6

fxe6 25 dxe6 ♘f6 26 ♖xd8+ ♖xd8 27 e7 with an advantage for White.

21 ♗f2 ♕xf4 22 ♕c1 ♕e5 23 ♗b5!

The point of this move will become clear at the next note.

23...♖ec8

If 23...♖e7 24 ♗d3± and 24...♘xe4? is now impossible due to 25 ♖xe4.

24 ♕a3 ♘xe4 25 ♗d3 f5 26 ♖ad1 ♖e8 27 ♗xe4 fxe4 28 ♗d4

White is clearly better.

b) 13...a6 14 a4 c4 15 ♗e3 ♕a5

After the inclusion of ...a7-a6 and a2-a4 the resource b2-b4! is not available to White any more and 16 ♗d4?! ♘c5 17 e5? ♘d3! is favourable for Black. White therefore has to choose between two other possibilities:

b1) The first is 16 ♕e2!? (Hitting the c4-pawn) 16...♖ac8 17 ♕f2 ♘c5 (Black waited passively, but without success, in Norwood-Westerinen, London 1988: 17...♖e7 18 ♖ad1 ♕b4?! 19 ♗d4 ♖ce8 20 ♖e2 b6?! [20...h6!? 21 ♕g3 ♘h7] 21 ♕g3 [21 ♔h1!?] 21...♘c5 22 e5 ♘fd7 23 e6 ♗xd4+ 24 ♖xd4 ♘f6? [24...fxe6 25 dxe6 ♘xe6±] 25 f5±) 18 ♗xc5 ♕xc5 19 ♕xc5 ♖xc5 20 e5 dxe5 21 fxe5 ♘d7 22 ♘e4! ♖xd5 (The only move. Otherwise 22...♖a5? 23 e6! fxe6 24 ♘d6± or 22...♖c7? 23 d6 ♖c8 24 ♗g4 ♖cd8 25 ♗xd7+-) 23 ♘f6+ ♗xf6 24 ♗xd5 with a clear advantage for White in the endgame, Lautier-Sutovsky, Tilburg 1996.

The second way is the prophylactic move:

b2) 16 ♔h1

This avoids a check after 16...♘c5 17 ♗xc5 ♕xc5. We consider three options for Black:

b21) 16...♘c5 17 ♗xc5 ♕xc5 18 e5 dxe5 19 fxe5 ♘d7

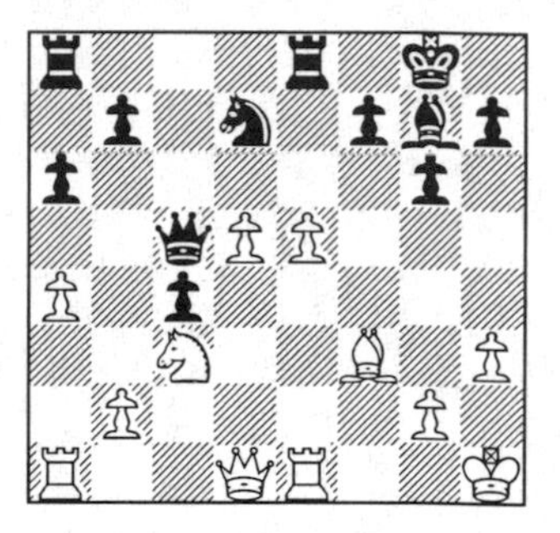

This is the critical position.

20 ♘e4

Often White plays 20 e6 first. The text move gives the additional possibility of playing 21 ♘d6 after 20...♕e7.

20...♕b4!? 21 e6 fxe6

If 21...♘e5 22 ♘g5!? gives White an initiative. On the other hand 22 exf7+ ♘xf7! 23 d6? is similar to the game Glek-Kaminsky, Odessa 1989, (where White was better) but in that example Black's queen was on b6 and the a-pawns on their starting positions, so this does not work here. Black can simply play 23...♖ad8 and if 24 ♕d5?

then 24...♖e5. Instead of 23 d6 White should play 23 ♗g4 ♘e5 24 ♗e6+ transposing to the text.

22 ♗g4!

22 dxe6?! ♘e5 23 ♕d6 was successful in the game Bode-Apicella, Paris 1990, after 23...♕a5? 24 e7! ♘xf3 25 ♕e6+ ♔h8 26 ♘d6! ♘g5 27 ♕d7+-, but Black's play was improved in the subsequent game Hensberger-Reinderman, Bussum 1993: 23...a5! 24 ♖ad1 ♘d3∓.

22...♘e5 23 ♗xe6+ ♔h8

This type of position is generally slightly better for White (in practice the queen is sometimes on e7 or c7 and the a-pawns on their starting squares). Here are two examples:

b211) Kakageldyev-Yurtaev, USSR 1983 (black queen on e7). 24 ♕d2 ♖f8 25 ♖f1 ♘d3? (25...h6!) 26 ♘g5! ♗f6 27 d6! ♕xd6 28 ♘f7+ ♖xf7 29 ♗xf7 ♗xb2 30 ♖ad1 ♕d4 (30...b5 31 ♕xb2!) 31 ♗xc4 ♕xc4 32 ♕xd3 ♕xa4 33 ♖b1±.

b212) Summerscale-Buckley, Hastings Masters 1995 (black queen on e7, pawns on a2 and a7 and one move less). 23 ♖f1 ♖f8 24 ♕c2 b5 25 b3 ♘d3 26 ♖ad1 ♕h4 27 ♕e2 ♖ae8 28 g3 ♕h5? 29 ♕xh5 gxh5 30 ♘d6±.

b22) 16...h6?! 17 ♗d4 (17 ♖e2!?) 17...♘c5 18 ♗xc5 ♕xc5 19 e5 dxe5 20 fxe5 ♘d7 (One might suppose that Black has won a tempo compared with variation b1, but in reality the move ...h7-h6 has just weakened the g6-pawn) 21 e6 ♘e5 22 exf7+ ♔xf7? (22...♘xf7!? 23 ♖e6!?) 23 d6!± ♘d3? 24 ♗d5+ ♔f6 (24....♕xd5 25 ♖f1+!) 25 ♕f3+ 1-0 Vaisser-Le Quang, Ostend 1992.

b23) **16...♖e7 17 ♖e2!**

An unfortunate manoeuvre by the white queen was met with a refutation in the game Peicheva-J. Polgar, Novi Sad Olympiad 1990: 17 ♕d2?! ♖ae8 18 ♕f2?! ♘xe4! 19 ♘xe4 ♖xe4 20 ♗xe4 ♖xe4 and Black is slightly better.

Also less precise than the text move is 17 ♗d4?! ♘c5! 18 ♗xc5 (18 e5? ♘d3!) 18...♕xc5 19 e5 ♖ae8.

17...♖ae8

17...♘c5!? 18 ♗xc5 ♕xc5 19 e5 is similar to variation b21.

18 ♗d4 ♘c5 19 e5! ♘fd7

In the case of 19...dxe5 20 fxe5 ♘fd7 21 d6 White simply wins an exchange.

20 e6!

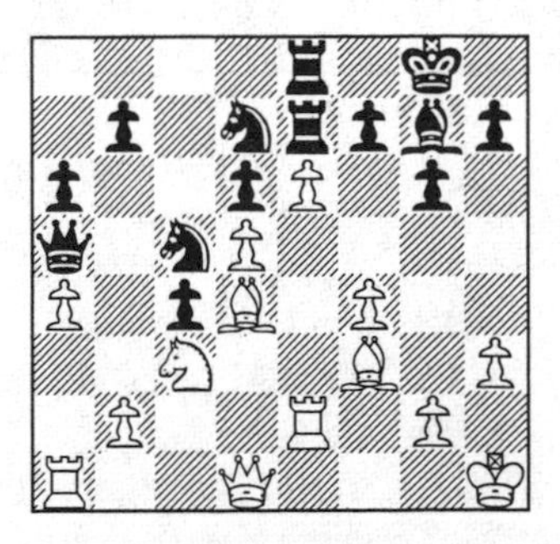

In this sharp position White has the better chances.

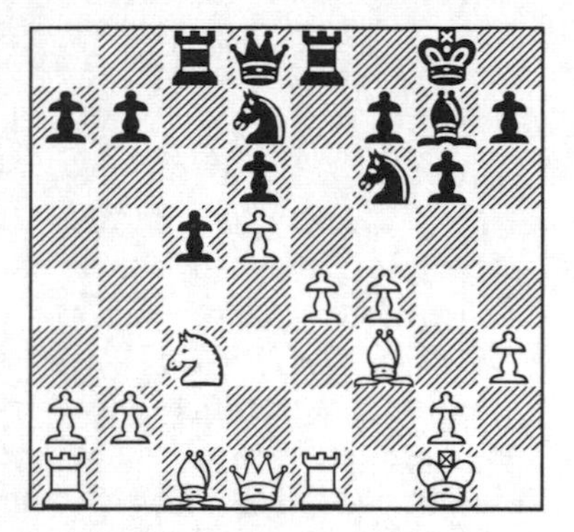

14 ♔h1!

Kasparov succeeded in equalising against Nogueiras (Barcelona 1989) after 14 ♗e3?! b5! 15 ♘xb5 ♘xe4 16 ♗xe4 ♖xe4 17 ♘xd6 ♖xe3 18 ♖xe3 ♗d4 19 ♕f3 ♖b8 20 ♔h2 ♘f6 21 ♘c4 (21 ♘e4 ♗xe3 22 ♘xf6+ ♕xf6 23 ♕xe3 ♕xb2=) 21...♗xe3 22 ♕xe3 ♕xd5=.

14 ... a6
15 a4 c4
16 ♗e3 ♘c5?!

It is better to take back with the queen on c5 rather than with the rook, as we have seen in other games. Therefore Black should try 16...♕a5!? 17 ♖e2 ♖cd8, preparing 18...♘c5, as in the game Vegh-Reinderman (Haarlem 1994).

17 ♗xc5 ♖xc5
18 e5 dxe5
19 fxe5 ♘d7
20 e6

This position is similar to that which arose in variation b21 above, but with the rook on c5.

20 .... ♘e5

If 20...fxe6 21 dxe6 ♘e5 22 ♕xd8 ♖xd8 23 ♗xb7 with an extra pawn for White (23...♘d3? loses to 24 e7 ♖e8 25 ♗d5+).

21 exf7+ ♔xf7

Christine Foisor had serious problems against Zsuzsa Polgar (Tilburg Candidates 1994) after 21...♘xf7 22 ♘e4 (22 ♖xe8+!? also seems strong: 22...♕xe8 23 ♘e4 ♖a5 24 d6! ♘e5 25 b4! cxb3 26 ♕xb3+±) 22...♖a5 23 ♗g4 ♔h8 24 ♗e6 ♘e5 25 ♕d2 h6 26 ♖ad1 ♘d3 27 ♖f1 ♖xd5? 28 ♗xd5 ♕xd5 29 ♘f6! ♗xf6 30 ♕xh6+ 1-0.

22 ♘e4! ♖c8

A very nice mate awaited Black after

22...♘d3

(see following diagram)

23 ♖f1 ♖xd5? (If 23...♖a5 White can choose between 24 ♗g4+ ♔g8 25 ♗e6+ ♔h8, transposing to the game Zsu. Polgar-C. Foisor in the previous

note, or the sharp 24 b3!?) 24 ♘d6+!! ♖xd6 25 ♗d5+ ♔e7 26 ♖f7 mate.

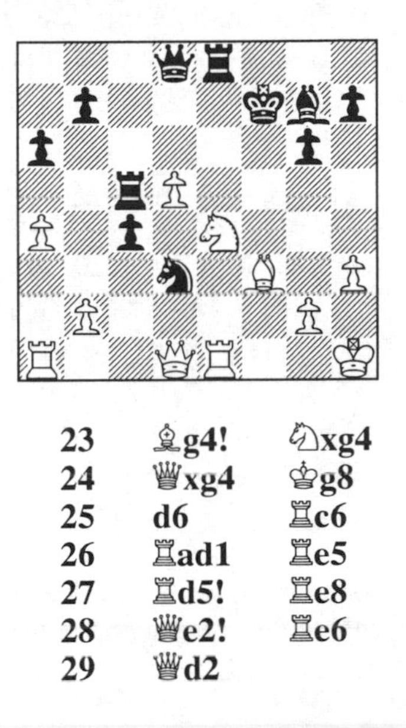

23 ♗g4! ♘xg4
24 ♕xg4 ♔g8
25 d6 ♖c6
26 ♖ad1 ♖e5
27 ♖d5! ♖e8
28 ♕e2! ♖e6
29 ♕d2

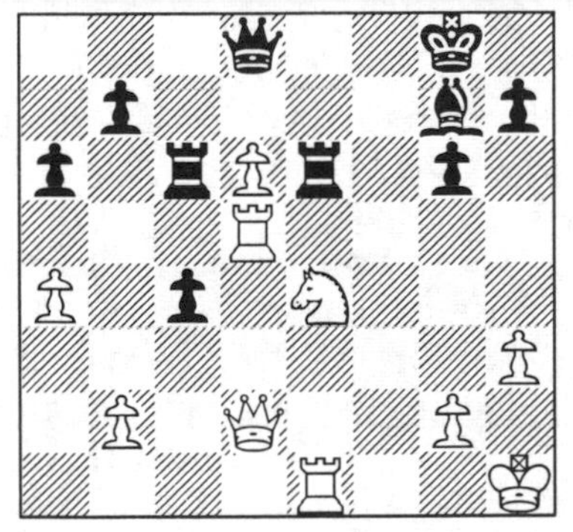

The desired construction has been built. White is winning thanks to the passed d-pawn.

29 ... h6
30 d7 ♖e7
31 ♘c5 c3
32 bxc3 ♗xc3
33 ♖xe7 1-0

Game 8
Vaisser-Smirin
PCA (rapidplay) Moscow 1996

1 d4 ♘f6 2 c4 g6 3 ♘c3 ♗g7 4 e4 d6 5 f4 0-0 6 ♘f3 c5 7 d5 e6 8 ♗e2 exd5 9 cxd5 ♗g4 10 0-0

10 ... ♘bd7

The most precise way of preventing e4-e5. Instead:

a) The consequences of the indifferent move 10...a6?! were grave in the game Vegh-Dambacher, Haarlem 1994: 11 e5! dxe5 12 fxe5 ♘fd7 13 e6 fxe6 14 ♘g5! ♗xe2 15 ♕xe2 e5 16 ♗e3 ♖xf1+ 17 ♖xf1 ♘f6 18 ♘e6±. We see a similar outcome after 10...♕a5?! 11 e5! dxe5 12 fxe5 ♘fd7 13 e6 fxe6 14 ♘g5! with a strong initiative.

b) 10...♗xf3?!

As we shall see in Game 9 (Monin-Shchekachev) the line 10...♘bd7 11 ♘d2 is harmless, so Black should not be in a rush to exchange this bishop. This move allows White to save the tempo h2-h3 and so cannot be recommended. If Black wants to play the system with ...♘bd7, ...♗xf3 and ...♘e8 discussed below, he should adopt the move order 10...♘bd7 11 ♖e1 ♗xf3 12 ♗xf3 ♘e8, as this cuts out one or two dangerous options for White.

11 ♗xf3 ♘bd7 12 ♖e1

White has another aggressive plan here: g2-g4-g5, ♗g4 or ♕c2, followed by the manoeuvre e4-e5! d6xe5, f4-f5. As an illustration the game Arencibia-Baron, Manresa 1996, continued: 12 g4!? h6 13 h4 ♘h7 14 g5 a6 15 ♗e3 b5 16 ♕d2 ♘b6 17 b3 b4 18 ♘e2 ♗xa1 19 ♖xa1 a5 20 ♘g3 a4 21 ♖b1 ♘d7 22 e5! dxe5 23 f5 axb3 24 axb3 ♖a6 25 ♗e4 ♕b6 26 ♖f1 with a strong initiative and full compensation for the exchange.

12...♘e8

12...♖e8 allows White the main line position without having wasted a tempo on h2-h3.

13 ♖e2

This is an important multifunctional move in the ...♗g4 system, but here 13 ♗e3!? preparing ♗e3-f2-g3 and eventually ♗g4 seems to me more precise.

13...a6?

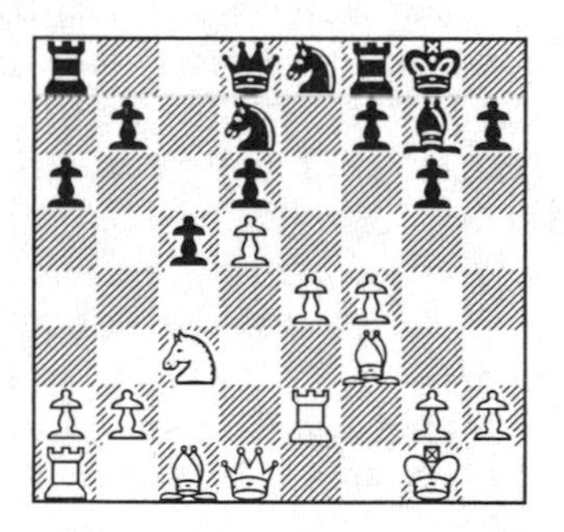

It was necessary to play 13...♘c7! 14 a4 a6 15 ♕e1 ♖e8 16 ♗e3 ♖b8 17 a5 with a complicated game, although White still has slightly better chances.

After the text move, White emerges on top with 14 ♕e1! ♕e7 15 a4 ♘c7 16 ♗e3 ♖fe8 (16...b5 17 e5!) 17 ♖d1 (again threatening 18 e5) 17...♕d8 18 ♗f2± Vaisser-Maki, Helsinki 1991. The manoeuvre ♗c1-e3-f2-g3 (or h4) is a typical one in this whole system.

c) 10...♖e8

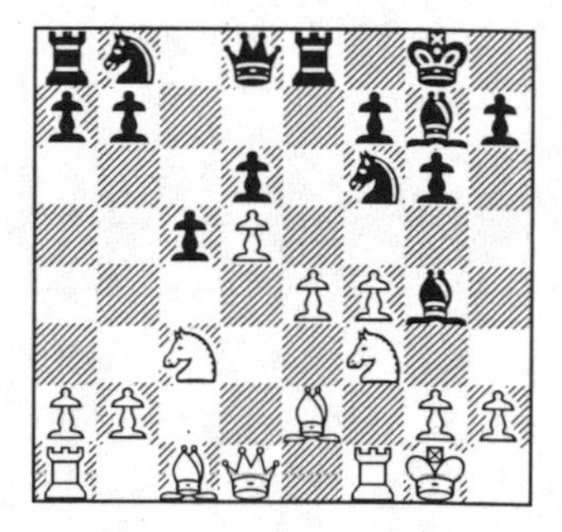

Now the solid 11 h3 ♗xf3 12 ♗xf3, trying to transpose to the main line after 12...♘bd7, can be met by 12...♘fd7!? or 12...♘a6!? 13 ♖e1 ♘d7. This is not bad for White, but is not to everyone's taste. It is more tempting to play:

11 e5! dxe5

In the game Jarovik-Mirovschikov, Russian Ch. Semi-Final 1996, White obtained a strong attack after 11...♘fd7?! 12 e6 fxe6 13 ♘g5 ♗xe2 14 ♘xe2 ♘f8 15 dxe6 ♘c6 (15...♘xe6? 16 ♕d5 ♕d7 17 f5 gxf5 18 ♘f4+-) 16 f5 d5?! (16...gxf5!?) 17 ♘f7 ♕e7 18 ♗g5 ♗f6 19 ♘f4 ♗xg5 20 ♘xd5.

12 fxe5 ♗xf3

If 12...♘fd7 13 ♗g5 f6 (13...♕b6!? 14 ♘a4!) 14 exf6 ♗xf6 15 ♕d2 with the better chances for White, Tozer-Lane, London 1988.

13 ♗xf3 ♖xe5 14 ♗f4

and now:

c1) 14...♖e7 15 ♕b3 ♘bd7?! (15...♖d7 seems better, but still after 16 ♗e2! White has more than enough compensation for the pawn) 16 d6 ♖e6 17 ♘d5! ♘xd5 18 ♗xd5 ♗d4+ 19 ♔h1 ♖f6 20 ♕xb7 ♖b8, Schon-Cvitan, New York open 1987, and now White should have played 21 ♕xa7! ♖xb2 22 ♕c7 with a clear advantage.

c2) 14...♖e8 15 ♕b3! ♕b6 16 ♕xb6 axb6

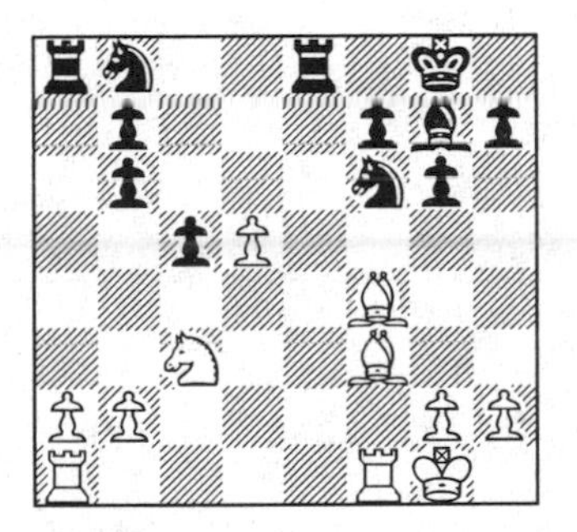

17 ♗c7!

The most precise. 17 ♘b5?!, Vaisser-Guyard, Aubervilliers (rapidplay) 1993, gave Black the possibility of 17...♖a4! with counterplay, while if 17 a4 then 17...♘fd7!

17...♘fd7

Or 17...♘a6 18 d6!

18 ♖fe1!

White is clearly better. For example: 18...♘a6 19 d6 ♖xe1+ 20 ♖xe1 ♗xc3 21 bxc3 ♘xc7 22 dxc7 ♖c8 23 ♖e7 ♖xc7 24 ♗d5±.

d) 10...♘fd7!? This clever move poses some problems for White:

d1) 11 a4 ♘a6 12 ♘b5 ♕e7 13 h3 ♗xf3 14 ♗xf3 ♘b4 15 e5 dxe5 16 d6 ♕h4 17 ♗xb7 ♖ab8 18 ♗d5, Piskov-Itkis, Kastel Stari 1988, and now 18...♘b6!? 19 ♗b3 c4 20 ♕d2 a5 would have given Black the better chances in a complex position.

d2) 11 ♘g5?! (If White wants to exchange bishops here, in contrast to variation b, it is better to achieve this with 11 ♘d2) 11...♗xe2 12 ♕xe2 h6 13 ♘f3 ♖e8 14 ♕c2 ♘a6 15 ♗e3 f5 16 ♘d2 ♘f6 17 h3 ♘b4 with an initiative, Piskov-Neverov, Podolsk GMA qualifier 1989.

d3) The interesting move ***11 ♘b5!?*** has never been tried. Black has three reasonable possibilities:

d31) 11...♘b6 12 a4 a6 13 ♘c3± (if 13 ♘a3?! ♖e8 14 h3 ♗d7! 15 a5 ♘c8 16 e5 ♕xa5 and White does not have enough compensation for the pawn).

d32) 11...♕b6 12 a4 c4+ 13 ♔h1 ♗xf3 (Otherwise 14 ♘d2! follows) 14 ♗xf3 ♘c5 15 ♕e2±.

d33) 11...♘f6 12 h3 (12 e5!?) 12...♗xf3 13 ♗xf3 ♖e8 14 ♖e1 a6 15 ♘c3 ♘bd7 16 a4 and we have arrived at a well-known position which favours White (see Game 7, Vaisser-Berelovich).

11 ♖e1 ♘e8!?

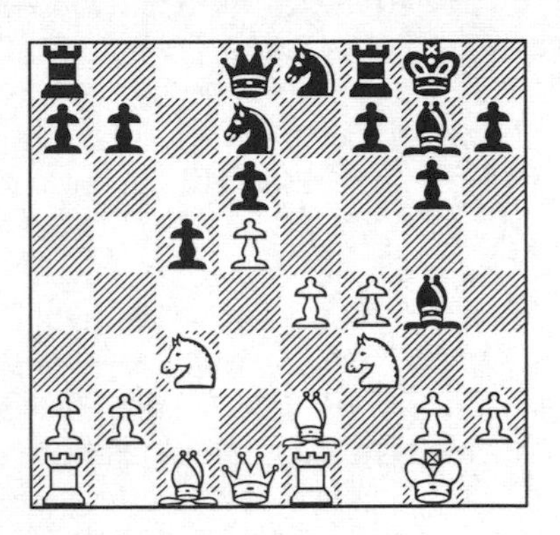

A rather unusual idea in this position.

12 a4

Instead:

a) 12 h3?! (It is not necessary to spend a tempo provoking this exchange) 12...♗xf3 13 ♗xf3 ♖b8 leads to Game 9, Monin-Shchekachev.

b) 12 ♘d2 is playable here. After 12...♗xe2 13 ♕xe2 (13 ♖xe2!?) 13...a6 14 a4 ♗d4+ 15 ♔h1 ♘ef6 16 ♕f3 ♖e8 17 ♘e2 ♕e7 18 ♘xd4 cxd4 19 b3 ♘xd5 20 ♗a3! ♘e3 21 ♖ec1 ♕e6 (21...♘c5!?) 22 ♗b2 ♖ac8 23 ♖xc8 ♖xc8 24 ♗xd4 ♘c2 25 ♖c1 ♘e5 26 ♗xe5 dxe5 27 fxe5 ♘d4 28 ♖xc8+ ♕xc8 29 ♕d1 ♕c3 30 ♘f3 ♘e6 the position is equal, Banikas-Beliavsky, European Club Cup 1995.

c) ***12 ♘g5!?*** ♗xe2 13 ♖xe2! seems to me the most unpleasant for Black. Compared to the game Piskov-Neverov from the previous note, the position of Black's knight on e8 instead of d7 is in White's favour.

12 ... a6
13 ♗e3 ♘c7
14 ♗f2 ♖b8
15 ♗h4 ♗f6
16 ♗g3 ♗xf3
17 ♗xf3 ♗h4?

Black should not permit e4-e5. It was necessary to play 17...♗d4+! 18 ♔h1 ♖e8 with counterplay.

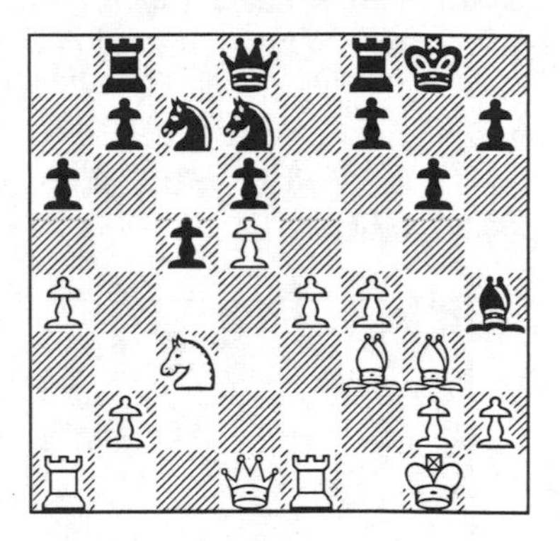

18 e5! ♗xg3
19 hxg3 dxe5
20 fxe5 ♕g5
21 ♘e4 ♕xe5
22 ♘xc5 ♕d6
23 ♘e4

White's pawn sacrifice to activate the d-pawn is the key to this position.

23 ... ♕b6+
24 ♔h2 ♕xb2
25 ♖c1 ♘e8
26 d6 ♘ef6
27 ♖c7 ♖fd8
28 ♘g5!

Preparing a decisive piece sacrifice.

28 ... h6

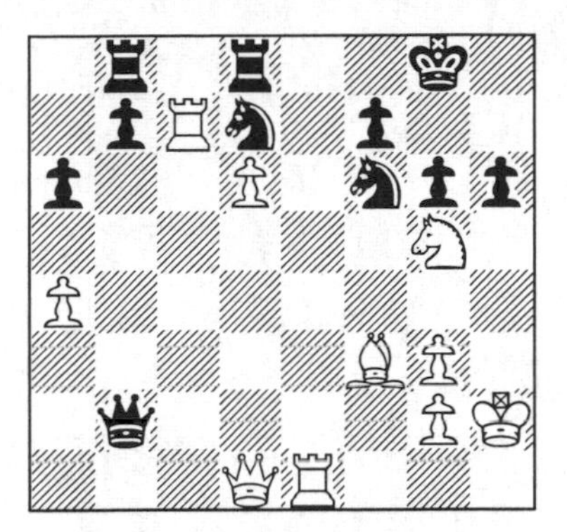

29 ♖e2!

First driving away Black's queen...

29 ... ♕b4

and now giving up the knight!

30 ♘xf7! ♔xf7
31 ♖e7+ ♔g8

31...♔f8 changes nothing. White plays 32 ♕d3 and after both 32...♘g4+ 33 ♗xg4 ♕xg4 34 ♕c3 ♕h5+ 35 ♔g1 ♕d1+ 36 ♔f2 ♘e5 37 ♖xe5 and 32...♘g8 33 ♕xg6! ♘xe7 34 ♕xh6+ ♔f7 35 ♗h5+ ♔g8 36 ♕e6+ ♔h8 37 dxe7 White wins.

32 ♕d3 ♘g4+

32...♘f8 doesn't help: 33 ♖g7+ ♔h8 34 ♕e3 g5 35 ♕e7 ♕d4 36 ♖g6 ♘g8 37 ♕f7 ♘d7 38 ♗e4 with mate in two.

33 ♗xg4 ♕xg4
34 ♕b3+ 1-0

Game 9
Monin-Shchekachev
St Petersburg open 1994

1 d4 ♘f6 2 c4 g6 3 ♘c3 ♗g7 4 e4 d6 5 f4 0-0 6 ♘f3 c5 7 d5 e6 8 ♗e2 exd5 9 cxd5 ♗g4

10 0-0

Instead White can play:

10 e5?!

This line is not very dangerous for Black. Nevertheless, he must play precisely. For example 10...♘fd7?! is suspicious: 11 e6! fxe6 12 ♘g5 ♗xe2 13 ♕xe2 exd5 14 ♕e6+ ♔h8 15 ♘xd5 ♘f6, Sutter-Wojtkiewicz, Bern open 1991, and now the simple 16 ♘f7+ ♖xf7 17 ♕xf7 ♘xd5 18 ♕xd5 ♕e8+ 19 ♔f2 ♗d4+ 20 ♔f3 would have maintained White's advantage.

10...dxe5 11 fxe5 ♗xf3 12 ♗xf3

Not 12 gxf3? ♘h5.

12...♘fd7

For 12...♖e8?! see the comments in variation c, Black's 10th move in Game 8.

13 e6 ♘e5

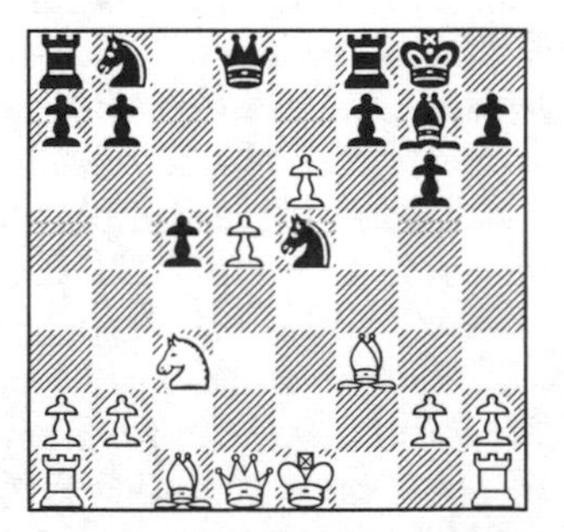

14 0-0

Weaker is 14 exf7+?! ♖xf7 15 0-0 ♘bd7 and now both 16 ♗e2 ♖xf1+ 17 ♕xf1 ♕b6!, Ludden-De Vries, corr. 1994, and 16 ♘e4 ♘xf3+ 17 ♖xf3 ♖xf3 18 ♕xf3 ♘e5, Knezevic-Gligoric, Yugoslavia 1970, give Black the better position.

After 14 0-0:

a) Warning – don't believe the published recommendation 14...♘xf3+ 15 ♖xf3 fxe6 16 ♖xf8+ ♕xf8 17 ♗e3! ♘a6! 18 dxe6 ♕e7 19 ♕b3 ♖e8 20 ♖e1 ♘b4 (20...♕xe6?? 21 ♗g5+-) 21 ♗f2 ♔h8 22 a3 ♘c6 23 ♘d5 ♕d6 24 e7, Schoen-Sherzer, New York open 1987, 24...♗e5! 'and Black is slightly better'. After ***25 ♗h4!*** White's threats are very strong. For example, 25...♗g7 26 ♘f6! ♗xf6 27 ♕f7 ♗d4+ 28 ♔h1 ♕b8 29 ♖d1! and Black is obliged to give back a rook.

b) 14...fxe6

and now:

b1) 15 ♗e4 ♖xf1+ 16 ♕xf1

and:

b11) 16...♔h8

The old Hort proposition 17 ♗e3? was tried in the game Hajenius-Le Quang, Brussels Zonal 1993: 17...exd5? 18 ♗xd5 ♘bd7 with a complicated game, but the simple ***17...♘g4!*** 18 ♗xc5 (18 ♖e1 ♘xe3 19 ♖xe3 ♗d4) 18...♕c7 19 ♕b5 ♘a6 would have won for Black.

Instead of 17 ♗e3? White should play 17 dxe6 and now Black has a choice between a draw after 17...♕d4+ 18 ♔h1 ♘g4 19 e7 ♘a6 20 ♗xb7 ♘f2+ and a complicated game after 17...♘bc6 18 ♗f4 ♕d4+ 19 ♔h1 ♘g4 20 ♗g3 ♖f8.

b12) 16...♘g4 seems attractive, but after 17 g3! ♗xc3 18 bxc3 exd5 19 ♗g2! ♘c6 20 ♕d1 White has good compensation for the two pawns.

b2) 15 ♗e3 ♘xf3+ 16 ♖xf3 ♖xf3 17 ♕xf3 exd5 18 ♘xd5 ♘c6

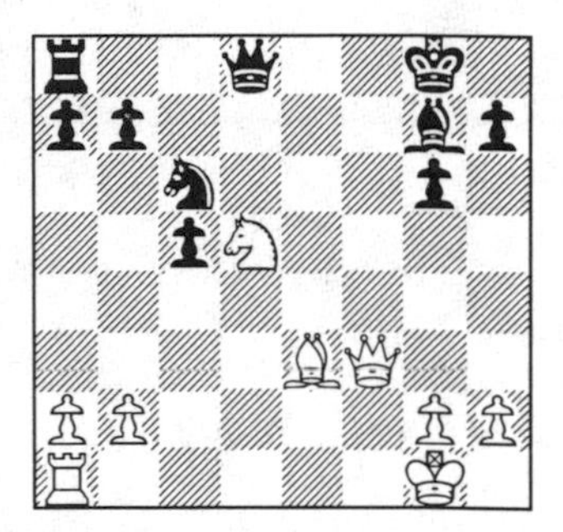

and now:

b21) 19 ♖f1?! ♘e5 20 ♕e4 ♕d6 21 ♗g5 ♘c6 22 ♗f6 ♖f8 23 ♕c4 ♔h8, when White's attack proved unsuccessful in Bischoff-Hellers, San Bernardino 1990.

b22) 19 ♗xc5 ♔h8 20 ♖d1 ♕a5 and Black has an edge.

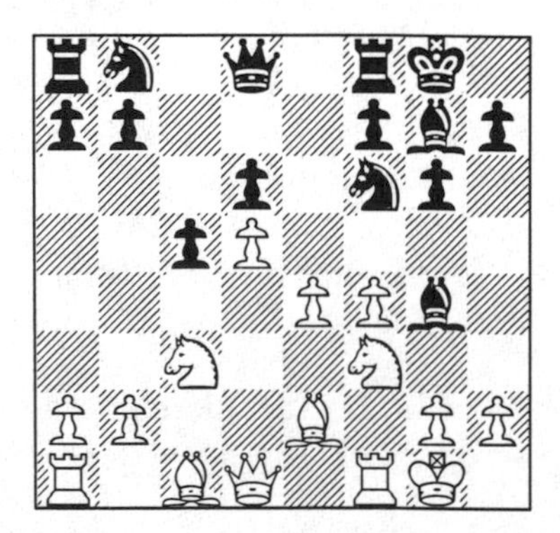

10 ... ♘bd7
11 h3

For the main line 11 ♖e1 see Game 6, Vaisser-Yrjola, and Game 7, Vaisser-Berelovich.

Instead:

a) 11 a4

This is not just a waste of time. It can be considered as a useful waiting move at the moment, as Black still has not chosen which piece is going to e8. White demonstrated some interesting ideas in Kahn-Mah, Budapest 1995: 11...♘e8 12 ♘g5!? ♗xe2 13 ♕xe2 ♘c7 (13...♗d4+!? 14 ♔h1 ♘ef6) 14 ♖a3 (An unusual way of preparing an attack on the kingside) 14...♕e7? (The combination of a queen on e7 and a knight on c7 is unfortunate, and White makes perfect use of this. Better was 14...h6 15 ♘f3 ♖e8) 15 e5! dxe5 16 ♘ge4! ♘e8 17 f5 gxf5?! 18 ♖xf5 ♘d6 (Black has helped a lot and now White's attack is very strong) 19 ♘xd6 ♕xd6 20 ♘e4! ♕xd5 21 ♖g3 ♔h8 22 ♕g4 ♖g8 23 ♕h5 ♕e6 24 ♘g5! ♕xf5 25 ♕xh7+! 1-0.

Black should try to obtain a position resembling that analysed in Vaisser-Berelovich where the move a2-a4 is often less useful than ♖e1:

11...♖e8!?

11...a6 12 ♖e1 ♖e8 13 h3 transposes to the main line of the 9...♗g4 variation, but with fewer options for Black.

12 h3 ♗xf3 13 ♗xf3 c4 14 ♗e3 ♕a5

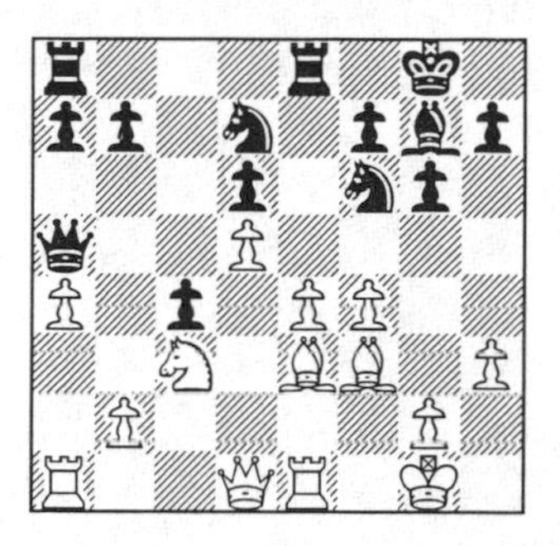

and now:

a1) 15 ♕e2?! was successful in Priehoda-Hass, Katowice open 1990, after 15...♕b4? (15...♖ac8? 16 ♘b5!) 16 ♕f2 ♖ac8 (16...a6 17 a5) 17 ♗xa7 ♘c5 (17...b6 18 a5 bxa5 19 ♖a4±) 18 ♗xc5 ♖xc5 19 ♖ae1 ♘d7 20 ♗g4 ♘f6 21 e5!±. Black should play actively: 15...♘c5! 16 ♕xc4 ♘fxe4 17 ♘xe4 ♘xe4 18 ♗xe4 ♖ac8! 19 ♕d3 ♕b4 with full compensation, e.g. 20 ♗f3? ♖xe3!

a2) The usual continuation is 15 ♗d4 ♖e7!

It is premature to play 15...♘c5?! 16 e5! ♘fd7 17 e6 fxe6 18 dxe6 ♘xe6 19 ♗d5 (19 ♔h1!?) 19...♗xd4+ 20 ♕xd4 ♕c5 21 ♖ad1 and White is slightly better, Fang-Zapata, Philadelphia 1994.

16 ♔h2!

This prevents the thematic exchange sacrifice that is possible in the case of 16 ♔h1 a6 17 g4 ♖ae8! 18 g5 ♘xe4 19 ♘xe4 (19 ♗xg7 ♘g3+) 19...♖xe4 20

♗xe4 ♖xe4 21 ♕f3 f5! and White is not better, Peev-Velimirovic, Sofia 1972.

16...♘c5! 17 e5 ♘e8!

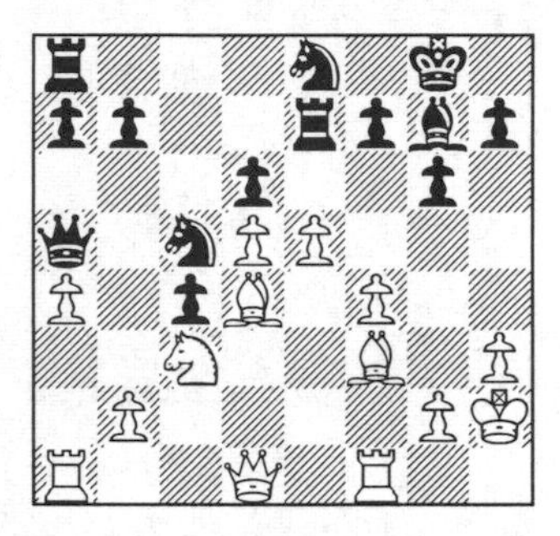

The game Hausner-Donchev, Pardubice 1994, continued 18 ♘b5 ♘b3 19 exd6 ♖d7 20 ♗xg7 ♔xg7 21 ♕e1 ♕xe1 22 ♖axe1 ♘xd6 23 ♘xd6 ♖xd6 24 ♖e7 ♘d2 with equality.

Other White 11th moves are not dangerous:

b) 11 ♔h1?! ♖e8 12 h3 ♗xf3 13 ♗xf3 b5! 14 ♕c2 b4 15 ♘d1 ♖c8 16 ♘e3 c4! with good counterplay, Krcmar-Felix, Karvina 1989.

c) 11 ♕c2?! ♖e8 12 ♗d2 a6 13 a4 ♖c8 14 a5 c4 15 ♖a4 ♘c5! 16 ♖xc4 ♘cxe4 17 ♘xe4 ♘xe4 18 ♗d3 ♖xc4 19 ♗xc4 ♕c7 20 ♗b4 ♘c3! 21 ♕b3 ♘e2+ 22 ♔h1? ♗xf3 23 ♖xf3 ♘d4 24 ♕a4 ♖e7 0-1 Holderried-Groszpeter, Andorra open 1995.

d) 11 ♗e3?! ♖e8 12 ♘d2 ♗xe2 13 ♕xe2 b5! 14 ♕f3 b4 15 ♘d1 ♕e7∓ Kaidanov-Lerner, Norilsk 1987.

e) 11 ♘d2?! ♗xe2 12 ♕xe2 ♖e8 13 ♕f3

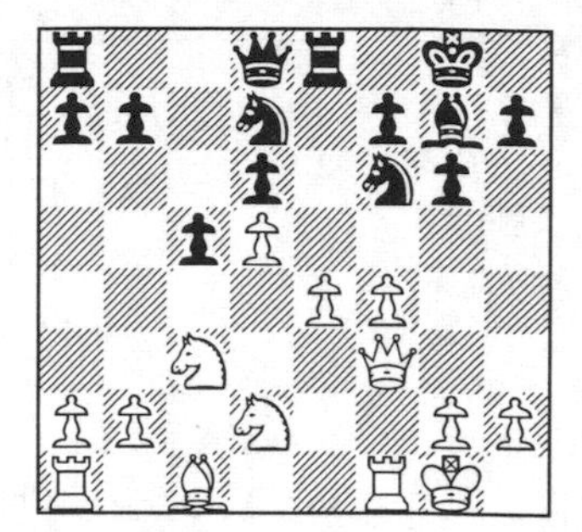

13...♖c8!?

This strong move, preparing 14...c4, was introduced by Nunn. Here White has tried a number of possibilities:

e1) 14 ♘c4?! ♘b6 15 ♘xb6 (Or 15 ♘xd6?! ♕xd6 16 e5 ♕d7 17 exf6 ♗xf6 18 f5 ♗d4+ 19 ♔h1 ♗xc3! 20 bxc3 ♘xd5 21 ♕g3 ♘f6!-+ Wells-Nunn, Borehamwood 1980) 15...♕xb6 16 ♔h1 ♕b4 17 e5 dxe5 18 fxe5 ♖xe5 19 ♗f4 ♖f5! 20 g4 ♘xg4 21 ♕xg4 ♕xb2 22 ♘e2 ♖e8 23 ♘g3 ♖xd5∓ Michaelsen-Maus, Hamburg 1987.

e2) 14 ♘b5?! ♕b6 15 a4 c4+ 16 ♕f2 ♖c5! 17 b4 cxb3 18 ♗a3 ♘g4! 19 ♗xc5 ♘xc5 20 ♘c4 ♘xf2 21 ♘xb6 ♘fxe4 22 ♘c4 a6 23 ♘bxd6 ♘xd6 24 ♘xd6 ♖d8 25 ♘c4 ♗d4+ 26 ♔h1 ♗xa1 27 ♖xa1 ♖xd5 0-1 Maier-Enders, Meisdorfer Schloturnier 1996.

e3) The most aggressive plan was demonstrated by Nogueiras against Cvitan (Novi Sad Olympiad 1990):

14 ♔h1 c4 15 g4?!

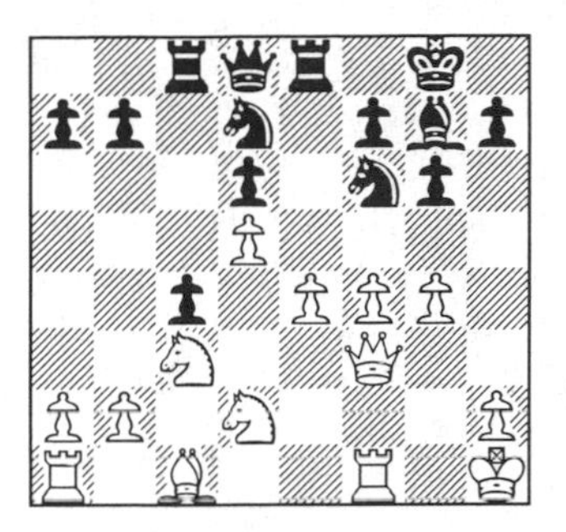

Cvitan immediately made a serious mistake with 15...♘c5? and White obtained a clear advantage after 16 e5! dxe5 17 fxe5 ♖xe5 18 ♘xc4 ♘cd7 19 ♘xe5 ♘xe5 20 ♕g3 ♘exg4 21 ♗f4. Black should have played ***15...h6!*** first. If White continues his plan with 16 h4, then 16...♘c5! and now 17 e5? dxe5 18 fxe5 ♘fd7! 19 ♕xf7+ ♔h7 is just bad for White. Black is also better after 17 g5 hxg5 18 hxg5 ♘h5.

11 ... ♗xf3
12 ♗xf3

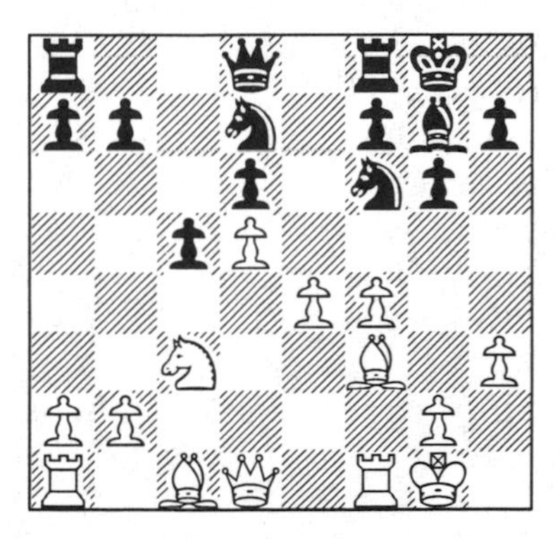

12 ... ♖b8!?

Black has a wide choice here:

a) The immediate 12...♘e8!? deserves attention. If White plays slowly then punishment is quick: 13 ♕e1?! ♘c7 14 a4 ♖e8 15 ♕g3 c4! 16 ♗e3 ♘a6 17 ♖ad1 ♘ac5 18 ♗d4 ♗xd4+ 19 ♖xd4 ♕b6 20 a5 ♕xb2 21 ♖xc4 b5! 22 ♖b1 ♕c2 23 ♖xb5 ♕d3 24 ♖bb4 ♘a6 with a large advantage for Black, Fors-Akesson, Stockholm 1990. White played more accurately in the game Adianto-Hulak, Jakarta 1986 (by transposition): 13 g4 a6 14 g5 ♘c7 15 h4!? ♘b5 16 ♗d2 ♘d4 17 h5 f6 18 h6 ♗h8 19 ♗g4 f5 20 exf5 ♘xf5 21 ♕e2 ♖f7 22 ♘e4 ♘b6 23 ♗c3±.

b) The following variation is rather popular, so it is useful to take a look at it:

12...♖e8 13 g4!?

13 ♖e1 leads to the main line of the 9...♗g4 variation.

13...h6 14 h4

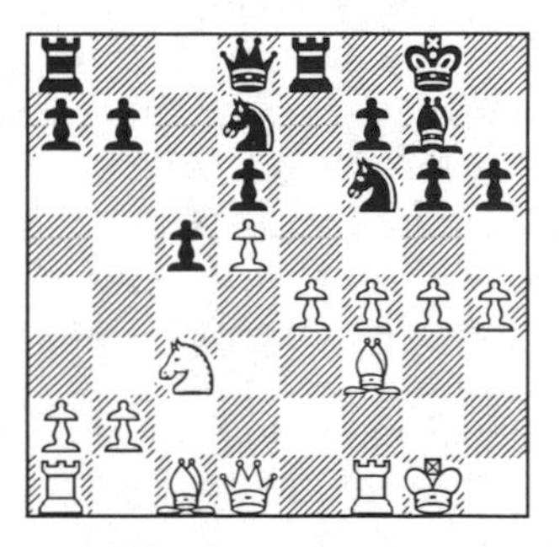

and now:

b1) The piece sacrifice is not well founded: 14...b5?! 15 g5 b4 (15...♘h7 16 ♘xb5±) 16 gxf6 ♘xf6 17 ♘e2!? ♘xe4 18 h5! and both of the following variations give a clear advantage to White:

b11) 18...gxh5 19 ♕d3 (19 ♗xe4!? ♖xe4 20 ♘g3±) 19...f5 20 ♗xh5 ♕h4? (20...♖e7!?±) 21 ♗xe8 ♖xe8 22 ♕f3 ♘f6 23 ♔g2 ♘h5 24 ♗e3 ♖e4 25 ♖ae1 ♗xb2 26 ♘g3+- Scholseth-Moen, Norwegian Ch. 1992.

b12) 18...♕h4 19 ♔g2 g5, Osmanbegovic-Rotstein, Maribor Pirc 1994, and now 20 ♗xe4! would have been strong: 20...♖xe4 21 ♖h1 ♕g4+ 22 ♘g3 ♕xd1 23 ♖xd1 ♖c4 24 ♘f5 ♖d8 25 ♔h3! (25 ♔f3?! ♗xb2!) with an edge for White.

b2) More solid is 14...♘h7 15 g5 hxg5 16 hxg5:

b21) Now 16...f6?! is not good, as has been shown twice: 17 gxf6 ♕xf6 (17...♘hxf6!?) 18 ♗e3 (Or 18 ♔g2 a6 19 a4 ♖e7 20 e5! dxe5 21 d6 ♖ee8 22 ♗d5+ ♔h8 23 ♘e4 ♕f5 24 ♘g5+- Moutousis-Hon Kah Seng, Thessaloniki Olympiad 1988) 18...♖e7 (18...g5 19 e5 ♕h6 20 ♗g4) 19 ♔g2 b5? 20 e5! ♘xe5 21 ♘e4 ♕h4 22 ♖h1 ♘c4 23 ♗c1 1-0 Arencibia-Gonzalez, Capablanca Memorial 1993.

b22) After 16...a6 17 a4 c4 18 ♗e3 ♖c8 White has a choice between the quiet 19 ♗d4 ♗xd4+ 20 ♕xd4 ♘c5 21 ♖ad1 with a roughly equal position, Monin-Purtov, Budapest 1993, and complicated play with 19 ♗g4!? ♗xc3 20 bxc3 ♖xe4 21 ♕f3! (Not 21 ♗d4? ♘xg5!∓) 21...♕e7 22 ♗d4 ♖e8 23 ♖a2 ♘df8, Stankovic-Paunovic, Cetinje 1992. Now instead of the continuation 24 ♕h3? ♖xd4! 25 cxd5 b5∓ White should have played 24 a5! with good compensation for the pawn.

b3) 14...h5!?

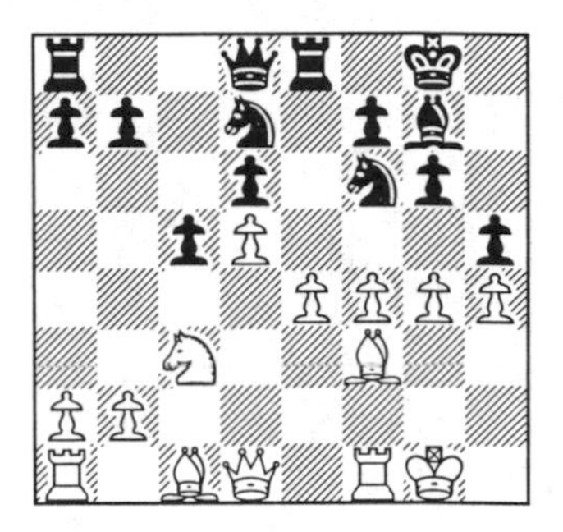

This actually seems to be Black's best:

b31) Existing theory gives the variation 15 gxh5 ♘xh5 16 ♗xh5 gxh5 17 ♕xh5 b5! 'with compensation'. This final evaluation can be accepted despite a spectacular White victory in the game Dekusar-Borulia, USSR 1990: 18 e5 dxe5 19 fxe5 ♘xe5? (It was necessary to play 19...♖xe5! 20 ♕xf7+ ♔h8 and if 21 ♗f4 then 21...♕xh4!) 20 ♗h6 ♘g6? (Also bad was 20...b4? 21 ♗xg7 ♔xg7 22 ♖ae1! f6 23 ♔h1! with a mating attack, but it was better to play 20...♕d6!? 21 ♗xg7 ♔xg7 22 ♘xb5±) 21 ♗xg7 ♔xg7 22 ♖xf7+! ♔xf7 23 ♕h7+ and mate was not far off. However, the problem is that the very first move of this variation is wrong! Let us rewrite it like this:

15 gxh5? ♘xh5 16 ♗xh5?!

16 ♕e1 is met by 16...f5∓. Now instead of 16...gxh5?? Black has a nice, practically winning improvement:

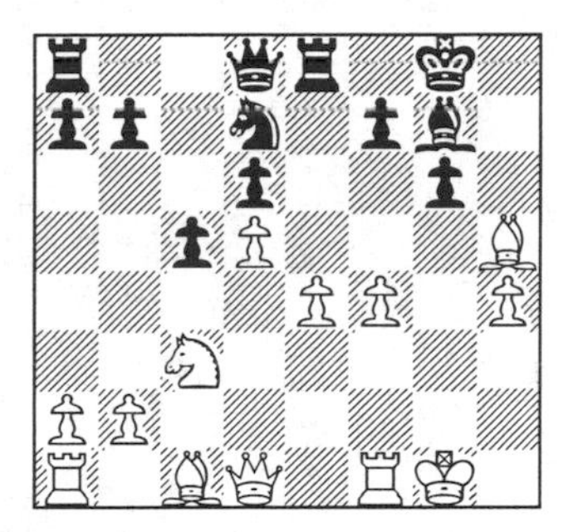

16...♕xh4!! 17 ♕g4 (Not 17 ♗g4? ♗xc3! 18 ♔g2 ♘f6 19 ♗f3 ♗d4-+) 17...♕xh5 18 ♕xd7? (18 ♕xh5 gxh5∓) 18...♖ad8 19 ♕b5 ♕g4+! 20 ♔f2 (20 ♔h2 ♗xc3 21 ♕d3 ♗d4-+) 20...♗d4+ 21 ♔e1 ♗xc3+ 22 bxc3 ♖xe4+-+.

b32) So White should try 15 g5 ♘g4 16 ♗xg4 hxg4 17 ♖e1 (Or 17 ♕xg4 ♗xc3 18 bxc3 ♖xe4 19 ♗d2 ♕e7 20 ♖ae1 ♘b6 21 ♕f3 ♖ae8 22 f5! ♘xd5 23 fxg6 fxg6 24 c4! ♘e3 25 ♗xe3 with a drawn ending, Bach-Trisic, Hamburg 1996) 17...c4 18 ♗e3 (It would be interesting to check out 18 ♕xg4 ♘c5 19 ♕f3) 18...♗xc3 19 bxc3 ♖xe4 20 ♕xg4 ♕e7 21 ♗f2 ♘c5 22 ♖xe4 ♕xe4 (Kouatly-Kindermann, Trnava 1987) and here, according to Kindermann, White has enough compensation after 23 ♖e1 ♕xd5 24 ♗d4 with the idea of h4-h5.

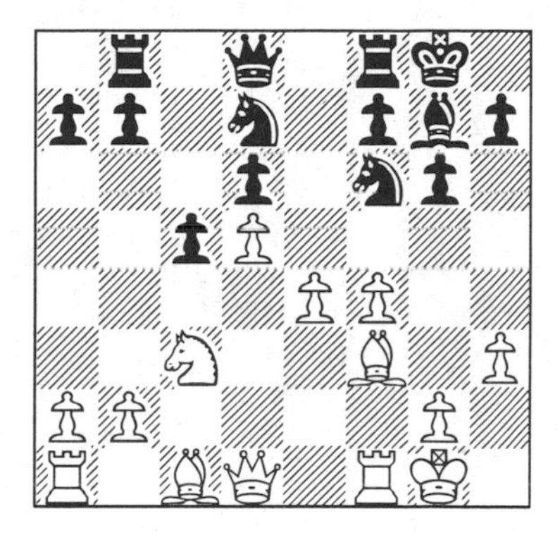

13 ♖e1 ♘e8

If 13...b5?! 14 e5±.

14 ♗g4?!

14 a4 a6 (14...♘c7!?) 15 a5 b5 16 axb6 ♖xb6 17 ♖e2± would have corresponded more with the spirit of the position.

14 ... f5

15 exf5

Or 15 ♗f3 b5!

15 ... gxf5

16 ♗e2 a6

Avoiding 16...♘c7 17 ♘b5!?

17 ♗d3!

Or 17 a4?! ♘c7 18 a5 ♗d4+ 19 ♔h2 ♕f6 with an initiative.

17 ... ♘c7

17...b5?! hands the initiative to White: 18 ♖e6! ♖b6 19 g4.

18 ♕c2

Now it is too late for 18 ♖e6?: 18...♘xe6 19 dxe6 ♘b6 20 ♕b3 ♕c7 21 ♘d5 ♘xd5 22 ♕xd5 ♕c6 with a clear advantage for Black.

18 ... ♕f6

With the threat of 19...c4.

19 ♘e2

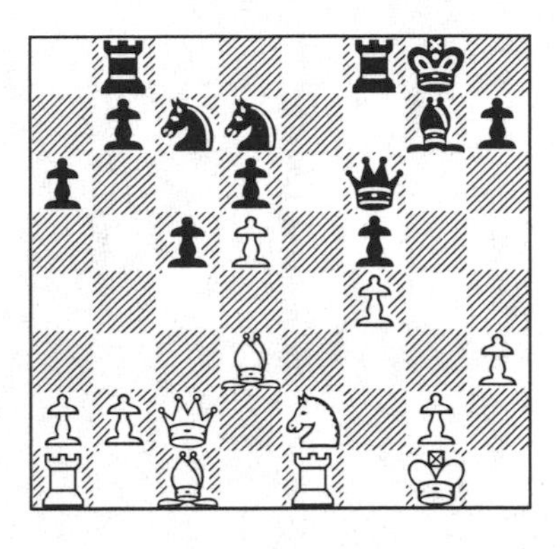

19 ... ♖be8?!

It would have been better to play 19...♘xd5!? 20 ♘g3 ♘e7!, when the exchange sacrifice doesn't work: 21 ♗c4+? d5 22 ♖xe7 ♕xe7 23 ♗xd5+ ♔h8 24 ♘xf5 ♕e1+ 25 ♔h2 ♖xf5! 26 ♕xf5 ♗d4 27 ♗e3 ♕xe3 28 ♕xd7 ♕xf4+ 29 ♔h1 ♗e5 30 ♔g1 ♕e3+ 31 ♔h1 ♕g3 32 ♔g1 ♖f8-+.

20 ♖d1

The inaccurate 20 ♗d2? just gives away a pawn after 20...♘xd5! 21 ♕b3 ♘7b6, and both attempts to justify it don't work: 22 a4? ♖xe2! 23 ♖xe2 (23 ♗xe2 ♕d4+) 23...c4-+; and 22 ♗a5? ♕xb2 23 ♕xb2 ♗xb2 24 ♖ab1 c4! 25 ♗c2 ♗a3-+.

20 ... ♕h4!

21 ♔h2

21 ♗xf5? ♖xf5! wins.

21 ... ♘f6

22 ♗xf5 ♘cxd5

23 ♘g3 ♔h8

24 ♕f2 ♘e7

25 ♕f3

Black's dream of a knight fork becomes real in the case of the stupid 25 ♗e6? ♘c6! 26 ♖xd6?? ♖xe6 27 ♖xe6 ♘g4+.

25 ... d5

26 ♗e3?

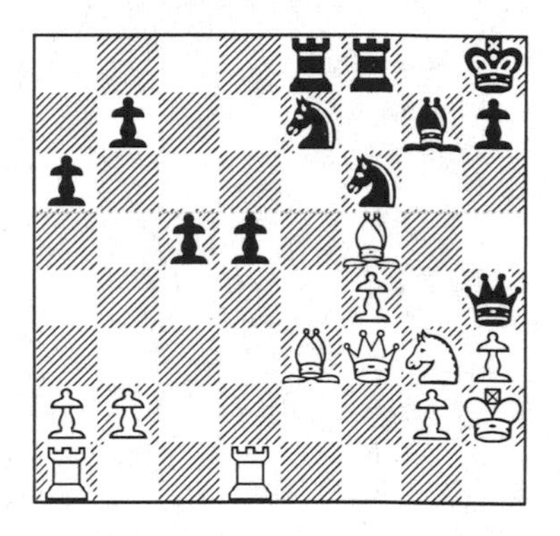

The decisive mistake. White would still have been okay after 26 ♗d2 d4 27 ♗e6!

26 ... ♕xg3+!

27 ♕xg3 ♘xf5

28 ♕g5

28 ♕f2? ♘xe3 29 ♖dc1 ♘fg4+-+.

28 ... ♘xe3

29 ♖e1 ♘e4

30 ♕h5 d4

31 ♖ac1 c4

32 ♕f3 ♖xf4!

33 ♖xe3 ♖xf3

0-1

3 Main Line: 9...b5 and rare moves

In this chapter we shall consider Black's alternatives to 9...♖e8 and 9...♗g4 in the main line.

Game 10
Komarov-Frolov
Kiev 1995

1 d4 ♘f6 2 c4 g6 3 ♘c3 ♗g7 4 e4 d6 5 f4 0-0 6 ♘f3 c5 7 d5 e6 8 ♗e2 exd5 9 cxd5

9 ... b5

First, let us take a look at Black's rare alternatives:

a) Black sometimes tries to prevent e4-e5 by 9...♘fd7?!, but this cannot be recommended, because White can play 10 ♘d2, when 9...♘fd7 is senseless. In Taimanov's 8 ♗b5+ (Chapter 7) White is even willing to play this position a tempo down. Here is a practical example: 9...♘fd7?! 10 0-0 ♘a6 11 ♔h1 (11 ♘d2 ♖e8 12 ♗f3 ♘c7 13 a4 a6 14 ♘c4 ♗f8 is also very attractive for White, Michaelsen-Ziger, Eger 1988) 11...♖e8 12 ♘d2 ♘b6 13 a4 ♗d7 14 a5 ♘c8 15 ♗f3 ♖b8 16 ♘c4 ♘b4 17 e5! ♗f5 18 ♗e4 ♗xe4 19 ♘xe4 dxe5 20 d6 and White is clearly better, Peev-Angelov, Bulgaria 1974.

b) 9...a6?! Now the simplest way for White to play is 10 a4 and after 10...♖e8, 11 ♘d2! transposing to an advantageous variation of the line 9...♖e8 10 ♘d2. It is worth bearing this in mind, because Black can practically force White to play a2-a4 earlier on, for example with 7...a6.

Instead White can also choose between 10 e5!? and 10 0-0!? b5 11 e5 with good prospects in both cases.

c) 9...♘a6?!, when White has a pleasant choice between:

c1) 10 0-0!? ♘c7 11 a4 b6 12 e5! dxe5 13 d6 ♘e6 14 fxe5 ♘d7 15 ♘d5 (A typical manoeuvre) 15...♗b7 16 ♘e7+ ♔h8 17 ♘g5 ♘xe5 18 ♘xh7! ♖e8 (18...♔xh7? 19 ♖a3!) 19 ♘g5 ♖xe7 20 dxe7 ♕xe7 21 ♕e1! and White is clearly better, Kaplun-Aarland, Riga 1982; and

c2) 10 e5!? dxe5 11 fxe5

♘g4 12 ♗f4 (12 ♗g5 f6!?) 12...♖e8 13 e6!? fxe6 14 d6 ♗d7 15 ♕d2 (15 h3!? also looks reasonable: 15...♘f6 16 ♘e5) 15...♘b4 16 0-0 ♖f8 17 h3 ♘f6 18 ♗c4 b5!? (Not 18...a6? 19 ♖ae1± Konikowski-Braune, corr. 1994) 19 ♘xb5 (19 ♗xb5!?) 19...♘bd5?! (It was better to play 19...♗xb5 20 ♗xb5 ♘e4 21 ♕e3 ♘d5 22 ♕xe4 ♘xf4 23 g3!, but White still enjoys a certain advantage due to the passed d-pawn) 20 ♗h2 ♘b6 21 ♗e2± Coo-Ciocaltea, Havana 1965.

d) 9...c4?! 10 ♗xc4 (10 0-0 is also quite possible, e.g. 10...b5 11 e5!) 10...♘xe4 11 ♘xe4 ♖e8 ***12 ♘fg5!*** (Less convincing is 12 0-0?! ♖xe4 13 ♗d3 ♖e8 14 f5 transposing to the variation 9 ♗d3 c4; while even worse are 12 ♘e5? ♗xe5! and 12 ♘d2? f5 in both cases with an advantage for Black) 12...h6 (12...♕b6? 13 ♕e2!±) 13 0-0 hxg5 14 ♘xg5 ♕b6+ 15 ♔h1 and the big question is whether or not Black has enough compensation for the pawn.

e) 9...♘bd7 and now:

e1) 10 e5 was dealt a strong blow in the game Lazic-Todorovic, Cetinje 1993: 10...dxe5 11 fxe5 ♘g4 12 e6?! (12 ♗g5!? ♕b6 is much like the main line of 9...♖e8 and needs further tests) 12...♘de5 13 ♘g5 fxe6! 14 ♗xg4 ♘xg4 15 ♕xg4 exd5 16 ♕h4 h6 17 ♘f3 g5 with a very strong attack for Black in the case of 18 ♕g3. Lazic preferred to give a piece back: 18 ♗xg5 hxg5 19 ♕xg5 ♕xg5 20 ♘xg5 ♗g4!, but the resulting ending is much better for Black.

e2) White doesn't need all these complications, because he can simply play 10 0-0 ♖e8 ***11 ♕c2!?*** (This seems even more interesting than 11 ♘d2, which transposes to the variation 9...♖e8 10 ♘d2 ♘bd7) White's knight stays on f3, supporting an eventual e4-e5 break.

We now consider the system with 9...b5.

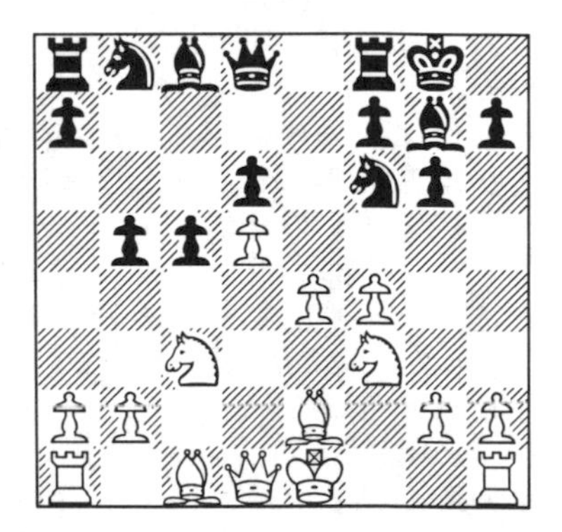

This old variation has had its 'ups' and 'downs' over the years. In the early 1990s, when 9...b5 was in crisis, the Ukrainian grandmaster A. Frolov gave it a new breath of life with 10...♘fd7!? This line is studied in the current game, while older lines are dealt with in Game 11, Blokh-Kitchev. Today we can again state that Black has no easy means of obtaining equality in this system.

10 e5!

10 ♗xb5?! ♘xe4 11 ♘xe4 ♕a5+ 12 ♔f2 ♕xb5 13 ♘xd6 ♕a6 doesn't promise much for White.

10 ... ♘fd7!?

After 10...♘g4?! 11 h3 ♘h6 12 ♗xb5 ♘f5 13 0-0 ♕b6, Skembris-Vuruna, Vrnjacka Banja 1989, ***14 a4!*** would have maintained a clear advantage for White; while for 10...dxe5 11 fxe5 ♘g4 see the next game, Blokh-Kitchev.

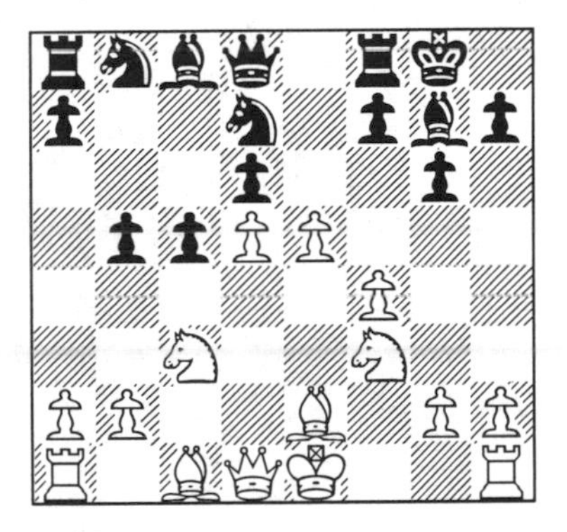

11 ♗xb5!

The only move to guarantee White an advantage. Here are some illustrations of the problems White has had with other continuations after 10...♘fd7!?:

a) 11 exd6?! a6!

b) 11 ♘xb5?! dxe5 12 0-0 e4 13 ♘g5 ♘f6 14 ♘c3 ♖e8 15 ♗b5 ♗d7 16 ♗xd7 ♘bxd7 17 ♖e1 ♘b6∓ Feldmann-Frolov, Sibenik 1989.

c) 11 e6? fxe6 12 dxe6 and now:

c1) 12...♘f6 13 ♘xb5 (13 ♗xb5 d5!) 13...d5 14 ♘g5 ♕e7 15 f5 a6 16 ♘c3 gxf5 17 ♘xd5 ♘xd5 18 ♕xd5 ♗b7 with a strong initiative, Zakharevich-Maximenko, Moscow 1991.

c2) 12...♘b6 13 0-0 ♘c6 14 ♘g5 b4 15 ♗f3 bxc3 16 ♗xc6 cxb2 17 ♗xb2 ♗xb2 18 e7 ♕xe7 19 ♕b3+ c4 20 ♕xb2 ♖b8∓ Purgin-Frolov, Smolensk 1992.

11 ... dxe5

12 0-0 ♗a6

Another possibility is

12...♕b6 13 a4!

and now Black has tried:

a) 13...♗a6 14 ♔h1 (14 ♖e1!?) 14...♗xb5 15 axb5 exf4 16 ♗xf4 ♘f6 17 ♘e5 ♘bd7 18 ♖a6 ♕b7 19 ♘c6 ♘b6 20 ♗d6 with a big advantage, Kahn-Kaeser, Budapest 1996.

b) 13...♖d8 was tried in Gerard-Hagege, French Team Ch. 1996. White's 14 d6 was not bad, but 14 fxe5!? seems better, since the variation 14...♘xe5 15 ♗g5 f6 (15...♖f8 16 ♗e7) 16 ♘xe5 fxg5 17 ♘f7 ♖f8 18 ♘xg5± is quite convincing.

c) 13...exf4

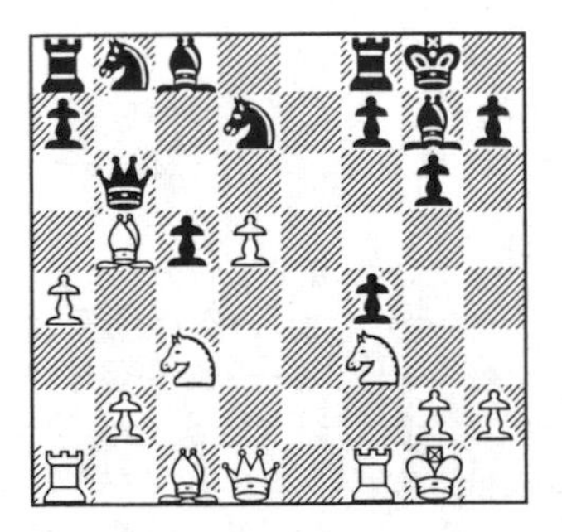

Now Lautier, White against Rogers at the Yerevan Olympiad 1996, lost a substantial part of his advantage by playing the natural:

c1) 14 ♗xf4?! a6 15 a5 ♕b7 16 ♗xd7 ♘xd7 17 ♕d2 ♘f6 18 ♗e5. Now instead of 18...♗g4? 19 ♖a4! Black should have played 18...♗f5!?, with no great problems for him.

It was better to play

c2) ***14 d6!***

For example, 14...a6 15 a5 ♕b7 16 ♗c4 ♘c6 17 ♘d5 ♘de5 18 ♘xe5 ♗xe5 19 ♗xf4 ♗xb2 20 ♖b1 ♗f5 21 ♘e7+! ♘xe7 22 dxe7 ♖fe8 23 ♗d5±. This was my preparation for my game against Frolov in Groningen 1993. Unfortunately, he declined to use his favourite King's Indian on that occasion.

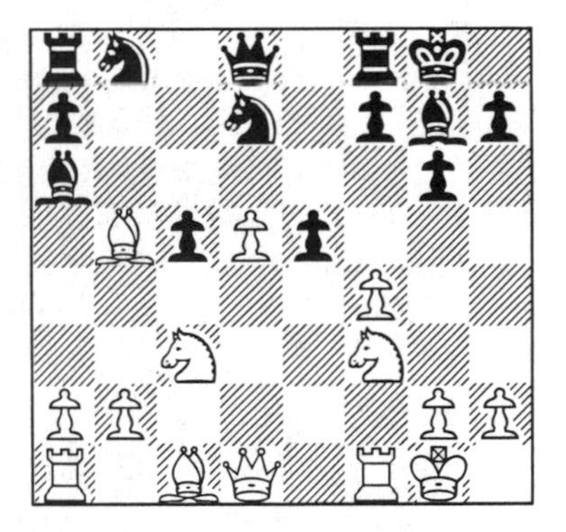

13 a4!

An improvement on 13 ♗xa6 ♘xa6 14 f5! c4! 15 ♘g5 ♘ac5 with a balanced game, Berkovich-Frolov, Alushta 1992.

13 ... ♗xb5

14 axb5 ♖e8

Or 14...exf4 15 ♗xf4 ♘b6 16 ♘e5! with an advantage.

15 ♖e1?!

More to the point was ***15 d6!*** exf4 (15...e4 16 ♘xe4!) 16 ♘d5! with a clear advantage.

15 ... exf4

16 ♗xf4 ♘f6?

The decisive mistake. Black simply forgot that the a7-pawn was pinned. 16...♘b6! was necessary, but after 17 ♗g5!? f6 (17...♖xe1+?! 18 ♕xe1 ♕d7 19 d6! ♕xd6 20 ♖d1±) 18 ♗f4 White is slightly better.

17 ♖xe8+ ♕xe8

18 b6 a6

18...♕d7 doesn't help: 19 bxa7 ♖xa7 20 ♗xb8 and White wins.

19 ♕b3 ♕d7

Or 19...♘bd7 20 b7 ♖b8 21 ♖xa6!+-.

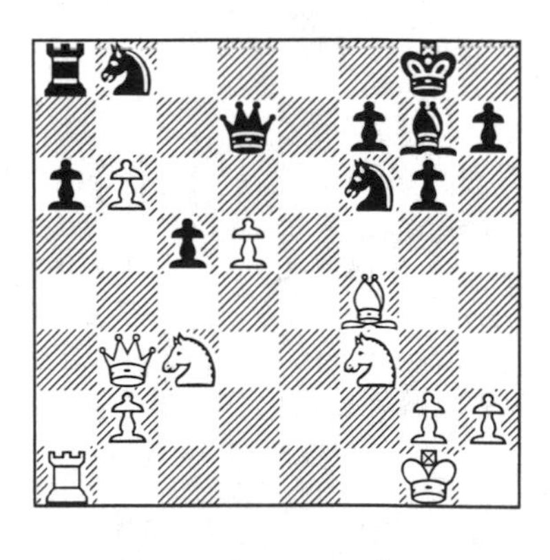

20 ♗c7! ♘e8

21 d6!

It was not late to let things slip: 21 b7? ♖a7 22 ♗xb8? (22 ♕b6±) 22...♖xb7 23 ♕a4 ♕xa4

24 ♖xa4 ♖xb8 and Black has no prospects of losing.

21 ... ♘c6
22 b7 ♖b8
23 ♗xb8 ♘xb8
24 ♖d1 ♘xd6
25 ♕d5 ♗f8
26 ♘e4 ♕xb7
27 ♘xd6 1-0

Game 11
Blokh-Kitchev
USSR (corr.) 1991

1 d4 ♘f6 2 c4 g6 3 ♘c3 ♗g7 4 e4 d6 5 f4 0-0 6 ♘f3 c5 7 d5 e6 8 ♗e2 exd5 9 cxd5 b5 10 e5

10 ... dxe5
11 fxe5 ♘g4
12 ♗g5

Although 12 ♗f4 is not recommended by theory, it is better than its reputation. Keres surprised Spassky with this move in their Candidates match in 1965 and could have obtained an advantage. Black must respond actively:

a) 12...♘d7?! 13 e6! fxe6 14 dxe6 ♖xf4 (Or 14...♘b6 15 ♕xd8 ♖xd8 16 ♘g5) 15 ♕d5 ♔h8 16 ♕xa8 ♘b6 17 ♕xa7 ♗xe6 (The attacking 17...♘e3? 18 e7 ♘xg2+ is not justified and ended in a fiasco in the game Todorovic-Ilic, Yugoslav Ch. 1988: 19 ♔f2 ♗d4+ 20 ♔xg2 ♗h3+ 21 ♔xh3 [21 ♔g3!?+-] 21...♕c8+ 22 ♔g2 ♕g4+ 23 ♔f1 ♖xf3+ 24 ♔e1 ♗f2+ 25 ♔d1 ♖d3+ 26 ♔c1 ♖xc3+ 27 bxc3 ♕xe2 28 ♕b8+ ♔g7 29 ♕f8 mate) 18 0-0 (18 ♖d1!? deserves attention, e.g. ♗d4 19 ♘xb5 ♘e3 20 ♘bxd4, Pelikan-Quinteros, Buenos Aires 1966) 18...♘e3 19 ♖f2 b4 (19...♘g4? 20 ♘g5!) and now instead of 20 ♘b5? Keres should have tried 20 ♘d1! ♖f7! (Bondarevsky; if 20...♘g4? 21 ♘g5! ♖xf2 [21...♕xg5 22 ♕b8+] 22 ♘xf2 ♕xg5 23 ♗xg4 ♘c8 24 ♕a4+- Bartis-Szmetan, Argentina 1970) 21 ♕a5 ♘g4 22 ♕xc5±.

b) In 1967 Petrayev invented an improvement 12...b4! 13 ♘e4 ♘d7, when Keres's plan doesn't work anymore:

b1) 14 e6?! fxe6 15 dxe6 (After 15 ♗d6!? the line proposed by Petrayev as good for Black needs practical tests, i.e. 15...♘e3 16 ♕b3 ♘xg2+ 17 ♔f2 c4) 15...♖xf4 16 ♕d5 ♔h8 17 ♕xa8 ♘b6 18 ♕c6 ♘e3 19 g3 ♘c2+ 20 ♔f1 (20 ♔f2? ♕d4+ 21 ♔g2 ♕xe4 22 ♗b5 ♘e3+ 23 ♔g1 ♕c2-+ Walter-Schmidt, corr. 1968) and now Black can obtain an advantage with 20...♖xf3+! (20...♖f5!?) 21 ♗xf3 ♘xa1. Originally this was rejected by some commentators because of 22 ♘g5, but in reality this is harmless in view of 22...♕e7.

b2) It is better to play 14 ♗g5!? ♕b6 (14...f6!?) 15 0-0 c4+! 16 ♔h1 ♘e3 17 ♗xe3 ♕xe3 18 ♘d6 ♘xe5 19 ♘xe5 ♕xe5 20 ♘xc4 ♕g5 21 ♖c1

♗a6 with approximate equality, Rodriguez-Cuartas, Buenos Aires 1973.

b3) Another interesting try is 14 0-0!? ♘gxe5 15 ♘xe5 ♘xe5 16 ♘xc5 ♕b6 17 ♗e3 ♘d7 18 ♕c1.

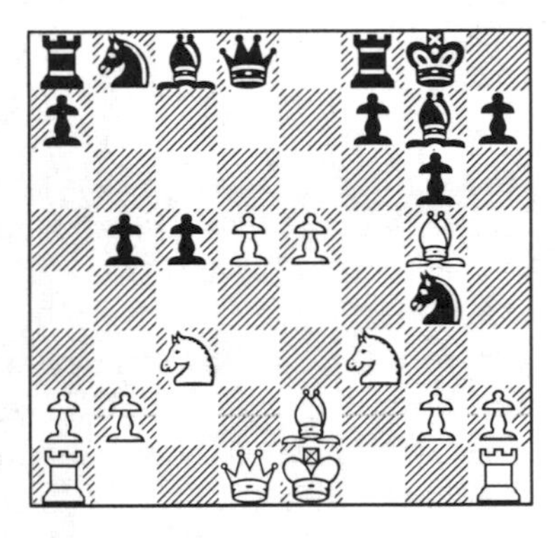

12 ... f6

Black can also move his queen, which is much better placed on b6 than on a5:

a) 12...♕a5?! 13 0-0 ♘xe5 (Or 13...b4 14 ♘e4 h6 15 ♗e7! ♘e3 16 ♕d2 ♘xf1 17 ♖xf1 ♗f5 18 ♘f6+ ♔h8 19 ♘h4 ♗c8 20 ♕d3! ♘d7 21 ♘xg6+! with a winning attack, Polikarpov-Zvorykina, USSR 1964) 14 d6 (14 ♘xe5!? ♗xe5 15 ♗e7 is also better for White) 14...♘bd7 (White obtains a clear advantage after both 14...♗b7 15 ♗e7 ♖e8?! 16 ♘xe5 ♗xe5 17 d7 ♘xd7 18 ♕xd7 ♕b6 19 ♗xb5, Summerscale-Rudd, British Ch. 1995, and 14...♗e6 15 ♘xe5 ♗xe5 16 ♗f3 ♘d7 17 ♗xa8 ♖xa8 18 ♕f3! ♖b8 19 ♖ad1, Blokh-Vexler, USSR 1978) 15 ♗e7 b4 (Better is 15...♗b7±) 16 ♗xf8 ♔xf8 17 ♘xe5! ♘xe5 18 ♕d5! ♖b8 19 d7 1-0 Bronznik-Majzlan, Bratislava 1992.

b) 12...♕b6!? 13 0-0

leads to the old and, I believe, the future main line of the 9...b5 system.

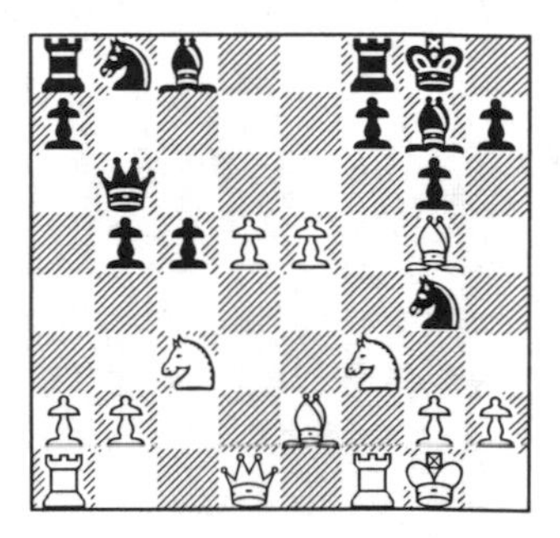

Black has a number of possibilities:

a) 13...h6?! 14 ♗e7 ♘e3 15 ♕d2 c4 16 ♔h1 ♖e8 17 d6± Sakharov-Tukmakov, Moscow 1963.

b) 13...♘xe5?! 14 ♘xe5! (More precise than the immediate 14 ♗e7?! c4+ 15 ♔h1 ♘bd7! 16 a4 b4 17 a5 ♕b8 18 ♘e4 ♘xf3 19 ♗xf3 ♗a6 20 ♕a4 ♕b5! with counterplay, Udovcic-Vasiukov, Yugoslavia-USSR 1963) 14...♗xe5 15 ♗e7 ♘d7 (Or 15...♖e8 16 d6 ♗e6 17 ♗f3 ♘c6 18 ♘d5 with a strong attack) 16 d6 ♗b7 17 ♘d5! ♕c6 18 ♗f3 ♔g7 19 ♘c7 ♕b6 20 ♘xa8 ♖xa8 21 ♔h1± Gorelov-Vasiukov, Moscow 1981.

c) 13...♘d7 (Without ...c5-c4+ either immediately or a little later, Black experiences more problems. The important developments in the theory of this line are due to Sosonko) 14 e6 (Note also Arencibia's idea: 14 d6 c4+ 15 ♕d4 ♘gxe5 16 ♕xb6 axb6 17 ♗e7) 14...fxe6 15 dxe6 ♕xe6 (15...♘df6? without ...c5-c4+ doesn't work: 16 e7 ♖e8 17 ♗xb5 ♖xe7 18 ♘d5+-) 16 ♘xb5 ♖b8 (Note that 16...♘e3?? loses immediately to 17 ♕c1!; 16...♗a6? 17 ♘c7! is also not good for Black due to 17...♗xe2?! 18 ♘xe6 ♗xd1 19 ♖fxd1 ♖f7 20 ♘d8!+- Sosonko-Hug, Geneva 1977; and 17...♕xe2 fails to the continuation 18 ♕xd7 ♗d4+ 19 ♔h1 ♖f7 20 ♕c6 ♖b8, Hovde-Schoppmeyer, corr. 1983, and now 21 ♘xa6!±) 17 ♘c7 ♕f7, and now instead of 18 h3 ♘gf6 19 ♕c2± Baumgartner-Lemaire, corr. 1994, 18 ♘e5!? is more promising.

d) 13...c4+ 14 ♔h1 ♘d7

14...h6?! and 14...♘xe5?! are analogous to variations a and b above respectively.

14...♘f2+?! 15 ♖xf2 ♕xf2 is even worse. Now 16 ♘e4 ♕b6 17 ♗e7, hoping for 17...♖e8? 18 ♘d6 ♖xe7 19 ♘xc8 ♕d8 20 ♘xe7+ ♕xe7 21 d6!±, can be met by 17...♘d7!, when the position is not at all clear. Therefore White must consider ***16 ♘xb5!*** and if 16...♘d7 17 e6! with a clear advantage.

After 14...a6 the game Rytov-Zhuravlev, Tallinn 1973, saw 15 d6! ♗e6 16 ♘d4 ♘xe5 17 ♗e7!? ♘bd7 18 ♘xe6 fxe6 19 ♗xf8 ♖xf8 20 ♖xf8+ ♗xf8 21 ♘e4 ♕e3 22 ♕c2 and White is better. In the recent game Kahn-Habibi, Balatonbereny 1995, White tried for even more with the combination 17 ♘xe6!? fxe6 18 ♘d5. The game continued 18...exd5 19 ♕xd5+ ♘f7 20 ♗e7 ♕c6 21 ♗f3 ♕xd5 22 ♗xd5 ♘d7 23 ♖xf7 ♖xf7, and now 24 ♖f1! instead of 24 ♗xa8? was promising. Black should have played 18...♖xf1+! 19 ♗xf1 exd5 20 ♕xd5+ ♘f7 21 ♗xc4! bxc4 22 ♖f1 ♖a7 23 ♗e7 ♕c6 24 ♕xf7+ ♔h8 with an unclear position.

15 e6

15 d6?! ♗b7! is less convincing.

15...fxe6 16 dxe6 ♘df6!

16...♕xe6? is worse, as shown by Zaltsman-Kalinsky, USSR 1964: 17 ♘xb5 ♖b8 18 ♘fd4! ♕d5 19 ♗xg4 ♕xg5 20 ♗e6+ ♔h8 21 ♘d6±.

17 e7 ♖e8

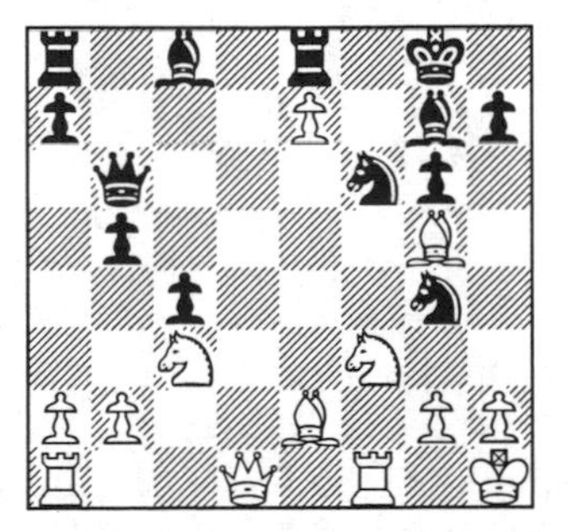

In this critical position White has two ways to a small plus, namely variations d2 and d3:

d1) Black can equalise with very precise play after 18 a4?! (18 h3?! h6 or 18...♘h6 promises nothing) 18...♗b7! 19 ♘d4 ♕c5! 20 ♗xg4 ♕xg5 21 ♗f3 ♗xf3 22 ♕xf3 ♕g4! 23 ♕xg4 ♘xg4 24 ♘c6, Gorelov-Gleizerov, USSR 1986, and now, as Gleizerov has shown, 24...♘e5! 25 axb5 ♘xc6 26 bxc6 ♗xc3 27 bxc3 ♖xe7 results in equality.

d2) 18 ♘d4!? ♕c5 (18...a6 19 a4!) 19 ♗xf6 ♘xf6 (19...♗xf6? is bad: 20 ♘dxb5 ♗xc3 21 ♘xc3 ♘e3 22 ♖f8+! ♖xf8 23 ♗xc4+! ♘xc4 24 exf8♕+ ♕xf8 25 ♕d5+ ♗e6 26 ♕xe6+ ♕f7±) 20 ♘dxb5! ♗e6! 21 ♕d4!? (Or 21 ♕d6 ♕xd6 22 ♘xd6 ♖xe7 23 ♗xc4 ♗xc4 24 ♘xc4 ♘e4!= Piskov) 21...♕xe7 (21...♕xd4? 22 ♘xd4 ♗f7 23 ♘c6 ♖ac8 24 ♗f3±) 22 ♗xc4 ♗xc4 23 ♕xc4+ ♔h8⩲ was Kharkova-Chelushkina, USSR Women's Ch. 1989.

d3) 18 ♕d4! ♗d7

An obligatory move. If 18...♕xd4?! 19 ♘xd4 b4 (19...a6 20 ♗f3±) 20 ♘cb5 ♘e4 21 ♗xc4+! ♔h8 22 ♗d5 ♘xg5 23 ♖ae1! ♗d7 24 ♗xa8 ♖xa8 25 h4 White gets a clear advantage, Blokh-Gunnas, corr. 1994.

19 ♕xb6!

19 ♖ae1 ♖ac8! 20 ♕xb6 axb6 21 h3 was Kaidanov-Gleizerov, Smolensk 1986, and now 21...h6! is unclear.

19...axb6 20 ♘d4 h6 21 ♗xf6 ♘xf6 22 ♘dxb5 ♖xe7 23 ♗xc4+ ♔h7

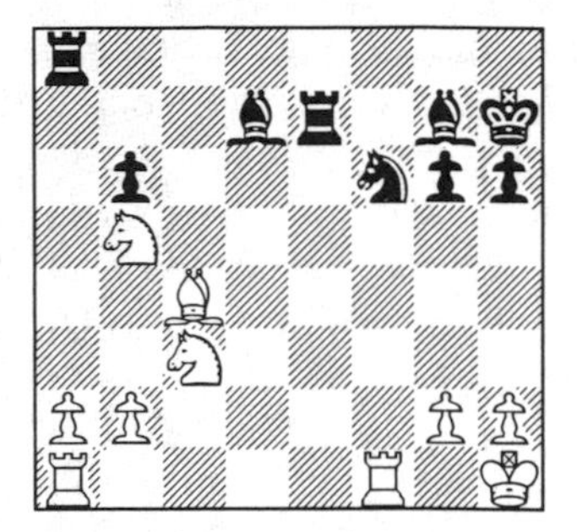

Here White is slightly better (Kaidanov).

13 exf6!

This move is good enough for White, so it is not necessary to investigate the huge complications which arise after 13 d6!? very deeply. Nevertheless, here is one fantasy variation: 13...fxg5 14 ♕d5+ ♔h8 15 ♕xa8 ♕b6 16 ♘d5! ♕a5+ 17 b4 cxb4 18 0-0 ♗f5 19 ♘xg5! ♘d7 20 ♘f7+ ♔g8 21 ♘e7+ ♔xf7 22 ♕d5+ with a winning attack.

13 ... ♗xf6
14 ♕d2

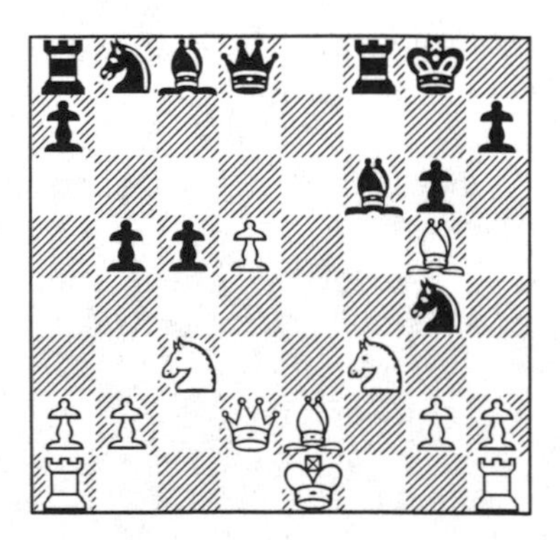

14 ... ♖e8!?

Before this game this was the only move that had posed any problems for White. The alternatives are:

a) 14...♗xg5?! 15 ♘xg5! (15 ♕xg5 is slightly better for White, but he wants more) 15...♘a6 (Or 15...b4 16 ♘ce4 ♕e7 17 0-0-0± Guidi-Troia, corr. 1991) 16 h3! ♘e5 17 d6! with a clear advantage for White, Blokh-Krasnov, USSR 1986.

b) 14...♗f5

Here Black has succeeded in neutralising a dangerous idea of Sosonko's:

b1) 15 ♘xb5 ♘d7

White maintains a clear advantage after 15...♕b6 16 d6! ♘c6 17 ♗c4+ ♔h8 18 0-0 ♘a5 19 b3! ♘xc4 20 bxc4 a6 21 ♘c7 ♖ad8 22 ♖ad1± Karlsson-Meyer, Uppsala-Bremen 1977, or after 15...a6 16 ♘c3 ♖a7 17 h3 ♘e5 18 ♗xf6 ♕xf6 19 0-0 ♘bd7 20 g4!, Konikowski-Stanojevic, Chianciano Team Ch. 1989.

16 0-0?! ♕b6 17 ♗c4 ♘de5 18 ♘xe5 ♘xe5 19 d6+ ♘xc4 20 ♕d5+ ♔g7 21 ♗xf6+ ♖xf6 22 ♕xc4

(see following diagram)

Now Reshevsky made a mistake against Sosonko (Amsterdam 1977): 22...♖b8? 23 ♖ae1! ♖f7 24 ♖e7 ♖xe7 25 dxe7 with a clear advantage for White. In the game Gornjak-Shemagonov, USSR Corr. Ch. 1992, Black improved on this and equalised after 22...♖af8! 23 ♖ae1 ♗e6 24 ♕d3 ♖xf1+ 25 ♖xf1 ♖xf1+ 26 ♔xf1 ♗d7 27 a4 a6 28 ♘c3 ♕xb2.

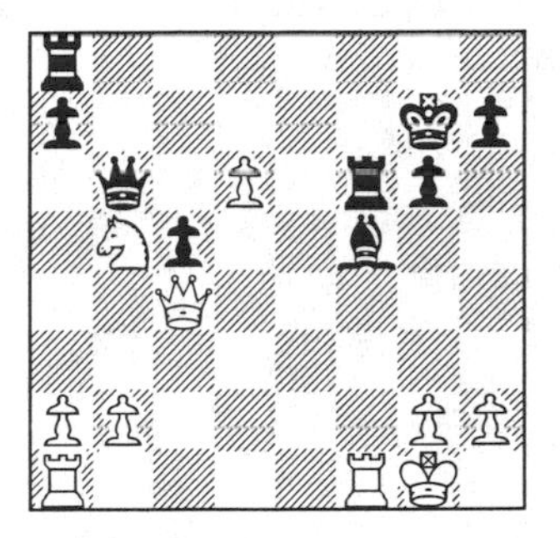

Still, White is better if he plays 16 d6!? before castling.

b2) Another good option for White is to avoid wasting time in grabbing the black pawn on b5, as in the game Semkov-Tasic, Cannes open 1989: 15 0-0!? b4 16 ♘d1 ♘d7 17 ♘f2! ♘xf2 18 ♖xf2 ♗e4 19 ♗xf6! ♘xf6 20 ♘g5 ♕xd5 (20...♗xd5 21 ♖d1±) 21 ♘xe4 ♕xe4 22 ♗f3 1-0.

15 0-0!

The active position of Black's rook makes 15 ♘xb5? inappropriate. After 15...♗xg5! 16 ♕xg5 (Even worse is 16 ♘xg5?! ♘e3! 17 ♘e6? ♗xe6! 18 dxe6 ♕h4+ 19 g3 ♕e4) 16...♖xe2+! 17 ♔xe2 ♕e8+ 18 ♔d2 ♕xb5 19 ♕d8+ ♔g7 20 ♕xc8 ♕xb2+ 21 ♔d3, when apart from the perpetual check (with 21...♕b5+), Black can play for the attack with 21...♘a6!? Here and later we have used and adapted some of Blokh's comments on his game.

15 ... b4

The game Neuman-Hallerova, Czech Republic Team Ch. 1996, continued 15...♗xg5 16 ♘xg5 ♘e3 17 ♘f7 (17 d6!?) 17...♕h4 (17...♘xf1!?) 18 ♖f3 ♕d4 19 ♕xd4 cxd4 20 ♘xb5 ♘c2 21 ♖c1 ♖xe2 22 ♘c7 with a clear plus for White.

16 ♘d1 ♗b7

17 ♘f2! ♗xg5?!

17...♕xd5? was bad: 18 ♕xd5+ ♗xd5 19 ♘xg4 ♗xg5 20 ♘xg5 ♖xe2 21 ♘f6+ ♔g7 22 ♘xd5 ♖e5 23 ♖f7+ ♔h6 24 h4+-. It was better to play 17...♘xf2 18 ♖xf2 ♘d7 (Again the d5-pawn is poisoned: 18...♗xg5? 19 ♘xg5 ♕xd5 20 ♕xd5+ ♗xd5 21 ♖d1 ♗xa2 22 ♗f3 ♗b3 23 ♖d6! ♗c4 24 h4 ♘a6 25 ♖xa6!+-) 19 d6 with an advantage for White.

18 ♘xg5! ♘f6

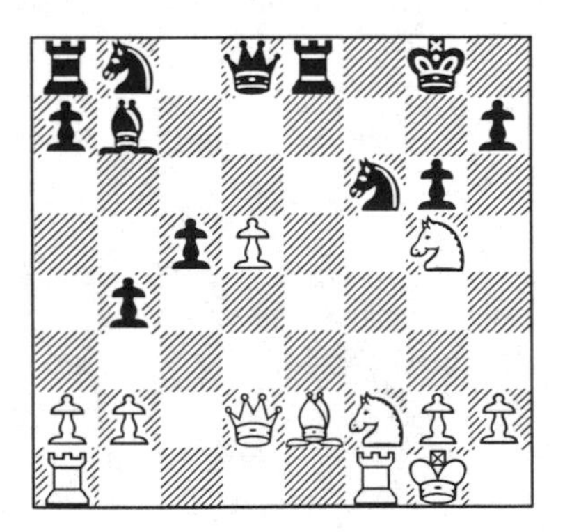

The following thematic variation is convincing enough: 18...♘e3 19 ♘fe4! ♘xf1 20 ♖xf1 ♖f8 21 ♘e6 ♖xf1+ 22 ♗xf1 ♕e7 23 ♘4xc5+-.

19 ♘g4! ♘xg4

19...♘bd7 loses immediately to 20 ♗c4!, or 19...♘xd5 20 ♘h6+.

20 ♗xg4 ♕xd5

21 ♕f2!

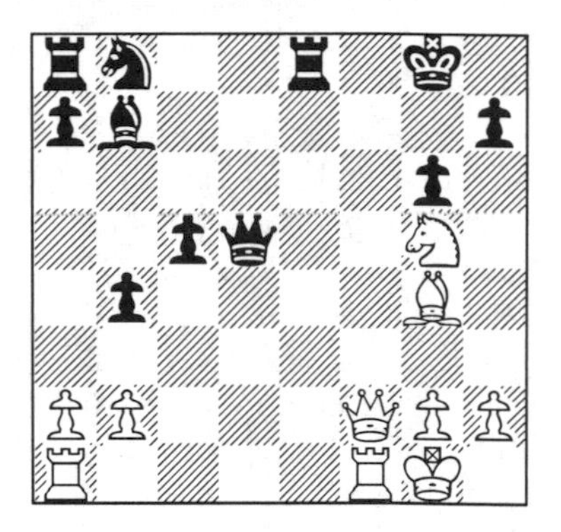

The threat of 22 ♗e6+ forces a transition into a winning ending.

21	**...**	**♕d4**
22	**♕xd4**	**cxd4**
23	**♗e6+**	**♖xe6**
24	**♘xe6**	**♘c6**
25	**♖f6**	**♘e5**
26	**♖af1**	**♘d7**
27	**♖f7**	**♗d5**
28	**♖g7+**	**♔h8**
29	**♖xd7**	**♗xe6**
30	**♖xd4**	**♗xa2**
31	**♖xb4**	**a5**
32	**♖b7**	**1-0**

4 Black plays 6...♘a6

Now we move on to examine early deviations along the way to the main line of the Four Pawns Attack after the first few moves of the King's Indian Defence. The material in this section is divided into three chapters: this chapter deals with 6...♘a6!?, Chapter 5 covers 6...c5 7 d5 b5, while Chapter 6 deals with other systems. The first of these is undoubtedly the best choice for Black.

1 d4 ♘f6 2 c4 g6 3 ♘c3 ♗g7 4 e4 d6 5 f4 0-0 6 ♘f3 ♘a6

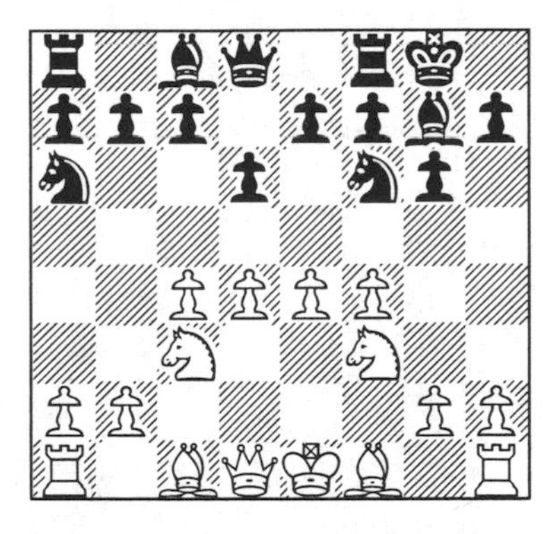

Now one of Black's main weapons against the Four Pawns Attack, 6...♘a6 was introduced into modern tournament practice by Igor Belov in 1987. Black prepares ...e7-e5 (immediately or after ...♗g4), while keeping open the option of playing ...c7-c5. This system has one advantage for died-in-the-wool King's Indian players: the resulting positions are often more in keeping with the spirit of that opening than are other variations of the Four Pawns Attack.

Initially I experienced problems after 6...♘a6 and my results were disastrous. I lost the first two games I played against it, and my total against 6...♘a6 (+2=5-2) is awful compared to my general results with the Four Pawns Attack in the period 1982-1996 (+31=10-2). Nevertheless, nowadays White has several ways of obtaining a pleasant position. The line with 7 ♗d3 is covered in the Game 12 (Zsu. Polgar-Chiburdanidze), while 7 e5!? and other lines are dealt with in Game 13, Vaisser-Golubev.

Game 12
Zsu. Polgar-Chiburdanidze
St Petersburg (match) 1995

1 d4 ♘f6 2 c4 g6 3 ♘c3 ♗g7 4 e4 d6 5 f4 0-0 6 ♘f3 ♘a6

7 ♗d3 ♗g4

Both this move and 7...e5 (considered in variation c below) are sound for Black. The alternatives are less precise:

a) After 7...♘d7?! 8 0-0 e5 9 fxe5 dxe5 10 d5 ♕e7 we reach a pawn structure typical of the ...♘a6 line, but in this case the d7-square is not a good place for Black's knight. The game Tsedev-Sammalvuo, Bratislava 1993, continued 11 a3 c6 12 b4 ♘c7 13 ♕b3 cxd5 14 cxd5 ♔h8 15 ♗g5 f6 16 ♗h4 with advantage to White.

b) 7...c5?! 8 d5 e6 9 0-0 (9 dxe6⩲) 9...exd5 10 exd5 transposes into the line 9 exd5 (see Game 16), but with an extra tempo for White (♗e2-d3). Furthermore, Black's move ...♘a6 would not be his first choice. These small differences swing the evaluation of the position in White's favour. One example: 10...♘c7 11 a4 ♘a6 12 f5! ♘b4 13 ♗b1 a6 14 ♕e1 ♘g4 15 ♗g5 f6 16 ♗d2 g5 17 ♕g3 h5 18 h3 ♘h6 19 ♘xg5! h4 20 ♕xh4 fxg5 21 ♗xg5± Tarasov-Krishilovsky, St Petersburg 1995.

c) 7...e5!? 8 fxe5

8 dxe5?! is weaker: 8...dxe5 9 ♘xe5 (9 fxe5?! ♘c5! 10 ♗c2 ♕xd1+ 11 ♔xd1 ♘g4 12 ♔e2 ♘xe5∓, Sokolin) 9...♘c5 10 ♗e3 ♘xd3+ 11 ♕xd3 ♕xd3 12 ♘xd3 ♖e8 13 ♘e5 (If 13 e5 ♘g4 14 ♗g1 ♗f5 15 ♘c5 b6 16 ♘a6 ♗xe5! with a fine initiative) 13...♘g4 ½-½ occurred in the game Ivanov-Sokolin, Leningrad 1991. The position is equal after 14 ♘xg4 ♗xc3+ 15 bxc3 ♗xg4 16 e5 f6.

8...dxe5 9 d5 c6

Black immediately tries to undermine White's strong centre. Another plan is to prepare counterplay on the kingside while restraining White's pawns on the opposite wing with 9...♕e7 (The immediate blockade with 9...♘c5 10 ♗c2 a5 is not a good choice, as White can prepare b2-b4 with an advantage: 11 0-0 ♘h5 12 ♗e3 ♕e7 13 a3 f5 14 b4, Kalousek-Jirovsky, Mlada Boleslav open 1995) 10 0-0 ♘h5. Black's plan worked relatively well in the game Parker-Volke, Copenhagen 1996, thanks to the help of his opponent: 11 a3?! ♘f4 12 b4 (12 ♘xe5?! ♕c5+ 13 ♔h1 ♘xd3 14 ♘xd3 ♕xc4∓) 12...c5! 13 b5 ♘c7 (13...♘xd3 14 ♕xd3 ♘c7) 14 ♖e1 (14 ♗xf4! exf4 15 e5 ♗xe5 16 ♖e1 f6 17 ♗xg6! hxg6 18 ♘xe5 fxe5 19 d6±) 14...♘xd3 15 ♕xd3 ♘e8 16 ♗e3 b6 17 a4 ♘d6 18 a5 ♖b8 19 axb6 axb6 20 ♖a4 f5 21 ♘d2 ♕h4 with an initiative. As an improvement I suggest 11

♖e1!? ♘f4 12 ♗f1.

After 9...c6 White has a choice:

c1) Black has comfortable equality after 10 ♗g5?! h6! (10...♕b6?! 11 ♘a4! ♕a5+ 12 ♗d2 ♕d8 13 0-0± 13...cxd5?! 14 cxd5 ♘e8 15 ♗xa6 bxa6 16 ♗b4 ♘d6 17 ♖c1 ♖b8 18 ♕e1± Garcia Palermo-Danailov, Alicante open 1992) 11 ♗xf6 (Not 11 ♗h4? ♕b6! 12 ♕e2 ♘c5 with an initiative) 11...♗xf6 12 ♖b1 ♘c7 13 0-0 cxd5 14 cxd5 ♘e8, as in the game Garcia Palermo-Comas Fabrego, Ibercaja open 1992.

c2) Interesting complications occurred in the game Arencibia-Pecorelli, Santa Clara 1996, with White coming out on top: 10 ♕e2 ♘c5 11 ♗c2 cxd5 12 cxd5 b6 13 b4 ♗a6 14 ♕d1 ♘fxe4 15 ♗xe4 ♘xe4 16 ♘xe4 f5 17 ♘eg5 e4 18 ♘e6 ♕e7 19 ♘fd4 f4 20 ♕b3 ♗d3 21 h4!+-.

c3) 10 0-0! cxd5

10...♕b6+ is also possible (Arencibia's 10 ♕e2!? allows White to avoid this possibility). After (10...♕b6+) 11 ♔h1 ♘g4 12 ♕e2 ♘c5 13 ♗c2 f5, however, White should not be too afraid of the attack, which is a little too direct and overly aggressive. Now, besides the modest 14 ♖b1 fxe4 15 ♘xe4 cxd5 16 ♘xc5 ♕xc5 17 cxd5 ♗f5 18 ♗xf5 ♖xf5 (18...gxf5 19 ♘h4!) 19 h3 ♘h6 20 ♗xh6 ♗xh6 21 ♖bd1 ♖e8 22 d6! ♖d8 23 ♕d3, Giardelli-De Souza, Mar del Plata open 1995, when 23...♔h8! would given Black an approximately equal position, White has a more energetic option at his disposal, namely ***14 exf5!*** gxf5 (14...♗xf5 15 ♗xf5 gxf5 [15...♖xf5 16 h3±] 16 ♘h4 ♘d3! [16...♘e4?! 17 ♘xe4 fxe4 18 ♘f5±] 17 ♕xd3 ♘f2+ 18 ♖xf2 ♕xf2 19 g3 with a White advantage) 15 h3! ♘f6 (15...e4 16 hxg4 exf3 17 ♖xf3±) 16 ♗e3 f4 (16...♘fd7 17 ♘a4 ♕a5 18 ♘xc5 ♘xc5 19 a3 ♘e4 20 ♘xe4 fxe4 21 ♘g5±) 17 ♗f2 (17 ♘a4!?) 17...♘h5 18 ♘e4 ♘xe4 19 ♕xe4 ♘g3+ 20 ♗xg3 ♗f5 21 ♕xf5! ♖xf5 22 ♗f2 and the conclusion is that White has picked up too many pieces for the queen.

11 cxd5

Now Black has three plausible continuations:

c31) After the exchange on d5, Black's attack from the previous note is senseless, as White's bishop has c4 available to it, e.g. 11...♕b6+ 12 ♔h1 ♘g4 13 ♕e2 ♘c5?! 14 ♗c4! ♗d7 15 h3 ♘f6 16 ♗g5 ♘h5 17 ♕f2 ♘a4 18 ♘xa4 ♕xf2 19 ♖xf2 ♗xa4 20 ♖e1± Pribyl-Beckhuis, German Bundesliga 1993/94.

c32) 11...b5?! is original, but weakens the queenside and cannot be recommended. In the game Parker-Burgess, English Team Ch. 1996, White was clearly better after 12 ♗g5 (12 ♗xb5? ♘xe4!) 12...b4 13 ♘a4 h6 14 ♗xf6 ♗xf6 15 ♖c1 ♗g7 16 ♕e2 ♗d7 17 b3 ♗xa4 18 bxa4 ♘c7 19 ♗b5! ♘e8 20 ♗xe8 ♕xe8 21 ♖c6.

c33) <u>11...♘e8</u>

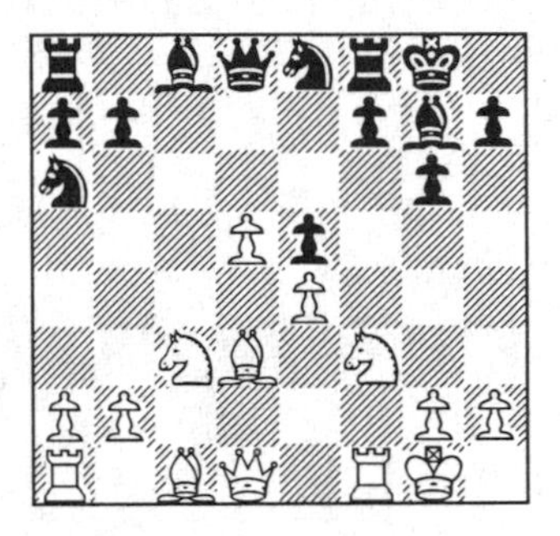

This is one of the critical positions of the 6...♘a6 system. White plans to break the blockade of the d6-square, thereby strengthening his passed d-pawn. Simultaneously he tries to diminish Black's counterplay on the kingside. I believe that White's prospects are slightly better.

Practical examples from this position are:

c331) White discourages his opponent from playing ...f7-f5: 12 ♕e2 ♘ac7 (After 12...♘c5 White should not allow his bishop to be exchanged: 13 ♗c2 b6 14 b4 ♗a6 15 b5±) 13 ♗g5 f6 14 ♗h4 ♕e7 15 ♔h1?! (The immediate 15 ♘d2 was more precise) 15...♘d6 16 ♘d2 ♗d7 17 a4 ♗h6 18 ♘c4 ♘ce8 19 ♗f2 ♘xc4 20 ♗xc4 ♘d6 21 ♗c5 ♖ac8 22 ♗a3 ♖f7 23 ♗b5 a6 24 ♗d3! ♔h8 25 ♕f2, Clement-Romero, Matalascanas 1995. Even after losing a tempo on move 15, White has a small advantage.

c332) White allows Black's counterplay: 12 ♗e3!? ♘d6 13 ♕b3 f5 14 ♘d2 (An interesting alternative was 14 ♘g5!? with the idea of 14...f4 15 ♘e6!) 14...f4 15 ♗f2 g5 16 ♘c4 g4, Ooi Chern Ee-Braga, Yerevan Olympiad 1996, and now White should have played 17 ♘xd6 ♕xd6 18 ♘b5 with good prospects in this complicated position.

c333) 12 ♗g5!? may transpose to variation b after 12...f6 13 ♗e3, but also sets a nice trap, since 12...♕b6+? is a mistake: 13 ♔h1 f6 (13...♕xb2? 14 ♘b5! ♕b4 [14...f6? 15 ♗d2! and 16 ♗c3±] 15 a3 ♕c5 16 ♖c1 winning the exchange) 14 ♘a4! ♕d8 15 ♗h4 ♘ac7 16 ♕b3 ♘d6 17 ♖ac1 (By playing ...♕d8-b6-d8 Black has lost two tempi and White is clearly better; the Black's next move allows a pleasing and decisive combination) 17...♕e7? 18 ♘xe5!! ♗h6! 19 ♘c4! b5 (Or 19...♗xc1 20 ♘xd6 ♕xd6 21 ♗g3 ♕d7 22 ♖xc1 with a large advantage) 20 ♘xd6 bxa4 21 ♘xc8 ♖fxc8, Lalic-Arakhamia, Staffordshire 1997. Now White could have obtained a winning ending after 22 d6+! axb3 23 dxe7 ♘e8 (23...♗xc1? 24 ♗c4+ ♔g7 25 ♗xf6+ ♔h6 26 ♖f3 g5 27 ♗f7 g4 28 ♖f5 mating) 24 ♖xc8 ♖xc8 25 axb3.

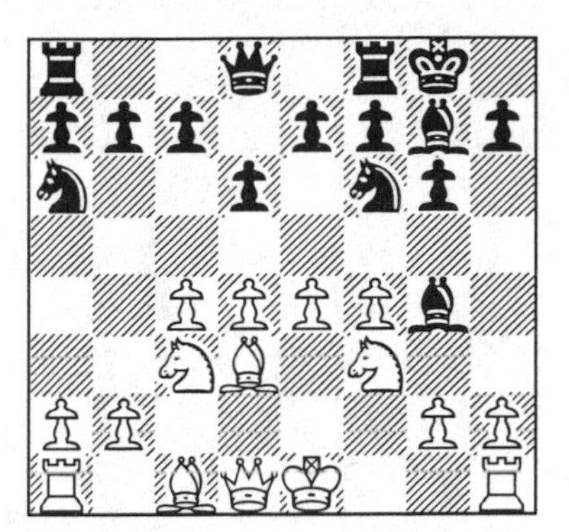

8 0-0

The most precise. Others:

a) 8 h3 ♗xf3 9 ♕xf3 e5! (Weaker is 9...♘d7?! 10 ♗e3 e5 11 dxe5 dxe5 12 f5 transposing to the game Braga-Comas – see note b1 below) 10 fxe5 ♘d7 11 0-0 c5 12 ♘d5 cxd4 13 ♘f6+ ♔h8 (13...♗xf6!?) 14 ♘xd7 ♕xd7 15 exd6 ♕xd6 16 ♗f4 ♕e6 17 a3 ♘c5 18 b4 ♘xd3 19 ♕xd3 ♖fe8 and Black has no problems, Weglarz-Kaminski, Gdansk 1994.

b) 8 ♗e3 and now:

b1) 8...♘d7?! 9 h3 ♗xf3 10 ♕xf3 e5 11 dxe5! dxe5 12 f5 ♘dc5 13 ♗e2±. Braga-Comas, Ibercaja open 1992, continued 13...gxf5 14 exf5 e4 15 ♕g3 ♔h8 16 ♖d1 ♘d3+ 17 ♗xd3 exd3 18 0-0 ♖g8 19 ♕f3 with advantage to White.

b2) 8...e5?! 9 fxe5 dxe5 10 d5 ♘h5 11 0-0± ♘f4?! 12 ♗c2 ♗h6?! 13 ♕d2 ♗xf3 14 ♖xf3 ♗g5 15 ♖d1 h6 16 h4! ♗xh4 17 g3 ♕g5 18 ♕h2 ♕g4 19 ♔f2 ♘b4 20 ♗b1+- Gretarsson-Meesen, European Club Cup, Eupen 1994.

b3) 8...c5!

The best way to exploit the vulnerability of the bishop on e3.

9 d5 e6 10 dxe6

Or 10 0-0 exd5 11 exd5 ♖e8 12 ♗d2 ♕d7! 13 a3 ♘c7 with equal chances, Vaisser-Gallagher, Swiss Grand Prix 1990.

10...♗xe6!

10...fxe6?!⩲ is worse.

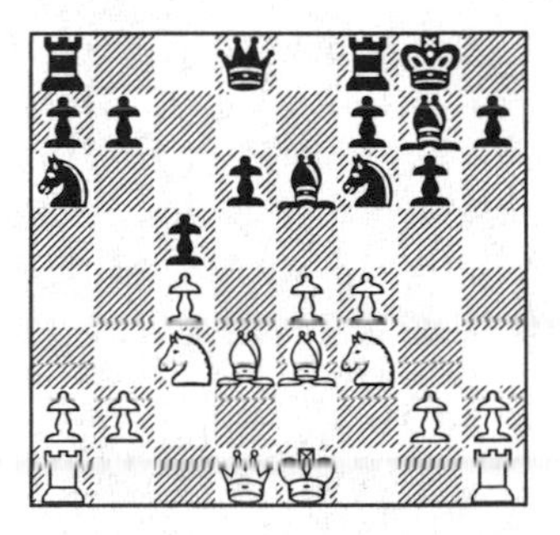

After 10...♗xe6 the Black threat is 11...♘g4 and 12...f5. He has enough counterplay after 11 h3 ♕b6, so the critical line is 11 f5 ♗xf5! 12 exf5 ♖e8 13 ♔d2 d5! 14 cxd5 ♘xd5 15 ♗g5 ♕a5 16 ♕b3 c4! with a very strong attack for the piece (Gallagher).

8 ... ♘d7

Instead the typical thrust 8...e5?! is premature after 9 fxe5 and now:

a) 9...♘d7 10 ♕e1! ♗xf3 (10...c5? [10...dxe5 11 d5⩲/±] 11 ♗g5! ♕a5 12 ♕h4 ♗xf3 13 ♖xf3 cxd4 [Or 13...dxe5 14 d5±] 14 ♘d5 with a decisive attack, for example: 14...♘xe5 15 ♖h3 h5 16 ♘e7+ ♔h8 17 ♕xh5+! gxh5 18 ♖xh5+ ♗h6 19 ♖xh6+ ♔g7 20 ♘f5+ ♔g8 21 ♗f6 ♘g6 22 ♘e7+ ♘xe7 23 ♖h8 mate, I. Belov) 11 gxf3 (Interesting is 11 ♖xf3 c5 12 ♘d5 cxd4 [12...dxe5 13 dxc5±] 13 exd6 with an unclear position. The game Gretarsson-Pedersen, Hallsdall open 1996, continued 13...♖e8?! 14 b4!? ♘e5 15 c5 f5 16 ♗b2 ♘xf3+ 17 gxf3 ♕g5+ 18 ♔h1 ♗e5 19 ♕f2 with a difficult position for Black) 11...dxe5 12 d5, Hubert-Belov, Porz 1995. Here Belov proposed as an improvement 12...♘f6!? 13 ♗e3 ♘h5 14 ♔h1 ♘f4 15 ♗c2 c5±.

b) 9...dxe5 10 d5 is also good for White. Compared with the 7...e5 line we can see that the move ...♗g4 is a waste of time. This difference changes the evaluation in White's favour. One example is 10...c6?! 11 ♗e3 cxd5 12 cxd5 ♗xf3?! 13 ♕xf3 ♘e8 14 ♘b5± Irzhanov-Doornbos, Bratislava 1993.

9 ♗e3

9 d5?! is ineffective: 9...c6 10 ♗e3 ♘ac5 11 ♗c2 ♕b6 12 ♖b1 ♕b4! 13 ♗b3 ♘xb3 14 ♕xb3 a5∓ Kahn-Panzer, Budapest 1993.

9 ... e5
10 fxe5 c5!

The point! Now White is obliged to play 11 d5 and Black gains control of the e5-square. Even so, the knight on a6 is a long way away from this key square, which allows White time to create problems for his opponent in the centre.

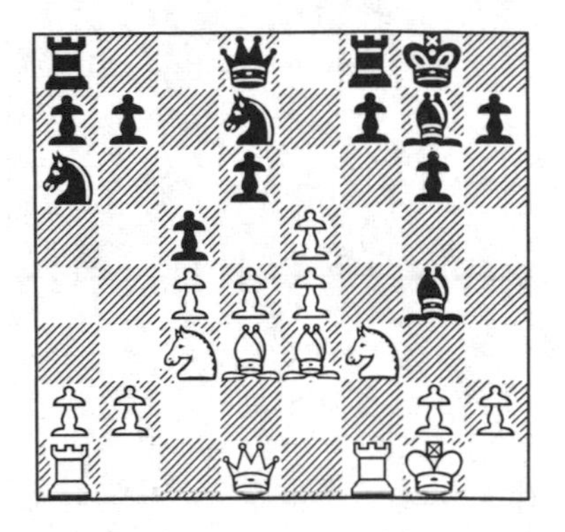

11 d5 ♘xe5
12 ♗e2 ♘xf3+!

Belov has tried several other options, but without much success:

a) 12...♗xf3 13 gxf3 f5 (13...♘c7!?±) 14 f4 ♘f7 (Or 14...♘d7!?) 15 exf5 gxf5 16 ♔h1 ♕e7 17 ♖f3 with an advantage for White, Petronic-Belov, Pravets 1989.

b) 12...♗d7 13 ♕d2 ♘c7 14 ♗g5 ♕e8 15 ♔h1 a6 16 a4 b6 17 ♕e1 f6 18 ♗d2 ♘f7 19 ♗d3 b5 20 b3 b4 21 ♘e2 ♕e7 22 ♕g3 ♖ae8 23 ♖ae1 ♘e5 24 ♗c2 and White has more space, Arkhipov-Belov, Moscow 1987.

13 ♗xf3 ♗xf3
14 ♕xf3

After the exchange of White's light-squared bishop, 14 gxf3 is no longer dangerous.

14 ... ♕e7

Black does not have enough time to bring her knight to e5: 14...♘b8?! 15 ♗f4! (This also follows 14...♘b4) 15...♗d4+ 16 ♔h1 f6 17 ♘b5 ♗e5 18 ♗xe5 dxe5 19 ♕h3! with a clear advantage for White.

15 ♗f4 ♘c7

Necessary to stop the unpleasant threat 16 ♘b5.

16 ♕g3 ♖ad8
17 ♔h1!

Preparing 18 ♗g5. The immediate 17 ♗g5?! is ineffective because of 17...♗d4+! 18 ♔h1 f6.

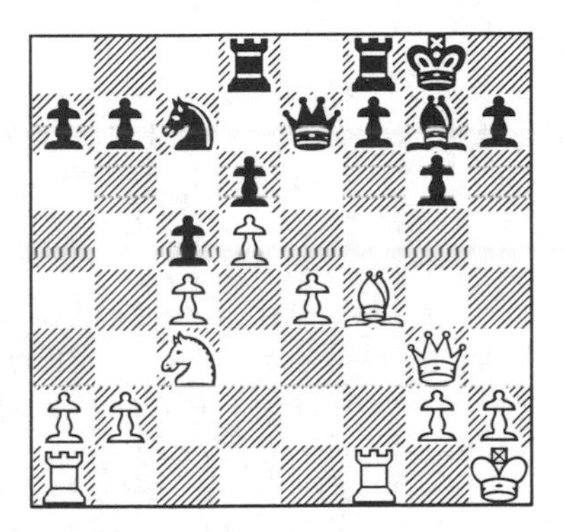

17 ... ♗d4!
18 ♖ae1 f6!

Black had to stop the threat of 19 e5!

19 ♘e2 ♗e5

Of course not 19...♗xb2? 20 ♖b1 ♗e5 21 ♖xb7±.

20 ♘g1

The knight heads for a more active post on f3. Both sides have played well up until now and White has succeeded in keeping a small initiative.

20 ... a6?!

An unnecessary move. It would have been better to advance with 20...b5!? (Zsu. Polgar) or play 20...♘a6!? 21 ♘f3 ♗xf4 22 ♕xf4 ♘b8, approaching the critical e5-square, with chances of equality.

21 ♘f3 ♗xf4

As shown by Zsuzsa Polgar, 21...b5? is bad because of 22 ♘xe5 fxe5 23 ♗h6!± (But not 23 ♗g5? ♖xf1+ 24 ♖xf1 ♖f8=).

22 ♕xf4 b5
23 b3 ♖b8?

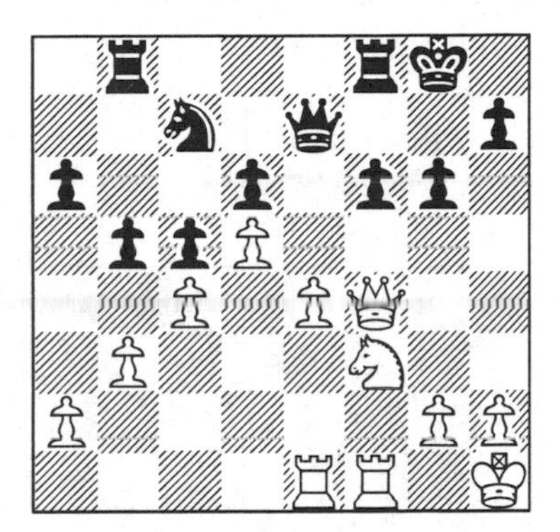

This allows a nice pawn break. White keeps a small advantage after both 23...bxc4 24 bxc4 ♖b8 25 ♖b1 ♖fe8 26 ♖b3 and 23...b4 24 g4, preparing g4-g5.

24 b4! cxb4
25 c5 ♖bd8

Or 25...dxc5 26 d6 ♕d7 27 dxc7 ♖bc8 28 ♖d1 ♕xc7 29 ♕xc7 ♖xc7 30 ♖d6±.

26 ♘d4

Also possible was 26 c6 with a stable advantage.

26	**...**	**dxc5**
27	**♘c6**	**♕d7**
28	**♘xd8**	**♕xd8**
29	**♖c1?!**	

A more straightforward path was 29 ♖d1 c4 (29...♕d7 30 e5! ♘xd5 31 ♕f3 ♖d8 32 exf6 ♔f7 33 ♖d2+-) 30 d6 ♘e6 31 ♕d2 a5 32 d7!±.

29	**...**	**c4**
30	**d6?!**	

30 ♖cd1!?

30	**...**	**♘e6**
31	**♕d2**	**♕d7?**

31...a5! (Ftacnik) was necessary: 32 ♕d5 (Not 32 d7? ♖f7 33 ♖cd1 ♘f8∓) 32...♕d7 and Black has managed to blockade the white pawns.

32	**♕xb4**	

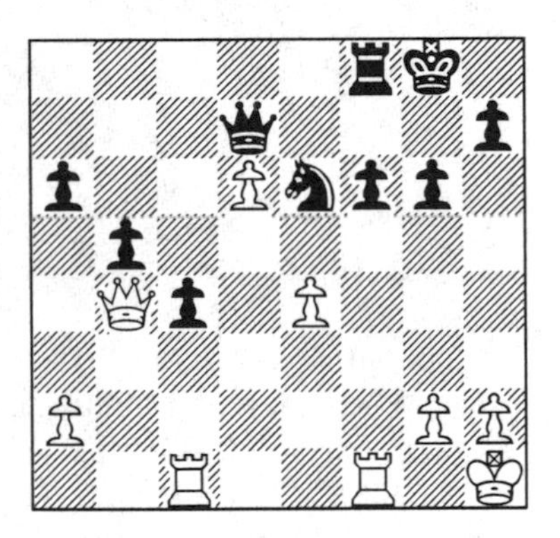

Now White is winning without any major problems.

32	**...**	**♘g5**
33	**♕c5**	**♖e8**
34	**♖ce1!**	**♖e6**
35	**e5**	**f5**
36	**a4!**	**♘f7**
37	**axb5**	**axb5**
38	**♕c7!**	**♕xc7**
39	**dxc7**	**♖c6**

Or 39...♖e8 40 e6 ♘d6 41 ♖d1 and White wins (Zsu. Polgar).

40	**e6**	**♖xc7**
41	**e7**	**♘d6**
42	**e8♕+**	**♘xe8**
43	**♖xe8+**	**♔f7**
44	**♖b8**	**c3**
45	**♔g1**	**1-0**

Game 13
Vaisser-Golubev
Biel open 1995

1 d4 ♘f6 2 c4 g6 3 ♘c3 ♗g7 4 e4 d6 5 f4 0-0 6 ♘f3 ♘a6

7	**e5!?**

Other possibilities for White on the 7th move (apart from 7 ♗d3, which was considered in the previous game) are:

a) 7 c5?! (An interesting idea of Riedel's which may, however, be dubious) 7...dxc5 8 d5 e6 9 ♗xa6 bxa6 10 0-0 exd5 11 e5 ♘e4 12 ♕xd5 ♕xd5 13 ♘xd5 ♗b7 14 ♘e3 ♖ad8 is slightly better for Black, Riedel-Held, Munich 1993.

b) 7 ♗e3?! (In this system the bishop is often vulnerable on e3. Here Black can take advantage of this by energetic play) 7...c5! 8 d5 e6! 9 dxe6 ♗xe6! (An idea of Prie's). Compared to the line with 7 ♗d3 we have a similar position but with the bishop placed on e3 instead of d3, a difference which favours Black. Black has excellent active play.

c) 7 ♗e2 e5!

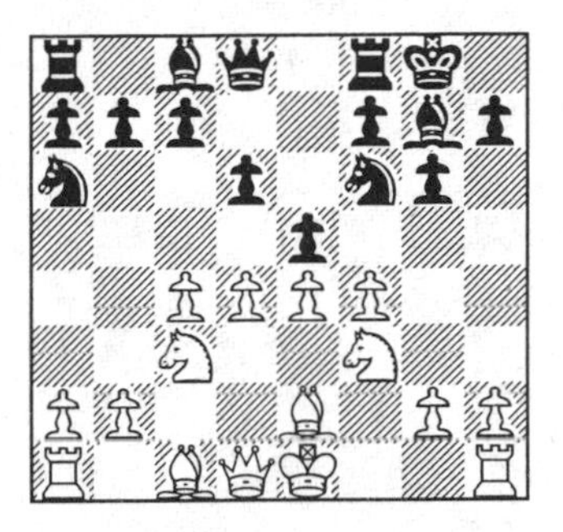

and now:

c1) 8 0-0 is harmless due to 8...cxd4 9 ♘xd4 ♘c5 10 ♗f3 ♖e8 11 ♖e1 ♗g4!? 12 ♘b3 ♗xf3 13 ♕xf3 ♘xb3 14 axb3 c6 15 ♗e3 with pleasant equality for Black.

c2) 8 dxe5

offers no more than equality

8...dxe5

and now:

c21) 9 ♘xe5 ♘c5 10 ♗f3 (10 ♕c2?! ♘fxe4! 11 ♘xe4 ♗f5 12 ♗d3 ♗xe4 13 ♗xe4 ♗xe5 14 fxe5 ♕h4+ 15 g3 ♕xe4+∓, Belov) 10...♕xd1+ 11 ♔xd1 ♖d8+ 12 ♔c2 (12 ♔e2?! ♗e6 13 ♗e3 ♘fd7! 14 ♘d5 ♘xe5 15 fxe5 ♘d7 16 ♗g5 ♗xd5! 17 cxd5 ♖e8 18 ♗f4 ♗xe5 19 ♗xe5 ♘xe5∓ Gorelov-Belov, Moscow 1987) 12...♘fxe4 13 ♘xe4 ♗f5 14 ♖e1 ♗xe5 15 fxe5 ♖d4 16 b3 (16 ♔c3 ♖d3+ 17 ♔b4 [17 ♔c2=] 17...♘a6+ 18 ♔a5 b6+ 19 ♔xa6 ♗c8+ 20 ♔b5 ♗d7+=) 16...♘xe4 17 ♔b2 ♘c5 18 ♔a3 ♘d3 19 ♖d1 c6 20 g4 ♗e6= Namgilov-Sepp, Rostov open 1993.

c22) 9 ♕xd8 ♖xd8 10 ♘xe5

An interesting alternative is 10 fxe5!? ♘g4 11 ♗f4 ♖e8 12 ♖d1 c6 13 h3 ♘xe5 14 ♘xe5 ♗xe5 15 ♗xe5 ♖xe5 16 ♖d8+ ♔g7 17 0-0 ♖b8 18 b4 ♗e6 19 ♖xb8 ♘xb8 20 c5 with approximately equality as in the game Belakovskaya-Winslow, New York 1993.

10...♘c5 11 ♗f3

Or 11 ♘d5 c6 12 ♘e7+ ♔f8 13 ♘xc8 ♖axc8 14 ♗e3 ♘fxe4 15 0-0 f6 16 ♘f3 f5 17 ♘e5 with equality, Chiburdanidze-Xie Jun, World Women's Ch., Manila 1991.

11...♗e6

This move gives White chances to go wrong. Black immediately forced a drawn position with 11...♘fd7 12 ♘xd7 ♗xc3+ 13 bxc3 ♗xd7 14 0-0 ♗c6 15 ♗e3 ♘xe4 16 ♗xe4 in Vera-Bass, Barcelona 1990.

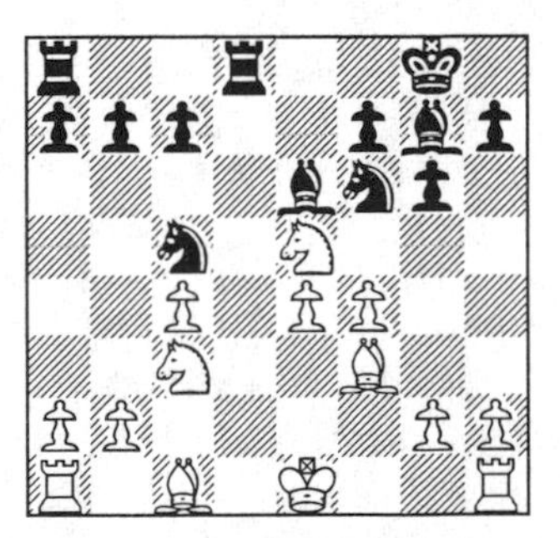

In this critical position White has tried:

c221) 12 ♗e3? ♘fd7! (Mistaken is 12...♘d3+? 13 ♘xd3 ♖xd3 14 ♔f2± 14...♗xc4? 15

e5!±) 13 0-0 (Or 13 ♘xd7 ♘d3+ 14 ♔f1 ♗xc4! and Black is better) 13...♘xe5 14 fxe5 ♘d3 15 ♘d5 ♗xe5∓ Sutter-Gallagher, Suhr 1992.

c222) 12 0-0 ♘fd7! 13 ♘xd7 ♗d4+! 14 ♔h1 ♖xd7 15 ♘d5 c6 16 ♗e3! cxd5 17 ♗xd4 dxe4 18 ♗xc5 exf3= Solovian-Belov, Podolsk 1990.

c223) 12 ♘d5 ♘fd7! 13 ♘xd7 (The interesting complications which arise after 13 ♘xc7 ♘xe5 14 fxe5 ♘d3+ 15 ♔f1 ♗xc4 16 ♗g5 ♘xe5+ 17 ♗e2 f6 18 ♘xa8 fxg5 are in Black's favour) 13...♖xd7, and now White should play 14 0-0, with a likely transposition to variation c222. 14 ♔e2?! is inferior due to 14...♖e8! 15 e5 c6∓ Vaisser-Weindl, Mendrisio open 1989.

c3) The most popular choice, and key to the evaluation of 7 ♗e2, is the line

8 fxe5 dxe5 9 d5

9 ♘xe5?! c5! 10 ♗e3 (10 d5 ♘xe4 11 ♘xe4 ♗xe5∓, Belov) and now the game Komarov-Vl. Georgiev, Benasque 1996, continued 10...♘g4? 11 ♘xg4 cxd4 12 ♘h6+! ♔h8 13 ♗f2 ♘b4 14 ♘d5 ♘xd5 15 exd5 ♕a5+ 16 ♔f1 ♗xh6 17 ♗xd4+ with a clear advantage for White. Instead Black should have seized the initiative by playing 10...♘b4!? or 10...cxd4 11 ♗xd4 ♘b4!? with threats of 12...♕xd4! and 12...♘c2!

After 9 d5 the position is similar to the corresponding one in the line 7 ♗d3, but with some differences.

Black has two good possibilities:

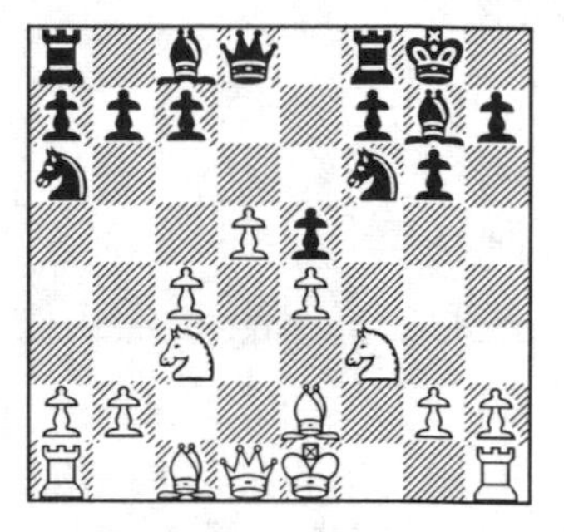

c31) 9...♘c5!? 10 ♗g5 (10 ♕c2?! ♘fxe4! 11 ♘xe4 ♗f5 12 ♗d3 ♗xe4 13 ♗xe4 f5 14 ♗xf5 gxf5∓ Kavalerov-Kochiev, St Petersburg 1994) 10...h6! (Not 10...a5? 11 ♘d2±) 11 ♗xf6 (11 ♗h4? g5 12 ♗g3 ♘fxe4 13 ♘xe4 ♘xe4 14 ♗xe5 ♗xe5 15 ♘xe5 c6! is in Black's favour) 11...♕xf6 12 b4 ♘a6 13 ♖b1 c5 14 a3 ♕b6 (Even world champions make mistakes in the Four Pawns Attack! Against Lautier, Amsterdam 1995, Kasparov played 14...♗d7? here and would have had big problems after the correct 15 d6!) 15 ♕d2 ♖d8 16 h4 h5 17 b5 ♘c7 18 ♕e3 ♕d6 19 0-0 and Black was at least equal in O. Rodriguez-Dorfman, Barcino 1994, though I believe that White's play could have been improved.

c32) 9...c6 10 0-0

Instead White can play 10 ♗g5 (10 dxc6 ♕b6! with good

counterplay or 10 ♗e3? ♘g4) 10...h6 11 ♗h4 ♕b6 12 ♕d2 ♘c5 13 ♗xf6 ♗xf6 14 ♕xh6 (14 ♖b1?! cxd5! 15 cxd5 ♗g7 16 b4 ♘a6 17 ♘a4 ♕d6∓ Bagaturov-Lukin, Frunze 1989) 14...♕xb2 15 ♖c1 ♗g7 16 ♕e3 f5 17 0-0 ♕a3! with complicated play, Armstrong-Milligan, corr. 1994.

10...cxd5 11 cxd5 ♕b6+ 12 ♔h1

At Linares 1995 Kaminski played 12...♘e8?! against me here. Play continued: 13 ♘d2 (13 b4!?) 13...♘d6 14 ♘c4 ♘xc4 15 ♗xc4 ♕d4! 16 ♕xd4 (Possible are 16 ♕e2!?± or 16 ♗b5!?±) 16...exd4 17 ♘b5 ♗d7 18 ♗f4 ♗xb5 19 ♗xb5 ♘c5 20 ♖fe1 d3. Now after 21 ♖ac1!? ♗e5 22 ♗d2 a6 23 ♖xc5 b6! White would have had a small advantage.

Six months later we met again in Biel, where he unleashed an improvement:

12...♘g4!? 13 ♕e1 ♘b4!

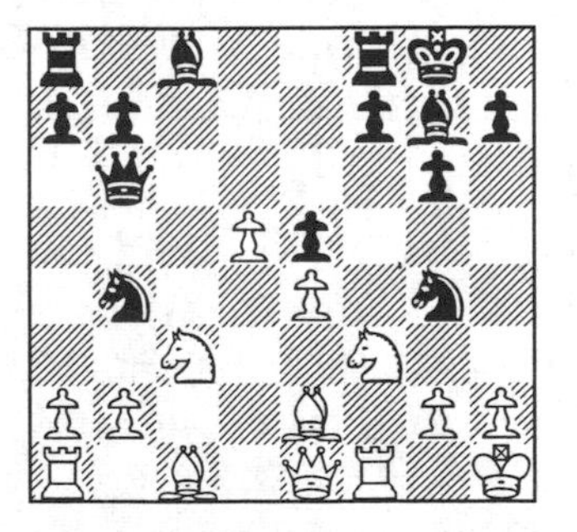

A strong novelty!

14 ♘a4 ♕d6

Now the critical line is 15 h3!? ♘c2 (15...♘f6? 16 ♕h4) 16 ♕c3 ♘xa1 17 hxg4 f5! 18 ♗e3! with a very complicated position, where White is probably not better.

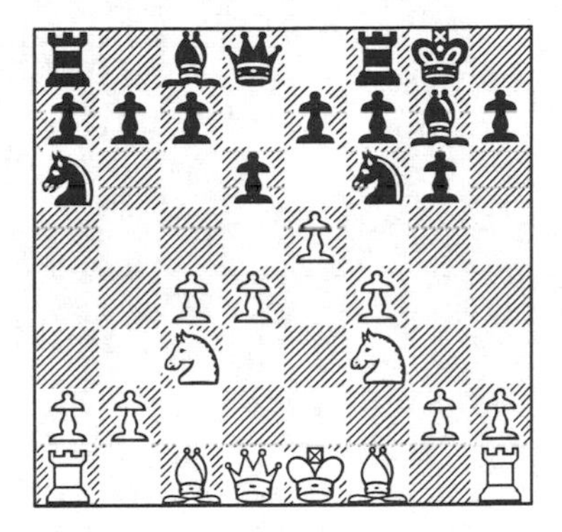

7 ... ♘d7

a) After 7...♘e8?! the reply 8 h3! (8 c5!?) highlights the passivity of Black's move and allows White to retain an advantage due to his strong centre.

b) Also 7...dxe5? cannot be recommended: 8 fxe5 ♘e8 (8...♘d7 9 ♗f4) Leitao-Ivanovic, Yerevan Olympiad 1996, and now 9 c5!?

c) 7...♘h5?! looks dubious but is not easy to refute. After 8 ♗e2 (8 ♗e3!?) 8...♗h6!? White should avoid the over-optimistic 9 f5?! ♗xc1 10 ♕xc1 ♗xf5 11 ♕h6 f6 12 g4 ♗xg4! 13 ♖g1 ♗xf3 14 ♗xf3 ♘g7 15 ♗xb7 ♕b8! with an unclear position, Vokac-Babula, Lazne Bohdanec 1996. Instead White should play 9 g3 f6 10 0-0 with a small advantage. For example: 10...dxe5 11 fxe5 ♗xc1 12 ♖xc1 ♗h3 13

♖e1± (Movsesian).

8 ♗e2!?

White has a number of other potential moves, but only one of them (8 h4!?) is playable:

a) 8 c5? dxc5 9 d5 ♘b6 10 a3 (If 10 ♗e3 ♘b4 White loses the d5-pawn for insufficient compensation) 10...e6!? (10...f6!?) 11 ♗xa6 (11 ♗e3? exd5 12 ♗xa6 d4!) 11...bxa6 12 ♗e3 and now Black is better after either 12...exd5, 12...♘xd5 or 12...c4!?

b) 8 e6?! fxe6 9 ♘g5 ♘f6 10 ♕e2 ♕d7 (Others are 10...e5!? or 10...♔h8!?) 11 ♗e3 (11 g3!?) 11...c5 12 0-0-0 and once again White does not have enough for the pawn, Sogaard-Kjeldsen, Odense 1993.

c) 8 ♕e2?! c5 9 d5 ♘b6 10 ♘e4 (No better is 10 h4 e6 11 h5 exd5 12 hxg6 hxg6 13 cxd5 ♘b4 14 a3 ♘4xd5 15 ♘e4 dxe5 16 fxe5 ♗g4 17 ♗h6 ♗xh6 18 ♖xh6 ♕e7 19 ♘eg5 ♕xg5 20 ♘xg5 ♗xe2 21 ♗xe2 ♖fe8 22 e6 f6∓ Vaisser-Hebden, London 1991) 10...♗g4 11 ♘eg5 (Or 11 ♘f2 ♗xf3 12 gxf3 e6 13 dxe6 dxe5! 14 fxe5 f5! 15 h4 ♖e8 16 f4 ♘c7 17 h5 ♘xe6 18 hxg6 hxg6 19 ♗g2 ♕d4!∓ Zakharevich-V. Ivanov, Moscow 1991) 11...f6 (After 11...♘c7 the knight sacrifice 12 ♘xh7 is not dangerous for Black: 12...♗xf3 13 ♕xf3 ♔xh7 14 ♗d3 ♘d7 15 h4 ♖h8 16 e6 fxe6 17 dxe6 ♘f6 18 f5 ♔g8∓ Rantanen-Sepp, Finnish Team Ch. 1996) 12 h3 ♗xf3 13 ♘xf3 e6! 14 dxe6 fxe5 15 fxe5 ♕e7∓ was Glek-A. Kuzmin, USSR Team Ch., Podolsk 1990.

d) 8 h4!?

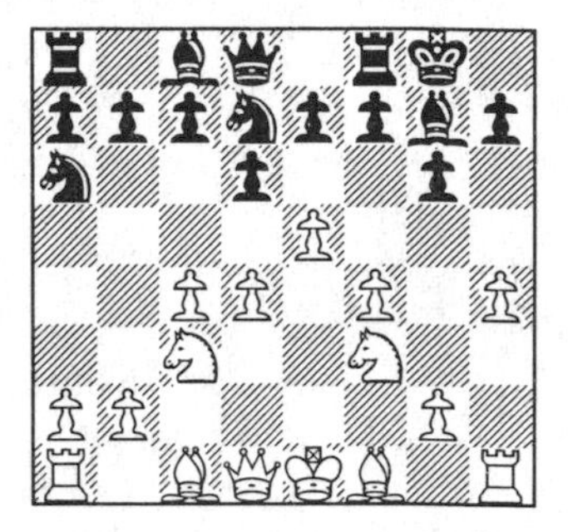

and now:

d1) 8...dxe5 9 dxe5?! (I like ***9 fxe5!?*** c5 10 ♗f4 cxd4 11 ♕xd4 ♘b4 12 0-0-0! with an initiative for White) 9...♘dc5 10 ♗e3 ♗f5?! (It was stronger to play 10...♗g4! 11 ♗e2 f6! with good counterplay) 11 ♘d4 ♕d7, Vaisser-Avrukh, Moscow (rapidplay) 1992, and now White should have played 12 ♗e2! with an advantage, for example: 12...♘b4?! 13 0-0! ♗d3 (13...♖fd8 14 ♘xf5 ♕xf5 15 ♘d5 ♘xd5 16 cxd5±) 14 a3 ♗xe2 15 ♘dxe2! ♘bd3 16 b4 ♘e6 17 ♘d5± or better 12...f6 13 ♘xf5 ♕xd1+! (13...♕xf5? 14 ♗xc5 ♘xc5 15 ♕d5+ ♘e6 16 g4+-) 14 ♖xd1 gxf5 15 e6! ♘xe6 16 ♗d3±.

d2) 8...c5 9 d5

White lost quickly in the game O.Rodriguez-Magem, Linares Team Ch. 1991: 9 e6?! fxe6 10 h5 cxd4 11 ♘e4? (It would have been better to play 11 ♘xd4) 11...♘f6 12 ♘eg5 h6 13 hxg6 hxg5 14 ♘xg5 e5 15 fxe5 ♕a5+ 0-1.

9...dxe5 10 h5! exf4

If 10...♕c7 then 11 hxg6 hxg6 (11...fxg6) 12 g3!?, preparing an attack along the h-file.

11 ♗xf4 ♘f6 12 hxg6

Usually White makes this exchange automatically. Nevertheless, ***12 ♘e5!?*** ♘xh5 (Or 12...♘d7 13 ♘g4!) 13 ♖xh5 gxh5 deserves further analysis. One sample variation: 14 ♗d3 ♗xe5! 15 ♕xh5! ♗xc3+ 16 bxc3 f5 17 ♕g5+ ♔h8 18 ♗e5+ ♖f6 19 d6! ♗d7 20 dxe7 ♕xe7 21 ♕xf6+ ♕xf6 22 ♗xf6+ ♔g8∓.

12...fxg6 13 ♕d2 ♗f5 14 ♗d3

If 14 0-0-0?! then 14...♘g4!? is an unpleasant answer. Alternatively ***14 ♗h6!?*** deserves attention but has yet to be tried in practical play.

14...♗xd3

Vaisser-Petit, French Team Ch. 1992, continued 14...♘h5 15 ♗xf5 (15 ♗h2!?) 15...♖xf5 (15...♘xf4 16 ♗g4) 16 ♗e3 b5?! 17 ♘xb5 ♖b8 18 0-0! ♘g3 19 ♖fe1 ♘e4 20 ♕d3 ♘d6 21 ♘xa7! ♖xb2 22 ♘c6 ♕d7 23 ♖ab1 and White obtained an advantage.

15 ♕xd3 b5?!

15...e6!?, 15...♘h5!?

16 ♘g5!

16 ♘xb5? ♘xd5!

16...♕b6

Not 16...♘b4?! 17 ♕e2 bxc4? 18 ♕e6+ ♔h8 19 ♖xh7+! ♘xh7 20 ♕h3 winning.

The complicated position after 16...♕b6 arose in the game Kahn-G. Horvath, Budapest 1996. White could now have continued ***17 cxb5!?*** ♘b4 18 ♕c4 ♘c2+ 19 ♔d2 ♘xa1 20 d6+ ♔h8 (Not 20...e6? which loses to 21 ♕xe6+ ♔h8 22 ♘xh7!+-) 21 dxe7 with the better chances.

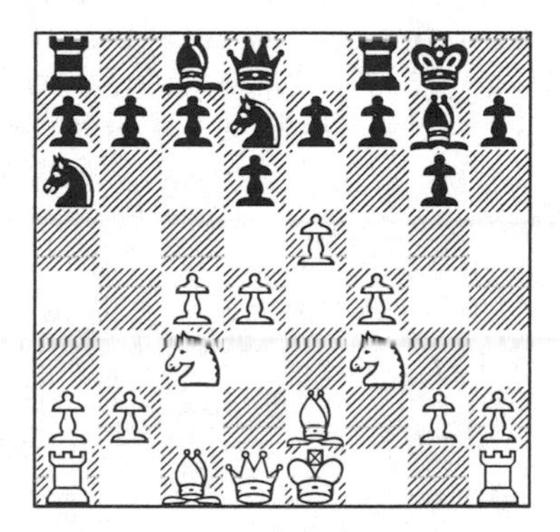

8	**...**	**c5**
9	**exd6**	**exd6**

Alternatively,

9...cxd4 10 ♘xd4

10 dxe7? gives Black a strong initiative after 10...♕xe7 11 ♘xd4 ♘b6.

10...♘b6!?

After 10...exd6 11 ♘db5 ♕h4+ 12 g3 ♕h3 13 ♗f1 ♖e8+ 14 ♔f2 ♕f5, Vokac-Spisak, Cappelle la Grande 1995, White could have taken a pawn: 15 ♘xd6!? ♕c5+ 16 ♔g2, when the threat of exchanging queens with ♕d5 keeps him out of trouble.

11 0-0 ♕xd6 12 ♗e3

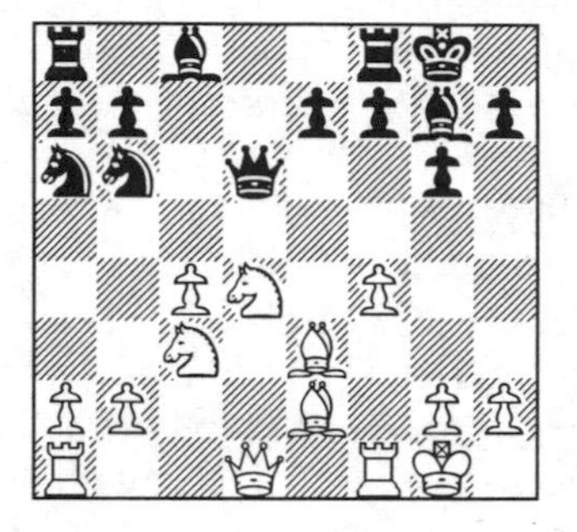

In this critical position Black has problems. For example:

a) 12...♖d8?! 13 ♘db5 ♕xd1 14 ♖axd1 ♖xd1 15 ♖xd1 ♗e6 16 b3 ♘b4 17 ♘c7 ♖c8 18 ♘3b5±.

b) 12...♕b4?! 13 a3 ♕xb2 14 ♘cb5 ♖d8 15 ♖f2 ♘c5 16 ♖b1 ♕a2 17 ♗d3!± ♕xf2+ 18 ♗xf2 ♘xd3 19 ♕xd3 ♗f5 20 ♕b3 ♗xb1 21 ♕xb1 ♘xc4 22 ♕b4± Knaak.

c) 12...♕c5 13 ♘e4 ♕c7 14 ♕b3! ♖d8 15 ♖ad1 (15 ♘b5!? ♕c6 16 ♘xa7 ♕xe4 17 ♗f3 ♕xe3+ 18 ♕xe3 ♗d4 19 ♕xd4 ♖xd4 20 ♘xc8 ♖xc8 21 ♗xb7 is good for White) 15...♗d7 16 c5! ♘xc5 (16...♘d5?! 17 ♕xd5 ♗c6 18 ♕c4 ♗xe4 19 ♘e6! [Less clear is 19 ♘b5 ♕c6 20 ♘xa7 ♕e6! 21 ♕xe6 fxe6 22 c6 ♘c7! 23 ♖xd8+ ♖xd8 24 ♗b6 ♖d2!] 19...fxe6 20 ♕xe6+ ♔h8 21 ♕xe4 ♘xc5 22 ♕c4 ♘a6 23 ♕xc7 ♘xc7 24 ♗f3!± Vokac-Kovalev, Ostrava 1993) 17 ♘xc5 ♕xc5 18 ♘b5 ♕f5 19 ♘xa7 ♘c8 20 ♘b5! (20 ♘xc8? ♖axc8 21 ♗b6 ♗e6 22 ♖xd8+ ♖xd8 23 ♕a3=) and, thanks to the pinned bishop on d7, White is better.

d) 12...♗e6 13 b3 ♖fd8 14 ♘cb5 ♕b8 (14...♕c5 15 ♕e1! ♖xd4? 16 ♕f2) 15 ♕e1 ♗d7 16 ♖d1±.

10 d5

This allows 10...♗xc3!? 11 ♗xc3 f5 with an approximately equal position (see the line 9 exd5 in Game 16).

White can try 10 0-0, waiting for 10...♘f6 before playing d4-d5. If instead 10...♖e8 then 11 f5 can be considered.

The immediate 10 f5?! is premature, however, due to 10...cxd4 11 ♘b5 d3! 12 ♕xd3 ♘dc5 13 ♕xd6 ♗xf5 14 0-0 ♖e8 15 ♖e1 ♖e6 with strong pressure for Black, Jagstaidt-Ad. David, Geneva 1996.

10 ... ♘c7
11 0-0 b5

Again 11...♗xc3!? 12 bxc3 f5 was possible.

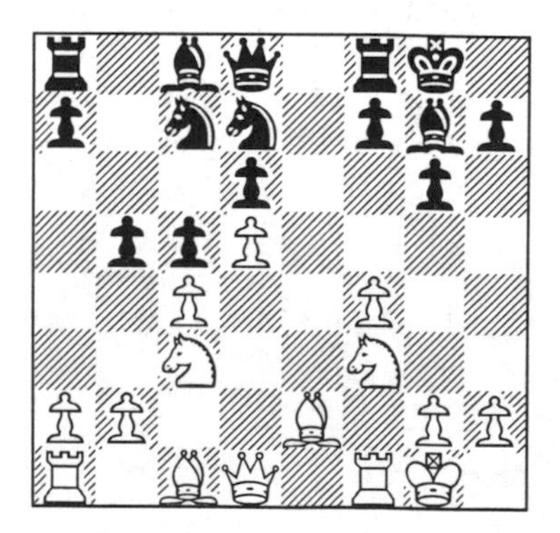

12 f5!?

12 cxb5!? was an alternative.

12 ... bxc4

13 fxg6

Or 13 ♗g5!? f6 14 ♗f4.

13 ... fxg6

This is more precise than 13...hxg6?!

14 ♗g5 ♘f6

Glek's 14...♕e8 is interesting. White can then play 15 ♗xc4 (15 ♕d2? ♘b6! 16 ♖ae1 ♕d7∓) 15...♘b6 16 ♖e1 ♕d7 17 ♖e7 ♕g4 18 ♖e4 with equality.

15 ♘d2! h6?

Golubev suggested that the alternative 15...♗f5!? 16 ♘xc4 ♕d7 might be an improvement. Now 17 ♗f3!? is nothing special and Golubev stated that 17 ♘e3 is harmless because of 17...♘e4! 18 ♘xf5 ♘xc3(?). If we continue this variation, however, with 19 ♘e7+! ♕xe7 20 ♗xe7 ♘xd1 21 ♗xf8 ♗d4+ 22 ♔h1 ♖xf8 23 ♖axd1 we can see that White wins an exchange without any compensation. Instead of 18...♘xc3 Black should play 18...gxf5 19 ♘xe4 fxe4 20 ♕c2 ♗d4+ 21 ♔h1 with an almost equal position.

16 ♗h4 a6?!

Here 16...♗f5 17 ♘xc4 ♕d7 18 ♘e3! ♘e4 19 ♘xf5 gxf5 is worse than on the previous move. White's bishop is not attacked and he can play 20 ♕c2 ♖ae8 21 ♖ae1 with a certain advantage.

17 a4

Strategically Black's position is very difficult, so Golubev tries to generate some tactical resources.

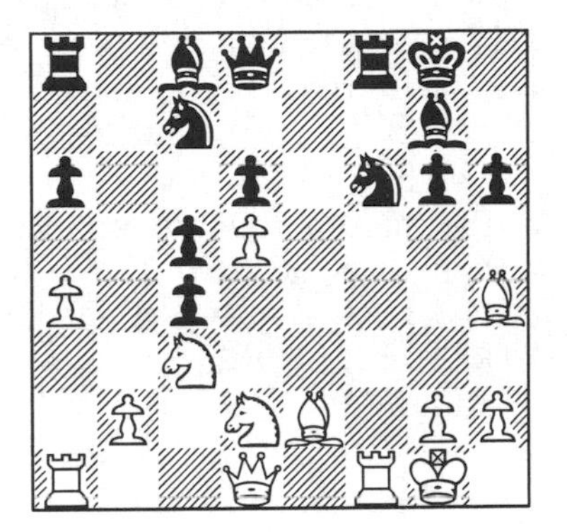

17 ... g5!?

18 ♗g3 ♘fxd5

19 ♘xd5 ♘xd5

20 ♗xc4 ♖xf1+?

After 20...♗e6 21 ♕b3 ♖b8 22 ♖xf8+! ♕xf8 (22...♔xf8? 23 ♕f3+) 23 ♗xd5 ♖xb3 24 ♗xe6+ ♔h8 25 ♘xb3 White's pieces are stronger than the black queen. The text move aims for an improved version of this continuation, but this fails tactically.

21 ♘xf1

If 21 ♕xf1 then Black can play 21...♗e6 22 ♕f3 ♕f6!, indirectly protecting the knight (23 ♗xd5 ♕d4+). The same trick works after 22 ♕d3.

21 ... ♗e6

22 ♗xd5?!

Instead of the text move, it would have been more convincing to play 22 ♔h1! ♗d4 23 ♕f3 ♘f4 24 ♗xe6+ ♘xe6

25 ♕d5 with a large advantage after both 25...♕e8 26 ♖e1 ♔f7 27 ♗xd6! and 25...♔f7 26 ♖e1 ♗e5 27 ♘d2.

Here 22 ♕b3 ♖b8 23 ♗xd5 is evidently worse than it was in the note to Black's 20th move.

22 ... ♗d4+
23 ♗f2

The three pieces are stronger than the queen after 23 ♕xd4 cxd4 24 ♗xe6+ ♔g7 25 ♗d5! ♖b8 26 ♗f2, but the text move is more solid.

23 ... ♗xd5
24 ♗xd4 cxd4
25 ♕xd4 ♗e6
26 ♖e1 ♕e7!

Putting up the toughest resistance.

27 ♘g3 ♖f8

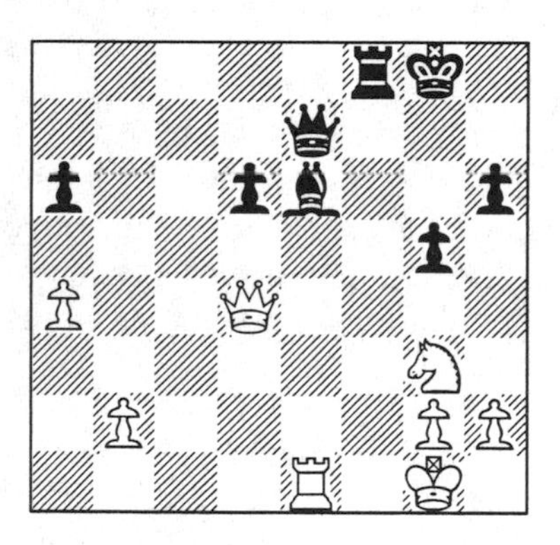

28 ♕e4?

A grave mistake. After 28 ♕e3! ♖f6 (Or 28...♖e8 29 ♕b6±) 29 ♘h5 ♖g6 30 ♕b6 White is clearly better.

28 ... ♕a7+
29 ♔h1 ♗b3
30 ♘f5 ♔h8!

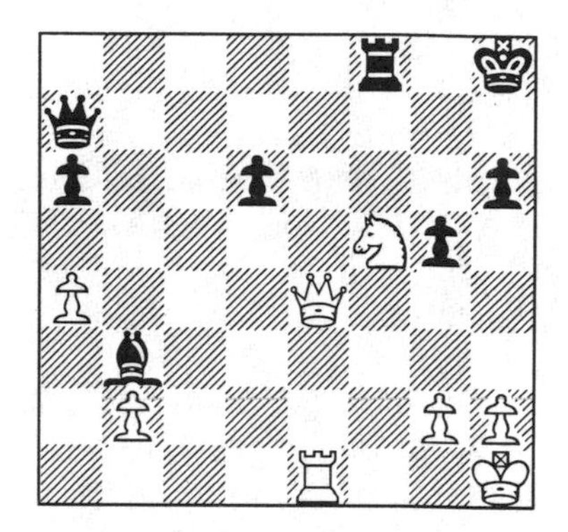

White had considered only 30...♕f2? 31 ♘e7+ ♔h8 32 ♘g6++-.

31 ♘e7?

Now the position becomes equal. It was better to play 31 ♕d3. The rest of the game was played in mutual time trouble.

31 ... ♖f6
32 ♕d3 ♕f2
33 ♕c3 ♔h7
34 h3 g4
35 hxg4 ♕h4+
36 ♔g1 ♕f2+
½-½

5 The Pseudo Benko Gambit 7...b5

1 d4 ♘f6 2 c4 g6 3 ♘c3 ♗g7 4 e4 d6 5 f4 0-0 6 ♘f3 c5 7 d5 b5

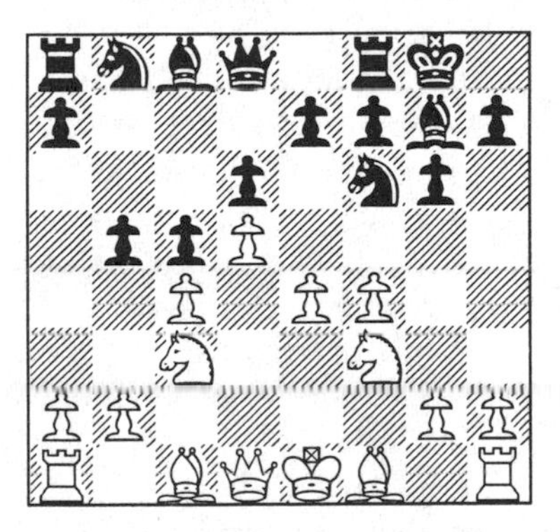

The idea of deploying the Benko Gambit structure against the Four Pawns Attack has both its pros and cons. Black's trump is that his opponent's position has been slightly exposed by e2-e4 and f2-f4. On the other hand, White has built a strong pawn centre without losing the right to castle and, additionally, has the constant threat of the break e4-e5. Black must keep a careful eye on this. Both the theory and the practice in this position promise slightly better chances for the White player.

Game 14
Nogueiras-Sax
Graz 1984

1 d4 ♘f6 2 c4 g6 3 ♘c3 ♗g7 4 e4 d6 5 f4 0-0 6 ♘f3 c5 7 d5 b5

8 cxb5

The safest course of action. After

8 e5?!

Black has two choices:

a) 8...♘fd7?! 9 ♘xb5! dxe5 10 ♗d3 a6 11 ♘c3 ♕c7 12 f5

and now:

a1) I cannot resist the temptation to show one old game with a nice combination at the end:

12...♘b6? 13 g4 ♘8d7 14 0-0 ♘f6 15 ♘g5 ♖b8± 16 ♘ge4 ♘bd7 17 ♕e2 ♘xe4 18 ♘xe4 ♘f6 19 ♗e3 ♘xe4 20 ♗xe4 ♗d7 21 ♕f2 a5 22 ♖ac1 ♖bc8 23 ♕h4 ♕d6 24 ♖f3 ♖b8 25 ♖c2 ♖b4

(see following diagram)

26 ♖h3! h5 27 gxh5! gxf5 28 h6 ♗f6 29 ♖g2+ ♔h8 (29...♔h7

30 ♕g3! fxe4 31 ♖h5!+-) 30 ♕g3! ♗g5 (Black has no good defence to White's threat 31 ♕g7+!) 31 ♕xg5 1-0 Vaisser-Loginov, Alma-Ata 1980.

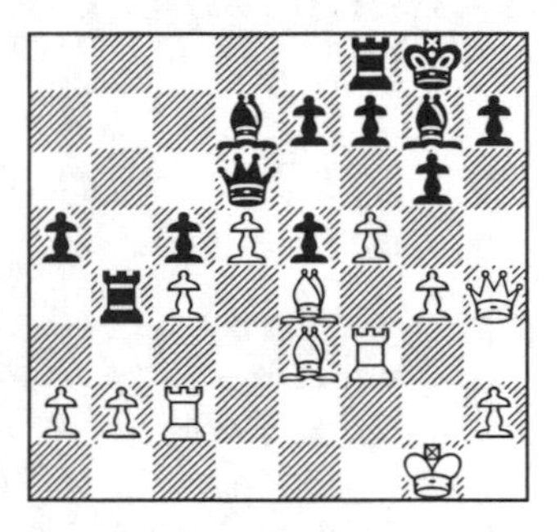

a2) 12...♘f6 13 ♕c2 gxf5 14 ♗xf5 e6 15 dxe6

15 ♗d3!? h6 is interesting.

15...fxe6

15...♗xe6, as recommended by Taimanov, is hardly better: 16 ♗xe6 (Or 16 ♘g5!?) 16...fxe6 17 0-0 ♘c6 18 ♗g5! ♘d4 19 ♕d1 ♖ad8 20 ♖e1!±, Wachsmuth-Jesch, corr. 1989.

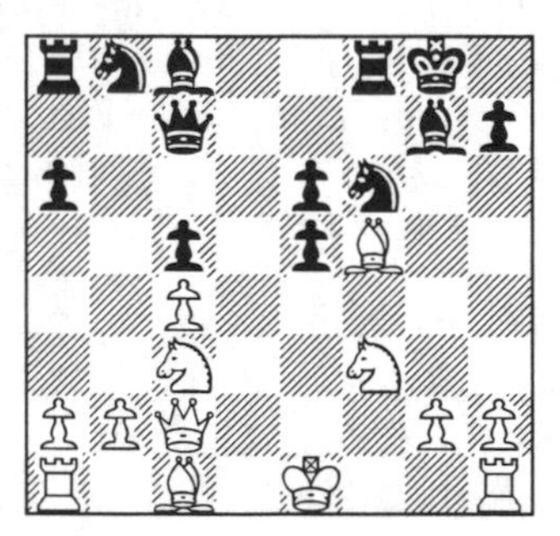

16 ♗d3 ♘c6 17 0-0 ♘b4?!

Or 17...♘d4!?±.

The encounter Ree-Ligterink, Leeuwarden 1976, now continued:

18 ♕e2 ♘xd3 19 ♕xd3 ♗b7 20 ♘g5 h6 21 ♖xf6!

with a clear advantage to White.

b) 8...dxe5! 9 fxe5 ♘g4 10 ♗f4

After 10 cxb5 ♘xe5 11 ♗e2 ♘bd7 12 0-0 a6 13 ♘xe5 ♘xe5 14 ♗e3 axb5 15 ♗xc5 b4! 16 ♘b5, Strating-Van de Mortel, Amsterdam 1994, Black should have played 16...♗a6! and if 17 d6 then 17...♕a5! 18 dxe7 ♖fc8 with the better chances.

10...♘d7 11 cxb5

Alternatively: 11 ♕e2 b4 12 ♘d1 ♕c7 13 d6 exd6 14 exd6 ♕c6∓; or 11 ♘xb5 ♘dxe5 12 ♘xe5 ♘xe5 13 ♕d2 e6 14 ♗e2 exd5 15 cxd5 c4 16 ♘c3 ♖b8 with enough counterplay for Black as in the game Schuh-Steinbacher, German Bundesliga 1987/88.

11...♘dxe5 12 h3

Another example went 12 ♘xe5 ♘xe5 13 ♗e2 ♗f5 14 0-0 c4! 15 ♕d2 a6 16 a4 and White is certainly not better, Kaidanov-Efimov, Sochi 1980.

12...♘xf3+ 13 ♕xf3 ♘f6

13...♘h6!? deserves attention, e.g. 14 g4 e5 15 ♗e3 f5 with complicated play, Kaplan-Vukcevic, Hastings 1976.

14 ♗c4 ♗b7 15 0-0 ♘d7 16 ♖ae1?! ♘b6 17 ♕d3 ♗d4+ 18 ♗e3

(see following diagram)

Schiller-Mohr, USA 1984, and now 18...♖c8! would have

given Black an advantage.

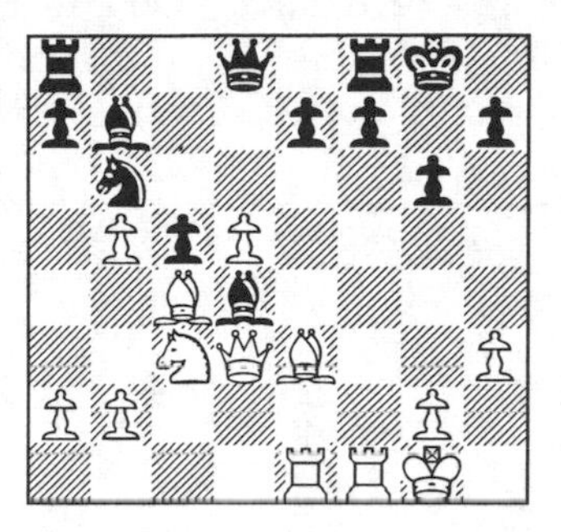

8 ... a6

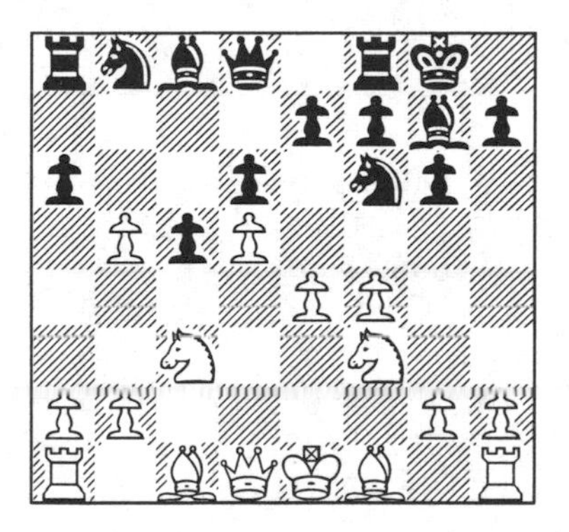

9 a4

The alternatives are:

a) 9 e5?! is a little more justified than on the previous move, but it does not offer more than equality: 9...dxe5 10 fxe5 Ng4 11 bxa6 (11 Bf4 Nd7 12 e6? fxe6 13 dxe6 Rxf4 14 Qd5 Ne3 15 Qxa8 Nb6 16 Qb8 Rb4∓ Kakageldiev-Acharya, Calcutta open 1994) 11...Nxe5 12 Nxe5 Bxe5 13 Bh6 Re8 14 Bb5 Bd7 15 Bxd7 Qxd7 16 Qd2 Rxa6 17 0-0 and Black has no problems, Moskalenko-Lukin, Lvov 1984.

b) 9 bxa6?! Qa5!

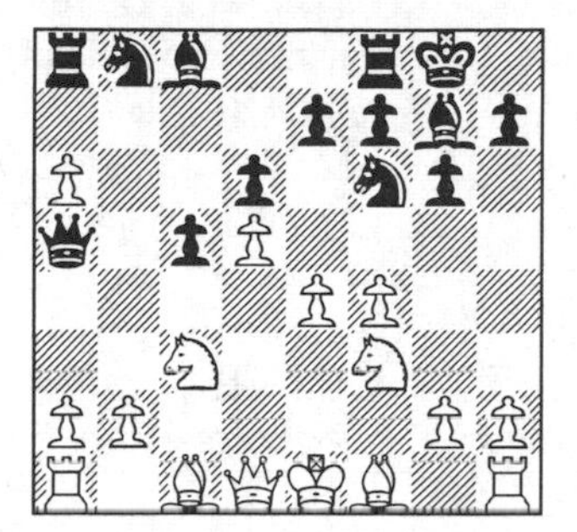

and now:

b1) 10 Qd2?! Bxa6 11 e5 Nfd7 12 e6 Nb6!? 13 exf7+ Rxf7 14 Ng5 Rf5 15 Qe3, Elbilia-Shirov, French Team Ch. 1993, when Black could have obtained a large advantage with ***15...Nxd5!*** 16 Qe6+ Kh8 17 Bd2 Bxc3! 18 bxc3 Nxf4.

b2) 10 Bd2?! Bxa6 (10...Nbd7!? 11 Qc2?! [11 Be2 Bxa6 12 0-0] 11...Bxa6 12 Nb5 Qb6 13 a4 c4! 14 Bxc4 Ng4 15 Rf1 Rfc8 16 Rc1 Bxb5 17 axb5 Ne3 18 Bxe3 Qxe3+ 19 Kd1 Qxf4 20 b3 Bh6∓ Herzog-Dzhindzichashvili, St Martin 1991) 11 Bxa6 (Or 11 Be2!? Qb4!? 12 e5! dxe5 13 fxe5 Ng4 14 Bxa6 Nxa6 15 Qe2 Qxb2 16 Rb1 Qc2 17 0-0!, Kozul-Kochiev, Palma de Mallorca 1989, with an unclear position) 11...Qxa6 12 Qe2 Qxe2+ 13 Kxe2 Nfd7 with a good version of the Benko Gambit for Black. For example: 14 Rhc1?! (14 Ne1!? Na6 15 Nc2 Rfb8 16 Rhb1!? with the idea of Nc2-e3-c4, Bangiev)

14...♘a6 15 ♘d1 f5! 16 ♘g5 fxe4 17 ♘e6 ♖fb8∓ Bangiev-Bologan, German Bundesliga 1993.

b3) 10 ♘d2 ♗xa6 11 ♗xa6 ♘xa6! 12 0-0 ♘c7 13 ♕e2 ♖fb8 14 ♘c4 ♕a6 15 ♗d2 ♘d7 16 b3 ♘b6 17 ♖ac1 ♘xc4 18 bxc4 ♖b4 with sufficient counterplay, Pr. Nikolic-Hoi, Esbjerg 1982.

c) 9 ♕b3!? (Threatening b5-b6) 9...♕b6 (9...axb5!? 10 ♗xb5 ♗a6; 9...e6!? 10 b6 ♕e7) 10 a4! axb5 11 ♗xb5, Piket-Shirov, Aruba (match) 1995, and now instead of 11...♗a6? 12 ♘d2 ♗xb5 13 ♘xb5 ♘a6, permitting 14 ♘c4 ♕b7 15 ♕f3 ♘b4 16 ♕e2!± (Korchnoi), Black should have played 11...♘a6! 12 ♘d2 ♘b4 with compensation for the pawn.

d) After 9 ♗d2 Black may transpose to the main line after 9...♕b6 10 a4 axb5 11 ♗xb5 (11 axb5?! ♖xa1 12 ♕xa1 e6 13 dxe6 ♗xe6 14 ♘g5?! ♗b3! is slightly better for Black, Arencibia-Tal, Manila Interzonal 1990).

Now we return to the main line 9 a4.

(see following diagram)

9 ... axb5

Other possibilities for Black in this position, which is critical for the 7...b5 line:

a) 9...♗b7 10 ♗e2!

White is slightly better after 10 bxa6 ♘xa6 11 ♗c4 ♘b4 12 0-0 ♘d7 13 ♗d2!? ♘b6 14 b3 ♗a6 15 ♗xa6 ♖xa6 16 ♕e2, Vaisser-Brito, Las Palmas 1993.

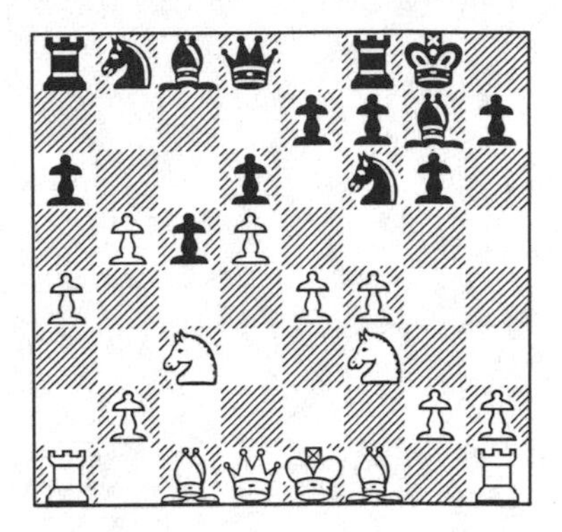

10...axb5 11 ♗xb5 e6 12 0-0 exd5 13 exd5 ♘bd7 14 f5!

A thematic move.

14...♘b6 15 ♗g5 ♕c7 16 fxg6

Also playable is 16 ♗xf6 ♗xf6 17 ♕d2!± (But not 17 ♘e4? ♗xb2! 18 ♖b1 ♗xd5!∓).

16...hxg6

Not 16...fxg6? 17 a5±.

17 ♗xf6 ♗xf6 18 ♕d2±

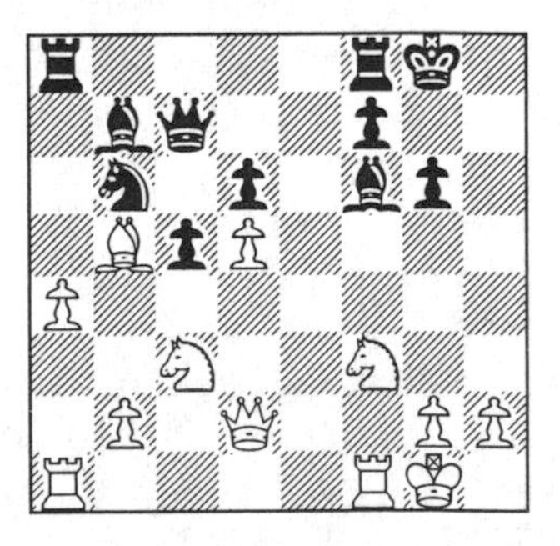

Here are two examples from this position:

a1) 18...♗a6 19 ♗xa6 ♖xa6

20 ♕f4 ♕d8 21 a5 ♘d7 22 ♘e4 ♗e5 23 ♕h6 ♗g7 24 ♕h3 and White developed a decisive attack on the kingside, Piskov-Friegrich, Berlin 1990.

a2) 18...c4 19 ♔h1! ♕d8 20 a5 ♘d7 21 ♘e4 and White is winning, Kishnev-Vukic, Pula 1988.

b) 9...♕a5 10 ♗d2

This is much more accurate than 10 ♘d2?! ♕b4!? 11 ♖a3 ♘g4! 12 ♕f3 f5! with the initiative.

10...♕b4

After 10...e6?! the simplest continuation is 11 dxe6! (Not 11 e5?! dxe5 12 ♘e4 ♕d8 13 ♘xf6+ ♗xf6 14 dxe5 ♗xe5!? 15 ♘xe5 ♕h4+ 16 g3 ♕e4+ 17 ♕e2 ♕xh1) 11...♗xe6 12 ♗e2 axb5 13 ♗xb5±.

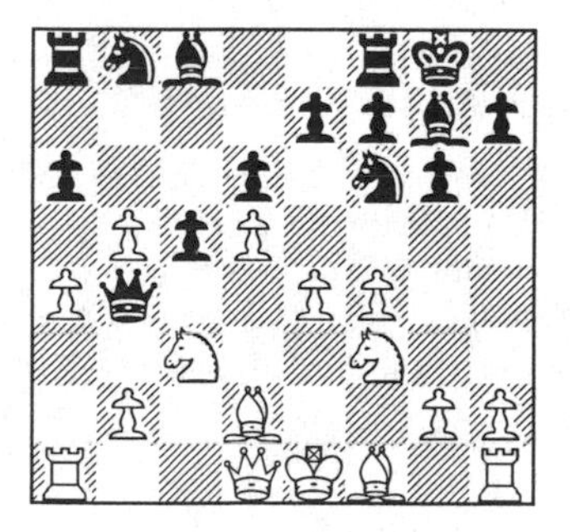

After 10...♕b4 White has three playable moves:

b1) 11 ♕c2 c4

The most critical move. After 11...axb5 (11...♗d7!? 12 e5 ♗f5) 12 ♗xb5 ♗a6? (The black bishop must control the f5-square. 12...♗d7!± was necessary, e.g. 13 e5? ♗f5! 14 ♕c1 ♘e4) 13 e5! ♘g4 (13...dxe5 changes nothing: 14 fxe5 ♘fd7 15 ♘e4+-) 14 ♘a2 ♗xb5 15 ♗xb4 and White went on to win, Barsov-Dostan, Budapest open 1989.

12 e5

Black has no real problems after 12 a5 axb5 13 ♘a4 ♕b3 14 ♕xb3 cxb3 15 ♘b6 ♖a7 16 e5 dxe5 17 ♘xe5, Lanchava-Van der Weide, Leeuwarden 1995, and now 17...♗a6!? is best.

12...♗f5!

But not 12...dxe5? 13 fxe5 ♘g4 (13...♗f5?! 14 ♘a2!+-) 14 ♘d1! ♕c5 15 ♕xc4±.

13 ♘a2 ♕c5 14 ♕xc4 ♘xd5

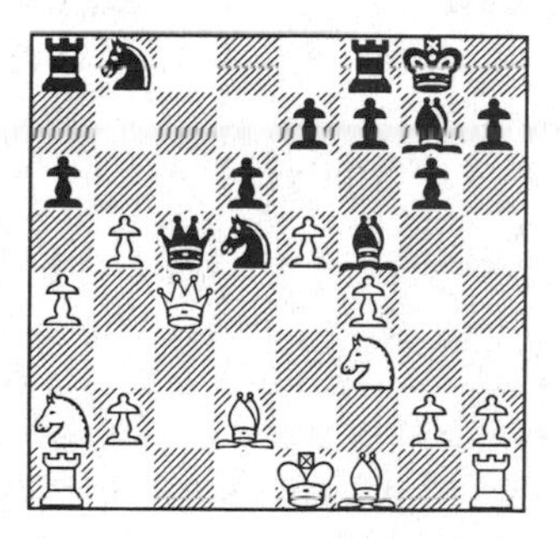

Compared with the variation covered in the previous comment, Black's queen is protected and this move becomes possible. However, White retains slightly better chances after

15 ♕xc5 dxc5 16 ♖c1 axb5!

This is much better than 16...♘d7?! 17 bxa6 ♖fb8 18 ♗c4 ♘c7 19 b4! ♘xa6 20 ♗b5 ♘c7 21 ♗c6 ♖a6 22 ♗xd7

♗xd7 23 a5± Blokh-Holthuis, corr. 1994.

17 ♗xb5±

Not 17 ♖xc5?! ♖xa4.

b2) 11 ♕b1!? is an interesting try:

b21) After 11...c4?! 12 a5! ♕c5 (12...axb5?! 13 ♘a4 c3 [Black cannot play 13...♕b3 as in the line with 11 ♕c2 because of 14 ♖a3] 14 ♘xc3±) 13 b6 ♘g4 14 ♕c1! ♗xc3 (14...f5 15 h3 ♕f2+ 16 ♔d1 ♗xc3 17 ♕xc3 fxe4 18 ♘d4 e3 19 ♗e1 e2+ 20 ♘xe2+-) 15 ♕xc3 ♕f2+ (15...♘f2? 16 b4!+-) 16 ♔d1 ♗b7 (16...♕c5 17 ♗xc4 ♘f2+ 18 ♔e2 ♘xe4 19 ♕d4 ♕xd4 20 ♘xd4±) 17 ♖a4! ♘d7 18 h3 ♘c5 19 ♖xc4 ♘f6 20 ♗e1 and White went on to win, Malinin-Sirota, corr. 1992.

b22) Probably Black should have played ***11...axb5!? 12 ♗xb5 ♗a6***. At least 13 e5 (which is winning with the queen on c2), doesn't work here: 13...dxe5 14 fxe5 ♘g4 15 ♘e4 ♕b3, attacking the d5-pawn.

b3) 11 ♗d3 c4 12 ♗c2 ♕c5

12...♘fd7 13 ♖a2 is not very promising for Black, but after the untried ***12...♕xb2?!*** it is not easy for White to prove an advantage. 13 ♖b1 ♕a3 14 b6! might well be the best way for White to continue, for example 14...♗b7 15 0-0 ♕c5+ 16 ♔h1 e6?! 17 dxe6 fxe6 18 ♘g5! ♕c8 19 f5±.

13 ♕e2 axb5

and now:

b31) 14 ♘xb5? ♘xe4! 15 ♗xe4 (15 ♕xe4 ♗f5 16 ♕xe7 ♗xc2∓) 15...♕xb5! 16 axb5 ♖xa1+ 17 ♔f2 ♖xh1 and Black is better, Balogh-Lechtynsky, Budapest 1986.

b32) 14 e5?! worked out well in the game Glek-Yanvarjov, USSR 1989, with Black's help: 14...dxe5? 15 fxe5 ♘fd7 16 ♗e3 ♕b4 17 ♗d4 bxa4 18 0-0 ♘c5? 19 e6! ♗xd4+ 20 ♘xd4 f6 21 ♗xg6!+-, but the move 14...♘g4! would have been very annoying.

b33) 14 ♗e3! ♕b4 15 0-0 bxa4

15...♕xb2?! is refuted by 16 ♘xb5 (Not 16 ♗d4? ♘xd5!∓; 16 ♖a2? ♕xc3 17 ♗d2 ♘xd5! winning) 16...♘xe4! 17 ♖a3! ♗f5 (17...♘c3? 18 ♖xc3! ♗xc3 19 ♖b1+-) 18 ♘fd4 ♘g3 19 hxg3 ♗xd4 20 ♘xd4! ♕xa3 21 ♗xf5±.

16 e5 ♘g4

Avshalumov-Smirin, USSR 1986 saw White develop a very strong attack after 16...♘h5 17 ♘g5! dxe5 (Or 17...♕xb2?! 18 ♘xa4 ♖xa4 19 ♖xa4 ♗f5 20 ♖xc4 with a clear edge for White, Ehlvest-Kochiev, Leningrad 1984) 18 fxe5 ♗xe5 19 ♘xh7! ♕xb2 (19...♗xh2+? 20 ♔xh2 ♕d6+ 21 ♔g1 ♘g3 22 ♕f2+-) 20 ♘xf8 ♕xc3 21 ♗xg6! fxg6 22 ♘xg6 ♗f6 23 ♘xe7+ ♗xe7 24 ♕xh5 (24 ♗f2!?) 24...♕xe3+ 25 ♔h1.

17 ♗d4

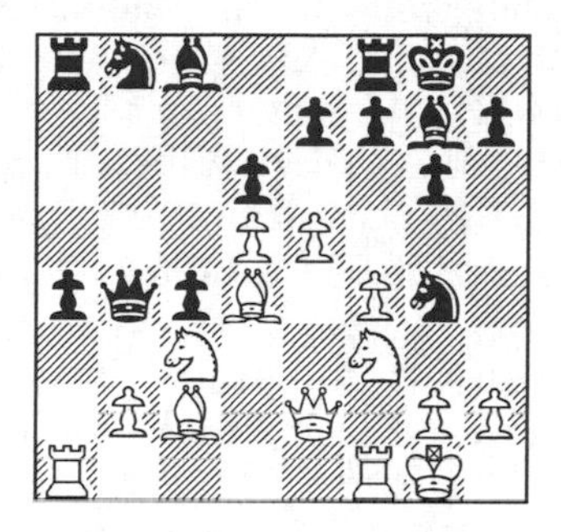

All White's pieces are well placed and he is clearly better. The game Glek-Sorin, Odessa 1989, continued 17...♘h6 18 ♘xa4 ♗f5 19 ♘b6 (19 e6!?; 19 ♗c3!? ♕b7 20 ♗xf5 ♘xf5 21 g4 ♘h6 22 ♘d4, Glek) 19...♖a6 20 ♘xc4 ♕b5! 21 ♖ac1! dxe5 22 ♗xe5! ♗xc2 (22...♗xe5 23 ♕xe5 ♕xc4 24 ♗xf5) 23 ♖xc2 ♕xd5 24 ♗xg7 ♔xg7 25 ♕xe7±.

c) 9...e6

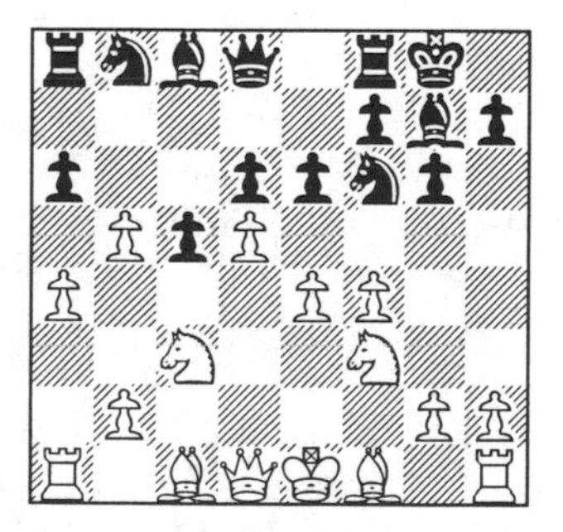

Here the possibility of transposing to the Benko Gambit with 10 b6 is not very convincing: 10...♕xb6 11 a5 ♕b7 12 ♗c4 exd5 13 ♘xd5 ♗e6 14 0-0 ♘xd5 15 exd5 ♗d7, Banikas-Herraiz, Cala Galdana 1996.

Instead White has two promising possibilities: 10 dxe6!? and 10 ♗e2!?

c1) 10 dxe6!? ♗xe6

10...fxe6?! is met by 11 e5 dxe5 (11...♘e8? 12 ♘e4±) 12 ♘xe5±.

11 ♗e2

Not 11 e5?! dxe5 12 ♕xd8 ♖xd8 13 fxe5 ♘g4 14 ♗f4 ♘d7! 15 ♗e2 axb5 16 ♘xb5 ♘gxe5 17 ♘xe5 ♗xe5! with an equal position, as in Karasev-Yuferov, USSR 1977.

11...axb5 12 ♗xb5 ♘a6

If instead 12...d5 (After 12...♕c7 13 0-0 ♘c6, Vaisser-Gufeld, Sochi 1981, 14 f5! would have seized the initiative) 13 exd5 ♘xd5 14 ♘xd5 ♗xd5 15 0-0 ♘c6 16 ♗e3! ♗xb2 (16...♗xf3?! 17 ♕xf3 ♘d4 18 ♕f2±) 17 ♖b1 (The spectacular 17 ♗xc5 ♗xa1 18 ♕xa1!? ♖e8 19 ♖d1 ♕a5! 20 ♖xd5 ♕xb5 21 ♕h8+! ♔xh8 22 axb5 is unclear) 17...♗d4 18 ♘xd4 cxd4 19 ♗f2 ♕f6 20 ♕d2 ♖fd8 21 ♖bc1 White is slightly better. The game San Segundo-Magun, Linares 1986, continued 21...♕e6?! 22 f5! ♕d6?! 23 ♗g3 ♕b4 24 ♕g5 and even after the accurate 24...♕e7! 25 ♕xe7 ♘xe7 24 ♗h4 ♖a7 25 ♖fd1 ♗e4 26 ♗xe7! ♖xe7 27 f6 ♖e6 28 ♖xd4! White has a large advantage.

13 0-0

and now:

c11) 13...♘b4?! is less circumspect than 13...♘c7. After the typical blow 14 f5! gxf5 15 exf5 ♗xf5 16 ♘h4 both 16...♗c2 17 ♕f3 ♘e4 18 ♘f5 ♘xc3 19 bxc3 ♗xf5 20 ♕xf5 ♗xc3 21 ♖a3 ♗d4+ 22 ♗e3, Bleis-Zuse, Mannheim 1987, and 16...♗g4 17 ♗e2 ♘fd5 18 ♘xd5 ♗xe2 19 ♕xe2 ♕xh4 20 ♘e7+ ♔h8 21 ♘f5 ♕f6 22 ♖a3!, Lalic-Zakic, Yugoslavia 1986, give White a strong attack.

c12) 13...♕b6 14 f5! gxf5 15 ♘g5!? (15 exf5 also deserves attention: 15...♗xf5 16 ♘h4 c4+ 17 ♔h1 ♗d3 18 ♖f4 d5 19 ♘f5, Iashvili-Gavrilov, Moscow 1990) 15...♘c7 16 exf5 ♗c8 17 ♗f4 ♘xb5 18 ♘xb5 h6 19 ♘h3 ♖d8 20 ♖a3 with the better chances for White, Semkov-Peev, Plovdiv 1988.

c13) 13...♘c7 14 ♗d3 ♕b8

I prefer White's position after 14...d5?! 15 e5 ♘d7 16 ♘g5!? ♕e7 17 f5!

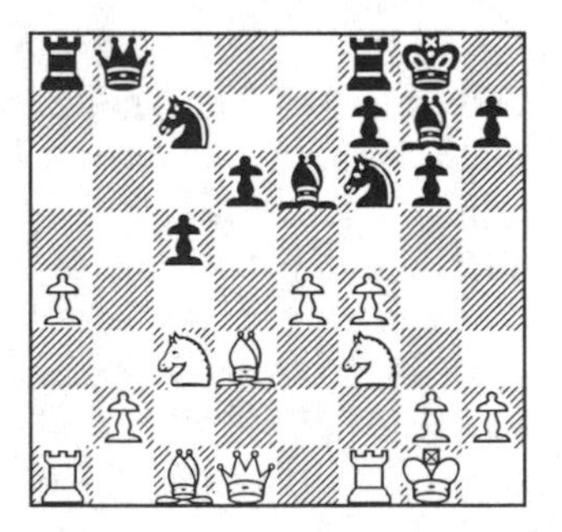

15 f5!

with a better position for White. In the game Ivanov-Kupreichik, Leningrad 1989, White missed this move and Black achieved full compensation for the pawn after 15 e5?! dxe5 16 ♘xe5 ♘fd5 18 ♕f3 ♘b4 19 ♗e4 ♖a6 20 ♕e2 ♖e8 21 ♗e3 f6 22 ♘c4 f5.

c2) 10 ♗e2!?

An idea originated by Uhlmann and developed by Piskov.

10...axb5

10...exd5 11 e5 normally just represents a transposition of moves after 11...dxe5 12 fxe5 ♘g4 13 ♕xd5 ♕xd5 14 ♘xd5 axb5 15 ♗xb5. Sooner or later Black must play ...a6xb5 in this line.

11 ♗xb5 exd5

A strange miniature occurred in Michaelsen-Binzenhoefer, Berlin 1993: 11...♗a6 12 ♗xa6 ♘xa6 13 dxe6 fxe6 14 0-0 d5 15 e5 ♘e8 16 ♘g5± ♕e7? 17 ♘xd5 1-0.

12 e5!

This is the point!

12...dxe5

Or 12...♘e8?! 13 ♘xd5 (13 ♕xd5 ♘c7 14 ♕xd6? ♕xd6 15 exd6 ♗xc3+ 16 bxc3 ♘xb5-+; 13 ♗xe8 ♖xe8 14 ♕xd5±) 13...♗b7 14 ♗c4 ♘c6 15 ♗e3! dxe5 16 ♗xc5 ♘d6 17 ♘e7+! ♘xe7 18 ♕xd6 ♗xf3 19 gxf3 ♘f5 20 ♕xd8 ♖fxd8 21 b3! and White is clearly better, Piskov-Savon, Norilsk 1987.

13 fxe5 ♘g4

Not 13...♘e4?! (13...♘e8? 14 ♕xd5±) 14 ♕xd5 ♘xc3 (If 14...♕xd5 15 ♘xd5 the black knight is badly placed on e4) 15

♕xd8 ♖xd8 16 bxc3 ♗a6 17 ♗g5! ♖c8 (17...♗xe5 18 ♘xe5 ♖d5 19 ♗f6 ♗xb5 20 c4 ♖d6 21 cxb5 ♖xf6 22 ♘f3±, Glek and Piskov. 22...♖f4 doesn't help: 23 0-0! ♖fxa4? 24 ♖xa4 ♖xa4 25 ♖d1!+-) 18 0-0 ♘c6 19 ♗f6!± Piskov-Vasyukov, Moscow 1987.

14 ♕xd5

14 ♗g5!? is complicated but seems to favour White, e.g. 14...♕a5 15 ♕xd5 ♗e6 16 ♕e4 ♘d7 17 ♗f4 (17 0-0? ♘dxe5 18 ♘xe5 ♗xe5!∓) 17...♘b6 (17...♕b4!?) 18 0-0 ♕b4 19 ♕xb4 (19 h3!? ♕xb2 20 ♖fc1) 19...cxb4 20 ♘e4 ♘d5 21 ♗g3 ♘de3 22 ♖fc1 b3!, Elbilia-Kaabi, Maghreb Ch. 1994.

14...♕xd5

14...♕a5?! is dubious. After 15 h3! ♗e6 16 ♕e4 ♘h6 17 g4 White is clearly better.

15 ♘xd5

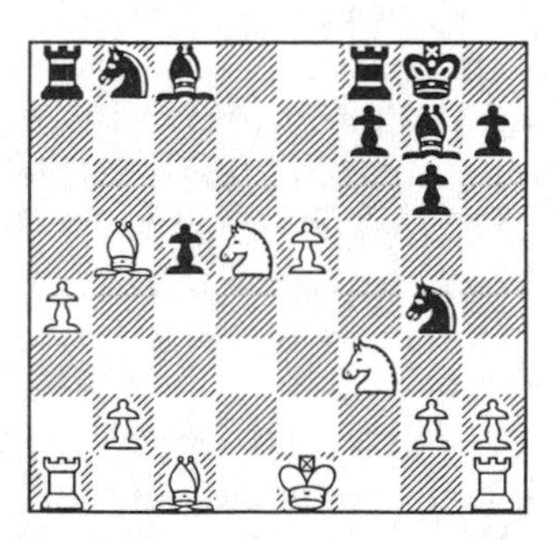

White has a small but secure advantage after both:

c21) 15...♘xe5 16 ♘xe5 ♗xe5 17 ♗h6 ♗g7 (17...♖d8 18 0-0-0!) 18 ♘e7+ (18 ♗xg7!? ♔xg7 19 0-0-0) 18...♔h8 19 ♗xg7+ ♔xg7 20 ♘xc8 ♖xc8 21 ♔d2 ♘c6 22 ♔c3 ♘d4 23 ♖he1; and

c22) 15...♗d7 16 ♘b6 ♖a7 17 ♘xd7 ♘xd7 18 ♗f4 ♘gxe5 19 ♘xe5 ♘xe5 20 0-0-0 c4 21 ♗xe5 ♗xe5 22 ♖d5, Destrebecq-Cortes, French Team Ch. 1991.

c23) Probably the best defence for Black was found in the very first game with this variation: 15...♗b7!? 16 ♘b6 ♖a7 17 ♘c4, Uhlmann-Votruba, Czechoslovakia 1978, and now Black should have played 17...♘c6 18 0-0 ♘cxe5 19 ♘fxe5 ♘xe5 20 ♘xe5 ♗xe5 21 ♗e3±.

10 ♗xb5 ♗a6

Black cannot be satisfied with his position after 10...♘a6?! 11 0-0 ♘b4 12 e5! ♘e8 13 ♕e2 (Or 13 ♗c4 immediately) 13...♘c7 14 ♗c4 ♗b7 15 ♖d1 ♖a7 16 ♗e3 ♕a8 17 ♕d2 ♖d8 18 f5!± Banikas-Karner, Cala Galdana 1996.

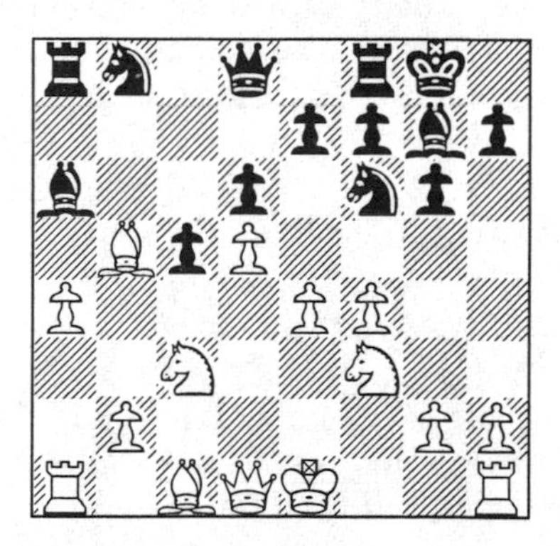

11 ♗d2!

This is more precise than 11 ♖b1?! ♗xb5 12 axb5 ♘bd7 13 0-0 ♘b6 14 ♕e2 ♕c8 15 ♔h1 e6 16 dxe6 ♕xe6 with enough counterplay for the pawn, Vaisser-S. Garcia, Bayamo 1985.

The evaluation of 11 ♕e2!? depends on the unclear position arising after 11...♘xe4! 12 ♕xe4 ♗xc3+ 13 bxc3 ♗xb5 14 ♗b2! In the game I. Horvath-Kiss, Zalakaros 1988, White succeeded in developing a strong attack after 14...♗a6?! (Better is 14...♗d7! 15 c4 ♕b6) 15 f5 ♘d7 16 fxg6 hxg6 17 c4 ♕a5+ 18 ♔f2 ♖ab8 19 ♖hb1 ♖fe8 20 ♕h4 f6 21 ♕h6 ♘f8 22 ♘h4 ♗xc4 23 ♘xg6 ♘h7 24 ♘xe7+! ♖xe7 25 ♗xf6! and went on to win.

11 ... ♗xb5

Instead:

a) The line which Hoi played against Peicheva (Copenhagen 1989) has not found a following: 11...e6?! 12 dxe6 fxe6 13 0-0 d5 14 e5 ♘e4 15 ♗e3 ♘xc3 16 bxc3 ♘d7 with an advantage for White. The game continued 17 ♘g5 ♕e7 18 ♕g4 ♖f5 19 ♕h3 h6 20 ♘f3 ♘f8 21 ♕g3 ♖f7 22 ♖fb1 ♕c7 23 ♕f2 ♘d7 24 ♗xd7! ♕xd7 25 ♕c2 and White won a second pawn.

b) After 11...♕b6 12 0-0 ♘e8, Galioto-Nepeina, Cappelle la Grande, White has the interesting try 13 a5!? ♕b7 14 ♗xa6 followed by 15 ♘a4±.

12 axb5 ♖xa1

After 12...♘bd7 13 0-0 ♖xa1 14 ♕xa1 we transpose to the next comment. It is less precise to play 13 ♖xa8, e.g. 13...♕xa8 14 0-0 ♘b6 15 ♕b3?! (15 ♕e2!? ♘e8 16 g4!?±) 15...♘e8 16 ♗e3 ♘c7 17 ♘e1? f5!∓ Lutskan-Krakops, Latvian Ch. 1993.

13 ♕xa1 ♕b6
14 0-0

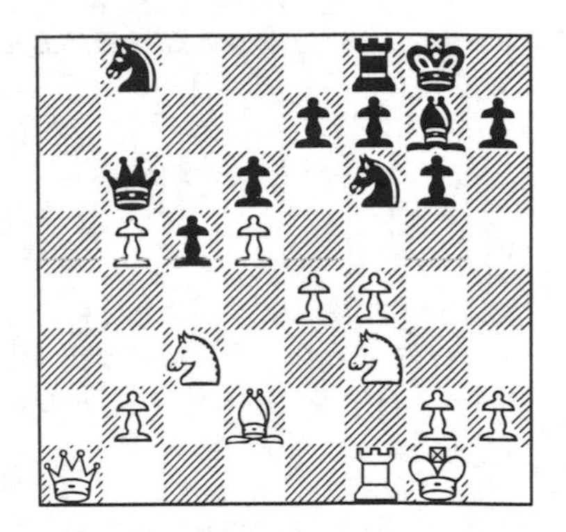

14 ... ♘e8?!

My first experience with the logical move 14...♘bd7!? was not successful:

a) 15 ♕a6?! (the queen does nothing on a6) 15...♖b8 16 ♖a1 ♘e8 17 ♕xb6 ♘xb6 18 ♖a7 ♔f8 19 ♗e1 ♘c8 20 ♖d7 ♘b6 ½-½ Vaisser-Lanka, Cappelle la Grande 1994.

b) White did better in the following game: 15 ♕e1! (Preparing 16 ♕e2 or 16 ♕h4) 15...e6 (15...♕b7!?) 16 dxe6 (Or 16 ♕h4!? exd5 17 e5) 16...fxe6 17 e5 ♘h5 18 exd6 ♕xd6 19 g3 with an advantage to White, Vaisser-Nataf, French Team Ch. 1996. The game continued 19...e5 20 fxe5 ♘xe5 21 ♘xe5 ♗xe5 22 ♖xf8+ ♔xf8 23 ♗h6+! ♔e7?!, and now the simplest way to play was 24 ♗f4! (24...♘xf4? 25 gxf4 ♕d4+ 26 ♔g2+-).

15 ♕e1! ♘c7
16 ♕h4!

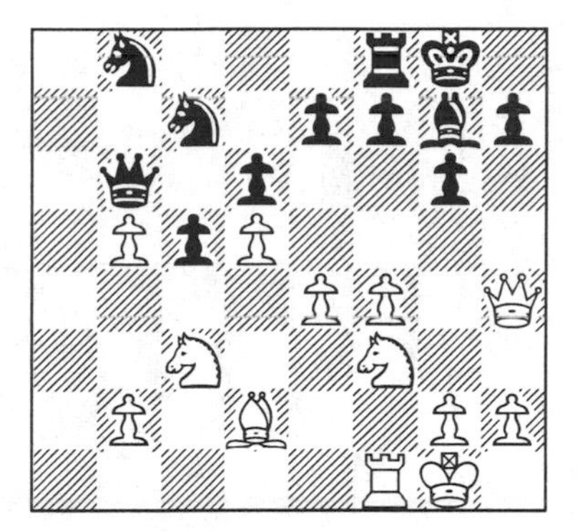

Another natural plan for White was shown in the game Lazarev-Yuferov, Naberezhnie Chelni 1988: 16 ♕e2!? ♘d7 (Or 16...♕b7!?) 17 e5 ♕b7 18 e6 fxe6 19 dxe6 ♘b6 20 ♘g5 with the initiative.

16 ... ♘xb5

Black's position is difficult. The choice is not easy: 16...♖e8 17 e5! and 16...e6 17 f5! exf5 18 exf5 ♘d7 19 ♘g5 both give White a strong attack.

17 ♘xb5 ♕xb5
18 ♕xe7

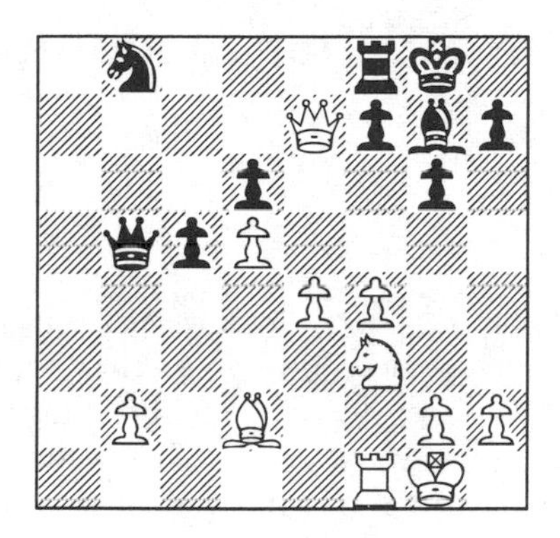

18 ... c4?

The decisive mistake. It was necessary to play 18...♗xb2! 19 ♕xd6 (19 e5? is weak. In the game Michaelsen-Kunsztowicz, Hamburg 1987, Black continued 19...dxe5! 20 fxe5 ♖e8 21 ♕h4 ♖xe5!∓) 19...c4 and the passed c-pawn offers Black some counterplay.

19 ♗c3 ♖e8
20 ♕xd6 ♖xe4
21 ♘e5 ♕e8
22 ♖a1 ♘d7
23 ♕c6 1-0

6 Other Systems for Black

In this chapter we consider other possibilities in the Four Pawns Attack from the King's Indian move order. The material is presented in two games. In Game 15, Vaisser-Krasenkov, we study sidelines without ...c7-c5, while in Game 16, Vaisser-Kr. Georgiev, we look at sidelines with …c7-c5.

Game 15
Vaisser-Krasenkov
Paris 1990

1	**d4**	**♘f6**
2	**c4**	**g6**
3	**♘c3**	**♗g7**
4	**e4**	**d6**

Overly-brave experiments in this opening can usually be punished, e.g. 4...0-0 5 f4 c6?! 6 e5! ♘e8 7 h4! with a strong attack.

5 f4

(see following diagram)

5 ... 0-0

The immediate 5...♗g4 is interesting. Now the attempt to deliver a direct refutation is dangerous for White:

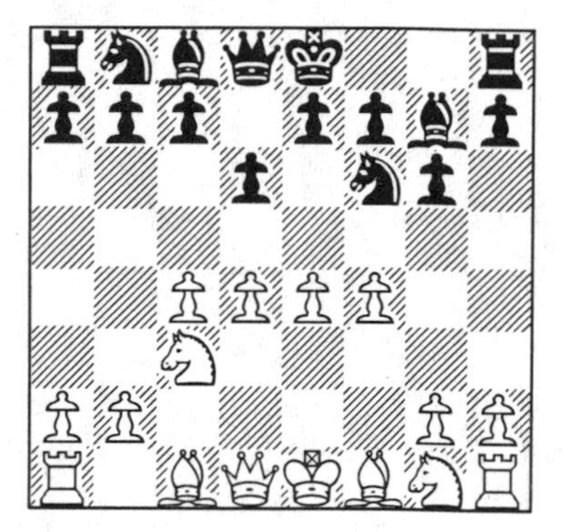

a) 6 ♕b3?! ♘c6! 7 ♗e3 e5 8 dxe5 dxe5 9 ♕xb7 ♗d7 with a strong initiative.

b) If White tries to transpose to the game continuation 5...0-0 6 ♘f3 ♗g4 7 ♗e2 by playing 6 ♘f3, Black can try 6...♘c6 7 d5 (7 ♗e3?! e5! 8 fxe5 dxe5 9 d5 ♘d4 10 ♗xd4 exd4 11 ♕xd4 0-0 gives a lot of play for a pawn) 7...♗xf3 8 gxf3 ♘b8 with complicated play.

c) 6 ♗e2!? looks best, e.g. 6…♗xe2 7 ♕xe2 (7 ♘gxe2 is also possible) and now:

c1) 7...0-0 8 ♘f3 c5 9 dxc5!

(An unclear position arises after 9 d5 e6 10 e5!? exd5! 11 exf6 ♖e8 12 fxg7 ♖xe2+ 13 ♘xe2) 9...dxc5 (9...♕a5? is incorrect: 10 cxd6 ♘xe4 11 ♕xe4 ♗xc3+ 12 ♔f1! ♗f6 13 dxe7 ♖e8 14 ♕xb7 ♘a6 15 ♗d2 ♕b6 16 ♕xb6 axb6 with a big advantage for White) 10 e5 ♘fd7 11 0-0 ♘c6 12 ♖d1 with pressure for White.

c2) 7...♘c6 8 ♘f3 e5 (8...♘d7?! 9 e5!) 9 dxe5 dxe5 10 fxe5 ♘g4 11 ♗g5 ♕c8 (11...♕b8!?) 12 ♘d5 0-0 (The capture 12...♘cxe5? does not work due to 13 h3, when now both 13...♘xf3+ 14 ♕xf3 ♘e5 15 ♕g3 and 13...h6 14 ♗f4 g5 15 ♗g3 ♘xf3+ 16 ♕xf3 ♘e5 17 ♕c3 are bad for Black) 13 0-0 ♖e8 14 ♗f6 ♘cxe5!? 15 ♘e7+ ♖xe7 16 ♗xe7 ♕e6 and Black has insufficient compensation for the exchange.

6 ♘f3

a) If White wants to get the most flexible version of the line 6 ♘f3 c5 7 d5 e6 8 dxe6 fxe6, he can play 6 ♗d3: 6...c5 7 d5 e6 8 dxe6 (8 ♘ge2 exd5 is not attractive for White; after 9 cxd5 ♕b6 or 9 exd5 ♘h5 Black has a good position) 8...fxe6 (8...♗xe6?! 9 f5! is in White's favour) 9 ♘ge2. Yuneev-Smirin, Daugavpils 1989, continued 9...♘c6 10 0-0 a6 11 a4 b6 12 ♘g3 ♘d7 13 ♕g4 ♘d4 14 ♗e3 ♕e7 15 ♖ae1 ♗b7 16 h4 ♔h8 17 h5 g5! with complicated play.

After 6 ♗d3 Black can also play 6...♘a6 7 ♘f3 transposing to the line 6 ♘f3 ♘a6 7 ♗d3 or try the interesting 6...♘c6!? 7 ♘f3 ♗g4 8 e5! (8 ♗e3 e5!) 8...dxe5!? 9 dxe5 ♘b4 10 ♗b1 ♕xd1+ 11 ♘xd1 ♗xf3 12 gxf3 ♘h5 with the idea of …f7-f5 and …♗h6.

b) After 6 ♗e2 the simplest for Black, depending on his taste, is to transpose to the line 6 ♘f3 ♘a6 7 ♗e2 with 6...♘a6 7 ♘f3 or to the line 6 ♘f3 c5 7 d5 b5 with 6...c5 7 d5 b5. In the latter line the position of the bishop on e2 instead of the knight on f3 usually favours Black. For example, after 8 cxb5 a6 9 a4?! axb5 10 ♗xb5 ♗a6 Black wins an important tempo compared to the 'normal' variation. In the case of 9 bxa6 ♕a5 10 ♗d2 ♗xa6 11 ♘f3 ♗xe2 12 ♕xe2 ♕a6! Black gets a Benko-like position with full compensation for the pawn, Welling-Hoeksema, Eindhoven 1988.

6 ... ♗g4

Let us consider other moves in this position apart from 6...c5 and 6...♘a6, which are studied elsewhere in this book:

a) 6...e5?! 7 dxe5!? (White can also play 7 fxe5 dxe5 8 d5 ♘bd7 9 ♗d3 with a position similar to that in the line 6...♘a6 7 ♗d3 e5) 7...dxe5 8 ♕xd8 ♖xd8 9 ♘xe5! (Less attractive is 9 fxe5 ♘fd7! [After 9...♘g4? 10 ♗g5 ♖e8 11 ♘d5

♘a6 ***12 c5!*** is bad for Black] 10 ♘d5 ♘a6 11 ♗g5 ♖e8 12 0-0-0 [12 ♘f6+?! ♗xf6 13 exf6 ♘ac5∓] 12...♘xe5 13 c5!? [13 ♘f6+?! ♗xf6 14 ♗xf6 ♘g4∓] 13...♗g4 with mutual chances) 9 ♘xe5 and now none of Black's three possibilities are enough to give Black equality:

a1) 9...♘xe4 10 ♘xe4 f6 11 ♘xf6+ ♗xf6 12 ♗d2 ♘c6 13 ♗c3 ♗f5 14 ♔f2 ♘d4 15 ♖d1 ♘e6, was the game Lingnau-Finke, RLNS 1989, and now White could have kept an advantage after 16 ♖xd8+ ♖xd8 17 ♔e3 ♖d1 18 g3.

a2) 9...♖e8 10 ♗d3 ♘fd7! (10...♘xe4? loses to 11 ♗xe4 f6 12 ♗d5+ ♔h8 [12...♔f8 13 b3 ♘d7 14 ♗a3+ c5 15 0-0+-] 13 ♗f7 ♖f8 14 ♘xg6+) 11 ♘xd7 ♗xc3+ 12 bxc3 ♘xd7 13 ♗e3 ♘f6 14 e5 ♘g4 15 ♗d2 f6 16 h3 ♘h6 17 0-0 fxe5, Stoy-Kuntzig, RLNS 1988, and after 18 fxe5! ♘f7 19 ♗f4 White could have achieved a small plus (19...♘xe5? 20 ♖ae1 ♖d8 21 ♖xe5 ♖xd3 22 ♖e8+±).

a3) 9...♘a6 10 ♗e3 reaches a position similar to that after 6...♘a6 7 ♗e2 e5 8 dxe5 dxe5 9 ♘xe5, except that instead of ♗e2 White has played ♗e3. But now the c5-square is controlled and this difference changes the evaluation of the position in White's favour. Two examples:

a31) 10...♗e6 11 ♗e2 ♘b4 12 ♖c1 ♘d7, Metge-Rogers, Auckland 1992, and now the simple 13 ♘xd7 ♖xd7 14 ♔f2 would have assured White a plus. For example: 14...♘d3+?! 15 ♗xd3 ♖xd3 16 ♘d5! c6 17 ♔e2± or 14...♖ad8 15 ♖hd1! ♖xd1 16 ♖xd1 ♖xd1 17 ♘xd1 ♘xa2 18 ♗xa7±.

a32) 10...b6 11 ♗e2 ♗b7 12 ♗f3 ♘b4 13 ♔e2 ♘c2 14 ♖ad1 ♘xe3 15 ♖xd8+ ♖xd8 16 ♔xe3 ♖e8 17 ♖d1 ♗f8 18 ♘d5± Gabriel-Steinbacher, Dresden open 1994.

b) After 6...♘bd7?! White has two ways to assume the advantage:

b1) 7 ♗e2 e5 8 dxe5 dxe5 9 fxe5 ♘g4 10 ♗g5 ♕e8 11 ♘d5 ♘dxe5 12 ♕d2!? (12 ♘xc7? ♘xf3+ 13 gxf3 ♕e5 14 ♘xa8 ♕xg5 15 fxg4 ♕h4+ 16 ♔f1 ♖d8 17 ♕b3 ♗xg4 18 ♗xg4 ♕xg4 gives Black a strong attack). The game Konikowski-Rechel, Bundesliga 1989/90, continued 12...f6? (Better was 12...♕d7) and now White could have obtained a clear edge with 13 ♘xc7! ♕e7 (or 13...♕c6 14 ♘xa8 fxg5 15 ♕d5+±) 14 ♘xa8 fxg5 15 ♖d1 ♗e6 16 ♕d6.

b2) 7 e5!? ♘e8 8 c5! (It is necessary to stop 8...c5) 8...c6 9 ♗e3 b6 (No better is 9...dxc5 10 dxc5 ♕a5 11 a3) 10 cxd6 exd6 11 ♗c4 b5 12 ♗b3 ♘b6 13 0-0 with advantage to White, Skembris-Kalesis, Greece 1994.

c) 6...a6. The main idea of this move is to prepare ...b7-b5, as for example in the case of:

c1) 7 ♗e2 c5 8 d5 b5!

c2) After 7 ♗d3 Black plays 7...♗g4 (Not 7...c5? 8 dxc5! dxc5 9 e5 and the weakness of the b6-square guarantees an advantage for White. If 7...c6?! 8 e5!? ♘fd7 9 ♕e2 b5 10 cxb5 axb5 11 h4 b4 12 ♘e4 ♗a6 13 h5 ♗xd3 14 ♕xd3 with a dangerous attack for White, O. Rodriguez-Gallego, Spanish Ch. 1993) 8 ♗e3 ♘fd7 attacking White's centre. Still the complicated position arising after the sequence 9 h3 (Also possible is 9 ♗c2!? ♗h6 10 ♕d2) 9...♗xf3 10 ♕xf3 ♘c6 11 ♕f2 e5 12 dxe5 dxe5 13 f5 ♘d4 14 0-0-0 (14 ♖d1!?) 14...b5 15 g4 c6 16 g5 f6 17 h4 must be better for White, Avshalumov-Loginov, Budapest 1990.

c3) A strange but perfectly playable move is 7 a3!?, preventing 7...c5? because of 8 dxc5! dxc5 (8...♕a5? 9 b4) 9 ♕xd8 ♖xd8 10 e5±. 7...♘bd7?! is also no good: 8 e5! ♘e8 9 c5 c6 10 ♗e3 as in variation b2 above. Black should play 7...♗g4 reaching a position very similar to that in the main game.

d) 6...♘fd7 7 ♗e3 e5 8 fxe5 dxe5 9 d5 a5 10 ♗e2 ♘a6. Now instead of the modest continuation 11 0-0 ♘ac5 12 b3 h6 13 a3 ♕e7 14 ♖b1 f5 15 exf5 gxf5 16 b4 axb4 17 axb4 ♘a6 18 c5 with complicated play, although White's chances might still be better, Vaisser-Hausrath, Baden Baden (rapidplay) 1995, I should have continued with the precise 11 a3!? ♕e7 12 ♖b1.

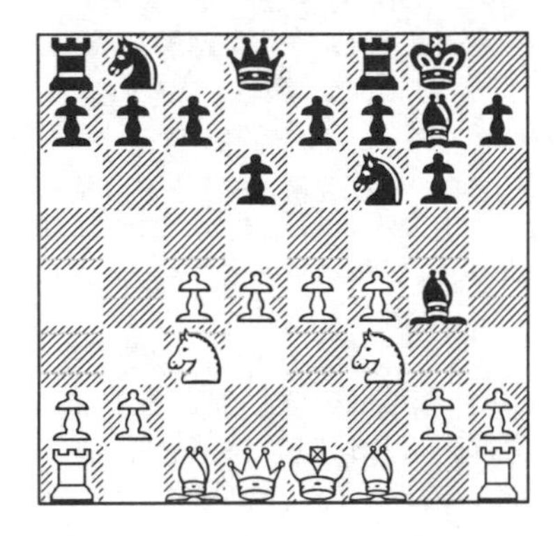

7 ♗e2

Alternatively:

a) 7 ♗e3!? is not bad either: 7...♘fd7 8 h3!? ♗xf3 9 ♕xf3 e5 (If 9...♘c6?! 10 e5! ♘b4 11 0-0-0!±) 10 dxe5 (10 fxe5? c5!) 10...dxe5 11 f5 ♘c6 (Or perhaps 11...♗h6!? 12 ♗f2 [12 0-0-0!?] 12...♘c6 13 ♖d1±) 12 0-0-0 ♘d4 13 ♕f2 c6 14 g4 ♕a5 15 g5 ♖fd8 16 h4 ♘c5 17 ♔b1! with advantage to White, Glek-Damljanovic, Belgrade 1988.

b) 7 h3?! is premature, however: 7...♗xf3 8 ♕xf3 ♘c6 9 ♗e3 e5! 10 dxe5 dxe5 11 f5 ♘h5! (An important difference compared to the previous note – a black knight comes to f4) 12 g4 ♘f4 13 ♖d1 ♕e7 14 ♕f2 ♖fd8 15 ♘d5 ♘xd5 16 exd5 ♘d4 and Black seized the initiative, Ruban-Krasenkov, Podolsk 1990.

7 ... ♘fd7
8 ♗e3 ♘c6?!

In the game Moskalenko-Ermenkov, Wijk aan Zee II 1992, Black played 8...e5?! 9 fxe5 dxe5 10 d5 ♗xf3 11 ♗xf3 ♗h6 12 ♗f2! ♕e7 13 0-0 a5 14 a3 ♘a6 15 ♖b1 b6 16 b4! axb4 17 axb4 with a clear advantage to White. 8...♗h6 deserves attention, preparing 9...e5.

9 d5

Also interesting is 9 e5!? e6 10 0-0 ♘e7 11 h3 ♗xf3 12 ♗xf3 ♗h6 13 ♕e1! ♘f5 14 ♖d1 c6?! (Better is 14...♘xe3!? 15 ♕xe3 ♖b8) 15 ♗c1 ♕b6 16 ♕f2 dxe5 17 dxe5 ♖fd8 18 ♘e4 ♕xf2+ 19 ♔xf2, Petronic-Markovic, Nis 1994, and White's space advantage was transformed into something more tangible.

9 ... ♗xf3
10 ♗xf3 ♘a5
11 ♕d3

11 ♗e2 with the idea of 11...c6 12 ♗d4 is not bad either.

11 ... c6!
12 ♖c1!

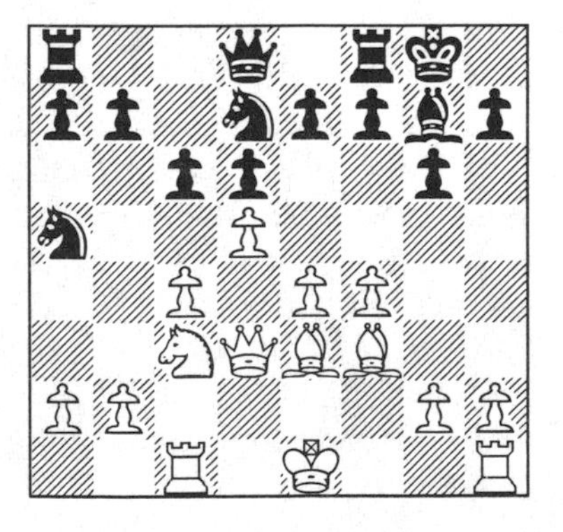

It is less precise to play 12 0-0?! cxd5 13 exd5 ♘c5!, while Black has good compensation for the piece after 12 b4? cxd5! 13 bxa5 ♕xa5 14 ♖c1 dxc4.

12 ... cxd5
13 exd5 ♖c8
14 b3 ♘c5
15 ♕d1

Now the queenside is well protected and White is better thanks to the two bishops and the bad position of Black's knight on a5.

15 ... e6

More precise was 15...e5.

16 0-0 exd5
17 ♗xd5 ♘c6

At last Black's knight re-enters the game, but now the d6-pawn cannot be defended.

18 ♘b5 ♔h8

19 ♘xd6 was a threat.

19 ♗f3 ♘b4
20 ♘xd6 ♘cd3

White's position is winning, so Black tries to create complications.

21 ♘xc8 ♕xc8
22 ♕d2!

The simplest solution.

22 ... ♘xc1
23 ♕xb4 ♘xa2
24 ♕d2! ♕e6

24...♘c3 25 ♗d4 does not save the knight.

25 ♗d5 ♕a6
26 ♗d4 ♗xd4+
27 ♕xd4+ ♔g8
28 ♖a1 ♖e8
29 ♕f2 ♕a3
30 h3

The knight is lost. Black resigned some moves later.

Game 16
Vaisser-Kr. Georgiev
French Team Ch. 1996

1 d4 ♘f6 2 c4 g6 3 ♘c3 ♗g7 4 e4 d6 5 f4 0-0 6 ♘f3 c5

7 d5

White can also play:

a) 7 dxc5 ♕a5

7...dxc5 8 ♕xd8 ♖xd8 9 e5 favours White. After 7...♕a5 White can choose between:

a1) If White is facing a stronger opponent and is happy to make a draw, he can try 8 ♗d2!? ♕xc5 9 b4 and now Black can choose between a draw by repetition after:

a11) 9...♕xb4 10 ♘a4 (The active 10 ♘d5?! is dubious because of 10...♕a3 11 ♗b4 ♕a6 12 c5 ♘xd5! 13 ♗xa6 ♘xb4 14 e5 ♘8a6∓) 10...♕a3 11 ♗c1 ♕b4+ 12 ♗d2; or the continuation

a12) 9...♕b6 10 ♗d3 (The complications after 10 e5?! were in Black's favour in Hamdouchi-Ehlvest, Lucern 1989: 10...dxe5 11 fxe5 ♘g4 12 ♕e2 ♕e6 13 ♘d5 ♘xe5 14 0-0-0 ♘bc6∓) 10...♗g4 11 ♖b1 ♘c6 12 h3 ♗xf3 13 ♕xf3 e5 14 ♗e3 ♕d8 15 f5 a5 16 b5 ♘b4 17 ♗g5 h6 with equality, Dorfman-Sznapik, Warsaw 1983.

a2) 8 ♗d3

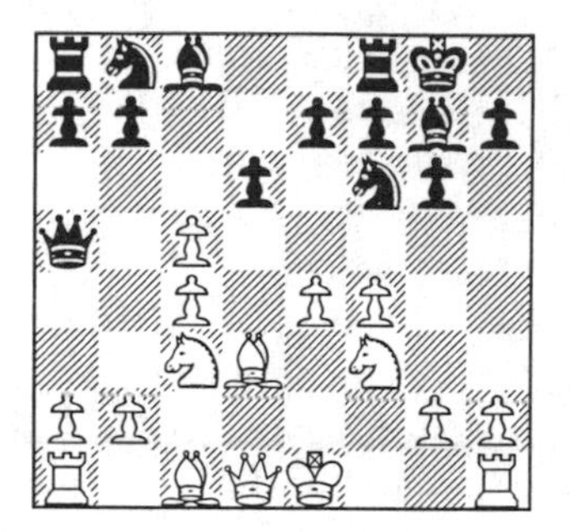

and now:

a21) 8...♘fd7!? is Van der Wiel's favourite move, but it now has the reputation of being very dubious. The game Gretarsson-Van der Wiel, Leeuwarden open 1995, is widely regarded as being the final refutation: 9 cxd6! ♗xc3+ 10 bxc3 ♕xc3+ 11 ♕d2 ♕xa1 12 dxe7 ♖e8 13 e5 ♘c6 14 0-0 ♘d4? 15 ♘g5! (An improvement on the original game Ljubojevic-Van der Wiel, Wijk aan Zee 1986, where after 15 ♗b2? ♘xf3+ 16 gxf3 ♕xa2 17 f5 Black could have stopped White's attack by playing 17...♖xe7! 18 f6 ♖xe5 19 ♕h6 ♖g5! 20 ♔h1 ♘xf6-+) 15...♘c5

16 ♗a3 ♘cb3 17 ♕f2! ♕c3 18 ♕h4 h5 19 ♘e4 ♕xd3 20 ♘f6+ ♔h8 21 ♘xe8 winning. A little-known correspondence game Szczepaniec-Stypka, corr. 1989, could change this conclusion. Instead of 14...♘d4? Black tried 14...♘c5! and won quickly after 15 ♗b2? ♕xa2 16 f5 ♗xf5! 17 ♗xf5 ♘e6 18 ♗xe6 fxe6 19 ♕h6 ♖xe7. The critical position, and one that needs practical tests, arises after 15 ♗a3! ♘b3! 16 ♖xa1 ♘xd2 17 ♘xd2 ♘xe7 18 ♘e4 ♖d8 19 ♘d6. White has good compensation for the exchange.

The courageous sacrifice 9 cxd6! is considered to be best, as the alternatives do not compare favourably, for example: 9 ♗d2?! (9 0-0?! ♗xc3!? 10 bxc3 ♕xc3) 9...♘xc5 10 ♗c2 ♕b4 (10...♘c6 11 a3?! ♕a6! 12 ♘b5 ♗g4 13 ♖b1 ♘d4 14 ♘bxd4 ♗xd4, Gorbatov-Bologan, Novgorod open 1995, is also in Black's favour) 11 ♘d5 (11 ♗b3?! ♕b6 12 ♕e2 ♘xb3 13 ♘d5? ♕a6-+ Johannessen-Tal, Reykjavik 1964) 11...♕xb2 12 ♖b1 ♕xa2 13 ♘c7 ♗g4 14 ♘xa8 ♘ba6∓.

a22) 8...♕xc5 9 ♕e2 ♘c6 10 ♗e3 ♕a5

An alternative is 10...♕h5 11 h3 ♘g4 (11...♘e8 12 ♖c1 e5 13 ♘d5 exf4 14 ♗xf4 ♘e5 15 0-0± Cifuentes-Herraiz, Benasque 1996) 12 ♗d2 ♘d4 (12...♘b4?! 13 ♘d5! ♘xd5 14 cxd5 ♗xb2 15 ♖b1 ♗a3 16 ♕f1 ♘f6 17 g4± Szily-Gereben, Hungary 1953) 13 ♕f1 ♘xf3+ 14 ♕xf3 ♗d4 15 ♔e2±.

11 0-0 ♗g4

A very interesting alternative is 11...♘g4!? 12 ♗d2 ♕b6+ (12...♘d4 13 ♘xd4 ♗xd4+ 14 ♔h1 ♕h5 15 h3 ♘f6 16 ♕f3 ♕xf3 17 ♖xf3± H. Gretarsson-A. Gretarsson, Icelandic Team Ch. 1995) 13 ♔h1 ♕xb2 14 ♘b5! (Stronger than 14 ♖b1) 14...♗d7 15 e5! dxe5 16 ♖fb1 e4 17 ♖xb2 exd3 18 ♕f1 ♗xb2 19 ♖e1 ♖ad8 20 h3 ♘h6 21 ♕xd3 and the complications were resolved with a slight edge for White, Leitao-Shaked, Cala Galdana 1996.

12 ♖ac1 ♘d7 13 ♕f2 ♗xf3

13...♘b4?! instead led to a strong White initiative after 14 ♗b1 ♖ac8 15 a3 ♘a6 16 ♘d2 ♗e6 17 f5! in the game Gabriel-Uhlmann, German Bundesliga 1995.

14 gxf3 ♘c5 15 ♗b1

Now White's natural plan is to attack on the kingside using the half-open g-file.

15...♘a4!

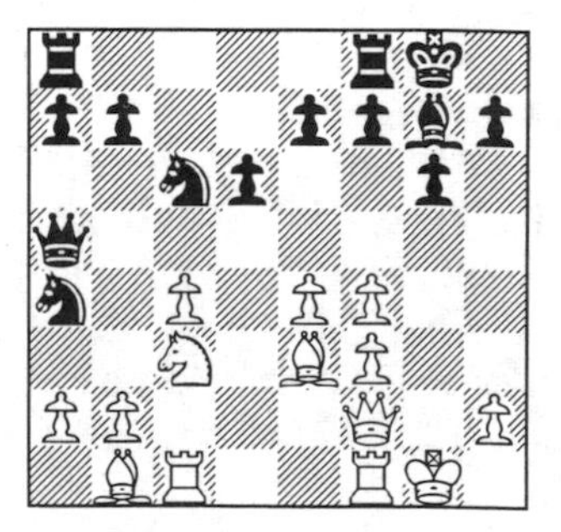

15...♕b4?! is very risky: 16 ♖fd1 ♕xc4 17 ♘d5 ♕a4 18 e5! b6 19 b4 ♘xb4 20 ♘xe7+ ♔h8 21 exd6± Cifuentes-Van Wely, Amsterdam 1995.

16 ♘d1!?

White has nothing special in the position after after 16 ♘xa4 ♕xa4 17 ♖fd1 (Or 17 b3 ♕a3 18 c5!? dxc5 19 ♗xc5 ♕xc5! 20 ♖xc5 ♗d4= Topalov-Kasparov, Linares 1994) 17...♖ac8 18 b3 ♕a5 19 ♖d5 ♕c7 20 ♖cd1 b6 21 a3 ♖fd8 22 h4 e6 23 ♖g5 ♕e7, Topalov-Dolmatov, Burgas 1995.

16...♕h5?!

16...♘c5!? is possible, ready to repeat moves after 17 ♘c3 ♘a4.

17 b3 ♘c5 18 ♘c3 ♘e6 19 ♘d5 f5 20 exf5 gxf5 21 b4 ♖f7 22 ♔h1 b6 23 ♖g1 ♔h8 24 ♖g3

White has a dangerous initiative, Leitao-Arduman, Yerevan Olympiad 1996.

b) It is worth saying a few words about a line that has almost fallen into disuse nowadays: 7 ♗e2 cxd4 8 ♘xd4 ♘c6 9 ♗e3 (If 9 ♘c2 ♘d7 10 0-0 ♘c5 11 ♗f3 f5 with counterplay). Now the simplest way to equalise may be 9...e5!? 10 ♘xc6 bxc6 11 fxe5 dxe5 12 0-0 (Or 12 ♗c5 ♖e8 13 ♕xd8 ♖xd8 14 0-0 ♖d2 15 ♖ad1 ♖xd1 16 ♖xd1 ♗e6 17 ♗d6 ♘g4= Uhlmann-Fisher, Varna 1962) 12...♕c7 13 ♕e1, Benko-Gligoric, Los Angeles 1963, and now 13...♗e6 14 ♕h4 ♘d7=.

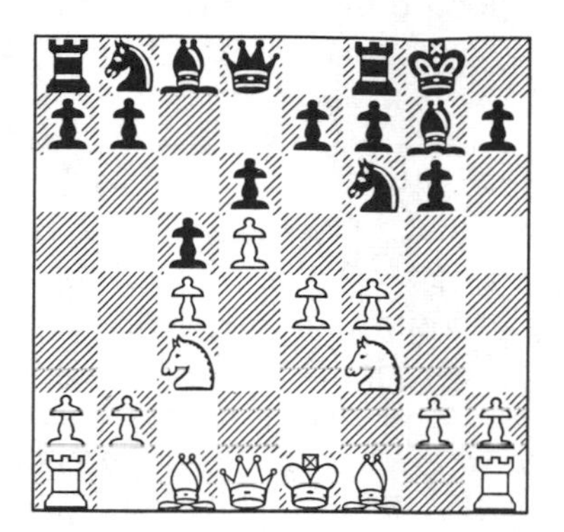

7 ... e6

7...b5 is seen in Game 14.

Right now 7...a6 can be met not only by the natural 8 a4, but also by the energetic 8 ♗d3!? b5 9 e5! dxe5 (After 9...♘e8!? 10 0-0 ♘c7 11 h3!? looks good, preventing 11...♗g4; while instead 9...♘fd7!? 10 e6!? fxe6 11 ♘g5 ♘f6 is unclear) 10 fxe5 ♘g4 11 ♕e2 ♘d7 12 ♗f4 ♕c7?! (Better is 12...b4!? first) 13 0-0 ♘gxe5 (13...♘dxe5 14 ♔h1) 14 ♖ae1 ♘xf3+ 15 ♖xf3 ♕b6 16 ♕xe7±. Now the continuation 16...bxc4?! 17 ♗xc4 ♕xb2 18 ♖b1 ♕c2 19 ♗b3 ♕f5 20 ♗d6 ♕g4 21 ♘e4 gives White a strong attack, Korchnoi-Gheorghiu, Vienna 1986.

8 ♗e2

8 ♗d3 exd5 9 cxd5 is not dangerous for Black. The simplest is 9...♗g4 (9...b5; 9...c4; 9...♖e8; 9...♕b6) 10 0-0 a6 11 a4 ♘bd7 transposing to an improved version of Chapter 2. If now Black can play ...c5-c4, ...♘c5 and ...♘fd7 he will have

a good position, while if White prevents this plan by playing 12 ♕c2 then Black gets active play with 12...♗xf3 13 ♖xf3 ♖c8 14 b3 ♘g4!?

After 8 dxe6 fxe6 (8...♗xe6 is met by 9 ♗d3, intending f4-f5) White can develop his bishop on either e2 or d3, but in both cases Black has some promising possibilities. The simplest way to equality is the universal manoeuvre ...e6-e5:

a) 9 ♗d3 e5!? 10 fxe5 (10 f5? is bad: 10...gxf5 11 exf5 d5! 12 ♗c2 [12 cxd5 e4!∓], Yuneev-I. Zaitsev, Chigorin Memorial 1994, and now Black should have played 12...d4 13 ♘e4 ♗xf5∓; while 10 0-0!? exf4 11 ♗xf4 ♘g4!? 12 ♗g5 ♗f6 is acceptable for Black) 10...dxe5 11 0-0 ♘c6. The position is equal, but look how White was outplayed in the game Dokhoian-Smirin, Sverdlovsk 1987: 12 ♗g5 h6 13 ♗h4 ♕d6 14 ♘d5 g5 15 ♗e1 ♗g4 16 ♗c3 ♘d4 17 ♗xd4 ♘xd5! 18 exd5 exd4 19 ♗e4 b5! 20 ♕c2?! bxc4 21 ♕xc4 ♗c8! 22 ♖fc1 d3! 23 ♗xd3 ♗xb2∓.

b) 9 ♗e2 ♘c6 10 0-0 e5!? 11 fxe5 dxe5 12 ♕xd8 ♖xd8 13 ♗g5 ♖f8=.

8 ... ♖e8

Black also has

a) 8...b5 when 9 cxb5 a6 (or 9...exd5 10 e5) 10 a4 exd5 11 e5 transposes into one of lines of the 7...b5 system which favours White.

b) 8...♘a6 can be met by 9 e5 dxe5 10 fxe5 ♘g4 11 ♗g5.

c) 8...exd5

and now:

c1) 9 cxd5 corresponds to the main lines considered earlier in the book (Chapters 1-3).

c2) 9 e5?!

This variation, attributed to Gunderam, is currently in crisis because of:

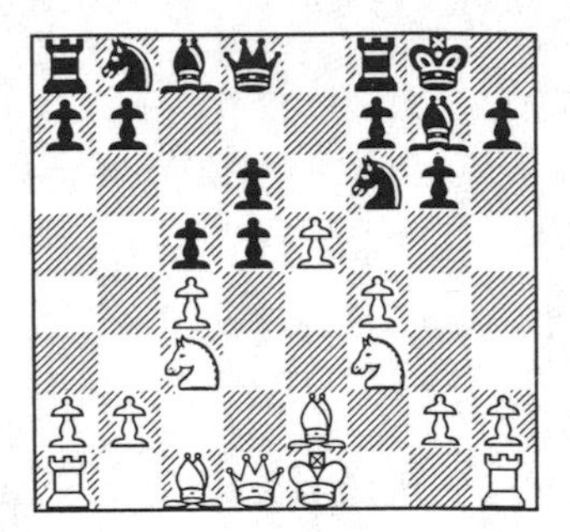

9...♘e4! 10 ♘xd5

No better is 10 cxd5 ♘xc3 11 bxc3 ♘d7 12 0-0 (Or 12 e6 fxe6 13 dxe6 ♘b6 14 0-0 ♗xe6 15 ♘g5, I. Ivanov-Hernandez, St John 1988, and now Black should have played 15...♗d5!∓ and if 16 ♖b1?! ♗xc3 17 ♗e3 ♗xa2-+) 12...dxe5 13 ♕b3 e4 14 ♘g5 ♘b6 15 ♖d1 ♗d7 16 a4 ♕e8 17 ♗b5 h6∓ Arencibia-Martin del Campo, Santa Clara 1990.

10...♘c6! 11 ♕c2

Or 11 ♗d3 f5 12 exf6 ♘xf6 13 0-0 ♘xd5 14 cxd5 ♘d4 15 ♘g5 ♗f5! 16 ♔h1 ♕d7 17 ♗e3 ♗xd3 18 ♕xd3 ♕f5 19 ♖ad1, as in Kantorik-Balogh, Slovakian Team Ch. 1995, and now

19...♘c2! 20 ♗c1 (Not 20 ♘e6? ♕xd3 21 ♖xd3 c4!-+) 20...♕xd3 21 ♖xd3 ♘b4 would have maintained Black's advantage.

11...f5 12 0-0 dxe5 13 fxe5 ♘xe5 14 ♗f4 ♘c6

14...♖e8!? also deserves attention, e.g. 15 ♖ad1 b6 with advantage to Black.

15 ♖ad1 g5 16 ♗c7 ♕e8 17 ♗d3 h6 18 ♖de1 ♕h5 19 ♗xe4 fxe4 20 ♕xe4 ♗f5 21 ♕e2 g4 22 ♘d2

This position arose in the game Reidel-Heinatz, Kecskemet 1989. Black could have won a pawn by 22...♖ae8 23 ♕d1 ♗xb2.

It was in this variation that I played a memorable game against Garry Kasparov in 1981. After 9 e5?! ♘g4?! 10 cxd5 dxe5 11 h3 e4 12 hxg4 exf3 13 gxf3 (This was a novelty at the time) 13...♖e8 14 f5 ♕b6? (Six years later Kalinin discovered an improvement: 14...gxf5! 15 ♗h6 ♗xc3+! 16 bxc3 fxg4, but White is still okay after 17 ♕d2 ♗f5 18 0-0-0 ♕b6 19 ♗d3 ♗xd3 20 ♕xd3 ♘d7 [∓ Kaplun] ***21 ♕f5!*** ♘f8! [21...♘e5? 22 d6! ♖e6 23 ♗g5+-] 22 ♕xg4+ ♘g6 23 ♕h5) 15 ♗h6! ♕xb2 16 ♗xg7 ♔xg7 17 f6+? (White could have secured a large advantage after 17 ♖c1! gxf5 18 ♖c2) 17...♔g8! 18 ♕c1! ♕b4!! 19 ♔f1? (19 ♕d2!=) 19...♘d7 20 ♗b5 ♕d4! Black was clearly better because the planned 21 ♕h6? is refuted by 21...♘xf6! 22 ♗xe8 ♕xc3 23 ♔g2 ♗xg4! 24 ♗xf7+ ♔xf7 25 fxg4 ♖e8-+. Some moves later Kasparov won the game.

c3) 9 exd5

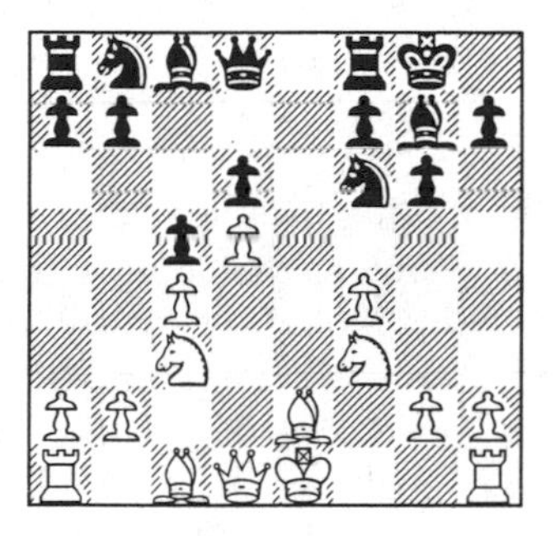

This line is much quieter than 9 cxd5 and not very popular nowadays. Black has a choice of solid continuations which give him comfortable equality.

9...♖e8

Black can try an interesting blockade idea 'à la Nimzowitsch': 9...♘h5!? 10 0-0 (10 ♗d2?! ♗d4! 11 ♘xd4 cxd4 12 ♘b5 a6! 13 ♘xd4 ♕h4+∓ as in the game Pribyl-Vukic, Kapfenberg 1970) 10...♗xc3 11 bxc3 f5! (A necessary move. If 11...♘g7?! then 12 f5! ♗xf5 13 ♗f4 with a strong initiative for the pawn) 12 ♘g5 ♘g7 13 ♗f3 ♘d7 14 ♗d2 ♘f6 15 ♗e1 ♗d7 16 ♗h4 ♕c7 with equality, Danner-Vukic, Austrian Team Ch. 1991.

10 0-0 ♗f5 11 ♗d3

A complicated and approximately equal position arises after 11 ♘h4!? ♘e4! 12 ♘xf5 gxf5 13 ♘xe4 fxe4 14 ♗e3 ♗xb2 15 ♖b1 ♕f6 16 ♕b3 ♗d4 17 ♗xd4 ♕xd4+ 18 ♔h1 b6, Antoshin-Boleslavsky, Leningrad 1956, 19 ♕a4!? ♖f8!

11...♕d7 12 ♘h4

White's king is in constant danger after 12 h3 ♘a6 13 a3 (Or 13 g4?! ♗xd3 14 ♕xd3 ♘b4 15 ♕d1 h5! 16 g5 ♘e4 with an edge to Black) 13...♘c7 14 g4 (The game Peng-J. Polgar, Novi Sad Womens' Olympiad 1990, saw 14 ♕c2 b5! 15 cxb5 [15 b3!?] 15...♘fxd5 16 ♘xd5 ♘xd5 17 ♗xf5 gxf5 18 ♖b1 ♖e4! with better chances for Black) 14...♗xg4!? 15 hxg4 ♕xg4+ 16 ♔h2 ♕h5+ 17 ♔g2 ♕g4+ 18 ♔h2 b5! 19 ♖g1 ♕h5+ 20 ♔g3? (20 ♔g2) 20...bxc4 21 ♗xc4 ♖e7 22 ♕d3 ♗h6! 23 ♔g2 (23 ♗d2 ♗xf4!+ 24 ♔xf4 ♕h3-+) 23...♖ae8. The game Conquest-Mestel, Hastings 1986, finished with a pleasant combination: 24 ♗d2? (24 ♘g5!?) 24...♗xf4! 25 ♗xf4 ♕g4+ 26 ♗g3 ♖e3 27 ♕f1 ♘h5 28 ♔h2 ♖xf3 29 ♕h3 ♕xc4 0-1.

12...♗xd3

The unclear position which arises after 12...♘e4 13 ♘xf5 gxf5 14 ♗xe4 fxe4 15 f5 ♗d4+ 16 ♔h1 e3 17 ♕g4+ ♔h8 18 ♘e2 ♗f6 19 ♖f3, Glek-Smirin, Minsk 1986, would not be to everybody's taste.

13 ♕xd3 ♘g4 14 ♘f3 ♘a6 15 a3 ♘h6 16 ♗d2 ♘c7 17 ♖fe1 ♕f5 18 ♕xf5 ♘xf5

with equality, Danner-Uhlmann, Graz 1991. If now 19 b4, Black has the powerful 19...b5! in reserve.

9 e5!?

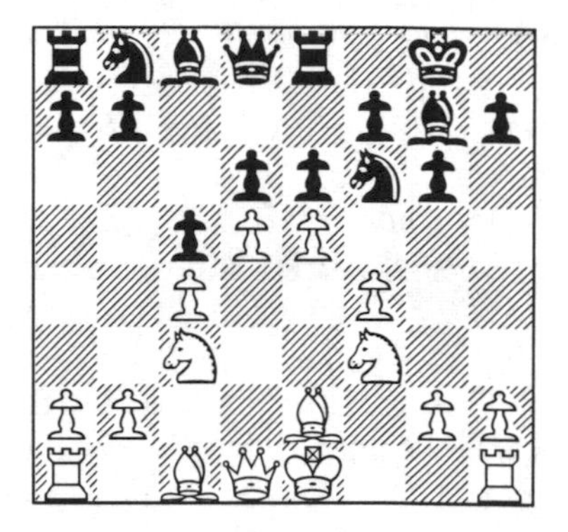

White can also play 9 dxe6. With the black rook on e8 this line is more attractive for White than the immediate 8 dxe6. Even Gunderam's variation 9 0-0 dxe5 10 e5 becomes playable.

9 ... dxe5
10 fxe5 ♘g4
11 ♗g5

11 ♗f4 resembles the line 8...exd5 9 cxd5 ♖e8 10 e5 dxe5 11 fxe5 ♘g4 12 ♗f4 ♘xe5 13 0-0 (Game 4).

11 ... ♕a5

More active is 11...♕b6 12 ♕d2 (12 d6?! ♘xe5 13 ♘b5 ♗d7 14 ♘c7 ♘bc6 15 0-0 ♘d4 16 ♘xa8 ♖xa8 17 ♗e7 ♘ec6 18 ♘g5 f5 and Black has more than enough play for the exchange, Bagaturov-Avshalumov, Yurmala 1982) 12...♘xe5 13 0-0 (13 ♘xe5!? ♗xe5 14

0-0) 13...♘bd7 14 ♖ad1 (14 ♔h1!?) 14...♘xf3+ 15 ♗xf3, Padevsky-Bilek, Bad Pyrmont 1970. Now instead of 15...♘f6? 16 d6! ♘d7 17 ♘b5 with advantage to White, Black should have played 15...♘e5! with an unclear position.

12 0-0 ♘d7?!

It was better to play 12...exd5 13 cxd5 ♘xe5 14 ♘xe5 ♖xe5.

13 ♘b5

Exploiting the offside position of the black queen, White's knight heads for d6. However, the more precise route was via e4, in order to keep open the option of playing ♘f6+.

13 ... ♘dxe5
14 ♘xe5 ♘xe5
15 ♘d6 ♖f8
16 ♗e7 ♗d7

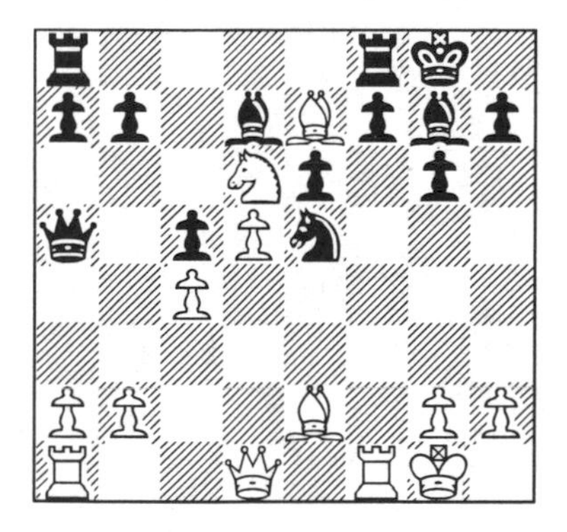

17 ♘e4

17 ♘xb7 would have been very unclear after 17...♕b6 18 ♗xf8 (18 ♕b3 ♖fc8; 18 dxe6? ♗xe6 19 ♗xf8 ♗xf8 20 ♕b3 ♕c7!∓) 18...♗xf8! 19 ♕b3 exd5 (19...♖b8? 20 ♘a5!) 20 cxd5 c4+ 21 ♕xb6 axb6 22 ♖f6.

17 ... f5!
18 ♗xf8 ♖xf8

We often meet this type of position in the Four Pawns Attack. The strong bishops and extra pawn provide almost full compensation for the sacrificed exchange.

19 dxe6 ♗xe6
20 ♘g5 ♗d7
21 ♗f3 ♘xf3+
22 ♕xf3 ♕d2

Interesting was 22...♗c6!? 23 ♕h3 h6 24 ♘e6 ♖e8 25 ♘xg7 ♔xg7 (Or 25...♖e2 26 ♘xf5 ♖xg2+ 27 ♕xg2 ♗xg2 28 ♘e7+ ♔g7 29 ♔xg2 ♕d2+ 30 ♔h1±) 26 ♕d3. White is better, but the strong bishop on c6 makes victory highly problematic.

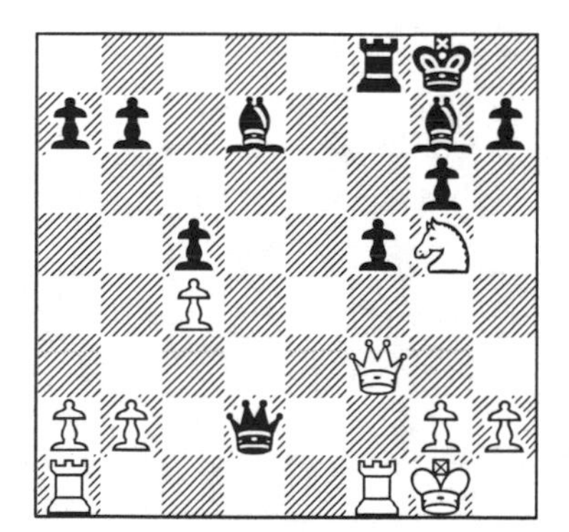

23 ♕xb7! ♗c8
24 ♕d5+ ♕xd5
25 cxd5 ♗xb2
26 ♖ab1 ♗d4+
27 ♔h1 ♗e3!

It is necessary to diminish the

activity of White's rooks. White wins after 27...♗a6? 28 ♖fe1 ♖d8 29 ♘e6 (Or 29 ♖e7!?) 29...♖xd5 30 ♘c7 ♖d6 31 ♖e7 ♔f8 32 ♖xh7 ♔g8 33 ♖e7 ♔f8 34 ♖e6.

28 ♘e6

Or 28 ♘f3!? ♗a6 29 ♖fe1 f4 30 ♘e5.

28 ... ♗xe6
29 dxe6 c4
30 ♖b7 ♖c8?

The decisive mistake. Black should have played 30...♖e8! 31 ♖d1 c3 32 ♖c7 ♗d2 33 ♖b1 ♔f8 34 ♔g1 ♗e3+! (34...♖xe6? 35 ♖b8+ ♖e8 36 ♖xe8+ ♔xe8 37 ♔f2±) 35 ♔f1 ♗b6! with real chances of a draw.

31 ♖d1! c3
32 ♖dd7 ♗d4

32...c2? loses immediately to 33 ♖g7+ ♔h8 34 ♖xh7+ ♔g8 35 ♖bg7+ ♔f8 36 e7+ ♔e8 37 ♖g8+.

33 ♖dc7 ♖e8
34 g3 h5
35 ♖d7 ♗f6
1-0

Here Black's flag fell, but after 36 ♖xa7 the result would have been clear in any case.

7 Taimanov System

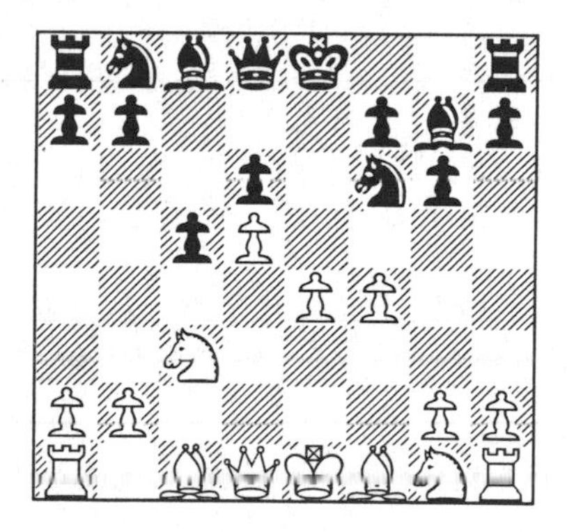

After the introductory moves of the Modern Benoni, 1 **d4 ♘f6 2 c4 c5 3 d5 e6 4 ♘c3 exd5 5 cxd5 d6 6 e4 g6 7 f4 ♗g7** we reach the diagrammed position. Here 8 ♘f3 leads to the Four Pawns Attack systems examined in the earlier chapters. White can also opt for two alternative moves: 8 ♗b5+ (the Taimanov System) and 8 e5 (the Mikenas Attack). The first of these lines is dealt with in this chapter and is particularly dangerous for Black, while the second one (covered in Chapter 8) is almost forgotten and could provide an unpleasant surprise for your opponent.

First we shall consider Taimanov's 8 ♗b5+.

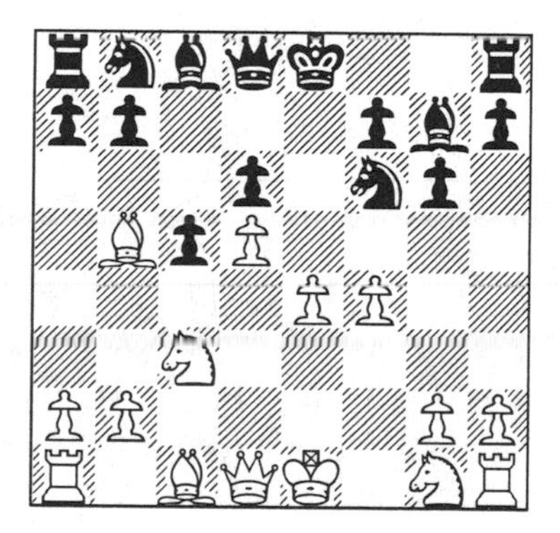

8 ♗b5+ introduces the aggressive Taimanov system. This bishop check aims to disturb the smooth development of Black's pieces and is rather unpleasant for Black. In fact, some of the leading Benoni players nowadays play 3...c5 only after 1 d4 ♘f6 2 c4 e6 3 ♘f3 in order to avoid this variation. The critical move to challenge White's approach is 8...♘bd7. The evaluation of this extremely sharp line has oscillated for many years between 'unclear' and 'White is better'. After the impressive game Sokolov-Topalov, Wijk aan Zee 1996, (Game 17) however, Black has hardly dared repeat this line, even though everything is not entirely clear. In the notes to this game you will also find 8...♗d7 and other deviations from the main move order. The alternative 8...♘fd7 has been considered slightly better for White for a long time now and this is examined in Game 18.

Game 17
Sokolov-Topalov
Wijk aan Zee 1996

1 d4 ♘f6 2 c4 e6 3 ♘c3 c5 4 d5 exd5 5 cxd5 d6

One way of avoiding the Four Pawns Attack is 5...♕e7. Unfortunately this is not the best place for the queen in several other systems of the Benoni.

6 e4 g6
7 f4 ♗g7

Other possibilities are not very attractive for Black:

a) 7...♕e7?! does nothing to combat White's build up: 8 ♘f3! ♗g4 (8...♘xe4? 9 ♕a4+) 9 h3 ♗xf3 10 ♕xf3 ♗g7 11 ♗d3 0-0 12 0-0 ♘bd7 13 ♗d2 is clearly better for White (*ECO*).

b) 7...a6?! 8 e5 and now:

b1) 8...♘fd7 9 ♘f3 ♗g7 10 ♘e4 dxe5 11 ♘d6+. We now have one of the principal positions of the Mikenas Attack with an extra tempo for White (because of 7...a6?!), and this changes the evaluation in White's favour. Look at the miniature Guseinov-Zaitchik, Volgodonsk 1983: 11...♔f8 (Or 11...♔e7 12 ♘xc8+ ♕xc8 13 ♗e2) 12 ♗e2!? ♕c7 (12...exf4 13 ♗xf4 ♕f6 14 ♗g3 ♕xb2 15 ♖b1±, Kapengut) 13 ♘xc8 ♕xc8 14 fxe5 ♘xe5 15 ♘xe5 ♗xe5 16 ♗h6+ ♗g7 17 ♕d2 ♕f5 18 ♕c3 ♗xh6 19 ♕xh8+ ♔e7 20 d6+ ♔xd6 21 ♖d1+ ♔c6 22 ♖f1 1-0.

b2) The game Nutu-S.Lupu, Romania 1993, saw 8...♕e7? 9 ♘f3 ♗g7 (9...♗g4 10 ♗e2 ♘fd7 11 exd6 ♕xd6 12 ♘g5! ♗xe2 13 ♕xe2+ ♕e7 14 ♘ce4±) and now White could have obtained a big advantage after 10 h3 ♘h5 11 ♘e4.

c) 7...♗g4?! 8 ♕a4+! ♗d7 9 ♕b3 ♕c7 10 ♘f3 ♗g7 11 e5±.

d)7...♘bd7?! 8 ♘f3 ♗g7 9 e5 dxe5 10 fxe5 ♘g4 11 e6 fxe6 12 dxe6 ♕e7 13 ♘d5! ♕xe6+ 14 ♗e2 ♕d6 15 ♗g5 ♗d4 16 ♗c4±.

8 ♗b5+ ♘bd7?!

The alternative

8...♗d7?

has proved unsuccessful. After

9 e5!

Black has:

a) Not many players are ready to suffer after 9...dxe5 10 fxe5 ♕e7 11 ♘f3 (11 ♕e2!?) 11...0-0 12 0-0 ♘g4 13 ♗f4 (13 ♗g5!?) 13...♘xe5 14 ♗xe5!

♗xe5 15 ♖e1 f6 16 ♗c4! ♔g7, Lau-Perenyi, Budapest 1981, and now the simplest was 17 ♘xe5 fxe5 18 ♕e2 with an evident advantage.

b) 9...♘h5 offers more resistance. 10 ♘f3 and then:

b1) After 10...dxe5 White was clearly better in the game O'Kelly-Diaz del Corral, Madrid 1957: 11 fxe5 0-0 12 ♗xd7! and now:

b11) After 12...♘xd7 Black loses a knight: 13 g4 ♘xe5 14 gxh5 ♘xf3+ 15 ♕xf3 ♖e8+ 16 ♔d1± Vaisman-Stcin, Odcssa 1958.

In 1993 the English international master Andrew Martin tried to revive this variation. He proposed here 16...♖e5 17 h6! ♗h8 (17...♖f5 18 ♕xf5! gxf5 19 ♖g1±) hoping that the threat of 18...♖f5 or quiet counterattack ...♕d7, ...b5-b4 would give Black good counterplay. White has nothing to be afraid of; two pawns instead of one for the bishop do not make Black's position any more enviable. The simplest solution is 18 ♗f4! ♖f5 19 ♕e4 ♕d7 (Other moves are no better: 19...♕h4 20 ♖e1!; 19...b5 20 d6! ♕e8 21 ♖e1 ♕xe4 22 ♖xe4 g5 23 ♗g3 ♖f1+ 24 ♖e2! ♖xa1 25 d7+-; 19...♗xc3 20 bxc3 ♕xd5+ [20...♖xd5+ 21 ♔c2+-] 21 ♕xd5 ♖xd5+ 22 ♔c2 f6 23 h4+-) 20 ♖e1 ♗xc3 (20...b5 21 d6! ♖d8 22 ♔c2 ♗xc3 23 bxc3 b4 24 a4! looks winning for White) 21 bxc3 ♖xd5+ 22 ♔c2 ♖d8 23 ♖e2 and, since 23...♖d4 does not work: 24 cxd4 ♕a4+ 25 ♔b2 ♕b5+ 26 ♔c1 ♕c4+ 27 ♕c2 ♕xd4 28 ♗e5+-, White has a practically winning position.

b12) 12...♕xd7 13 0-0 ♕f5 14 ♕a4 ♗xe5 15 ♘xe5 ♕xe5 16 ♗h6 ♖d8 17 ♖ae1 ♕d4+ 18 ♕xd4 cxd4 19 ♘b5 ♘a6 and now 20 d6! would have secured White's advantage.

b2) 10...0-0 11 ♗xd7 ♕xd7 12 0-0 ♘a6 13 ♖e1 ♖ae8 14 a3 b6 15 b3 ♘c7 16 ♖a2 ♖d8 17 g3, when Black can hardly create sufficient counterplay with the knight out of business on h5, but after 17...dxe5?! 18 fxe5 h6 19 d6 ♘e6 20 ♘d5 White is much better, Hertneck-Vlahopoulos, Katerini 1993.

9 e5!

Without this key move the check 8 ♗b5+ would represent a loss of time, as Black has developed his queen's knight to the natural d7-square.

9 ... dxe5

The immediate 9...♘h5? is bad because of 10 e6 ♕h4+ (10...fxe6 11 dxe6 ♕h4+ 12 g3 ♘xg3 13 ♘f3 ♕h3 14 ♕xd6!+- as in the game Schakis-Farron, Creil 1975) and now both 11 g3 ♘xg3 12 ♘f3 ♕h3 13 ♖g1! ♗xc3+ (13...♘f5 14 exd7+ ♗xd7 15 ♕e2+ ♔d8 16 ♗xd7 ♔xd7 17 ♕g2) 14 bxc3 ♘e4 ***15 ♕d3!*** and 11 ♔f1 ♗d4 12 ♕e1! are winning for White.

10 fxe5 ♘h5

Of course not 10...♕e7? 11 ♕e2+-.

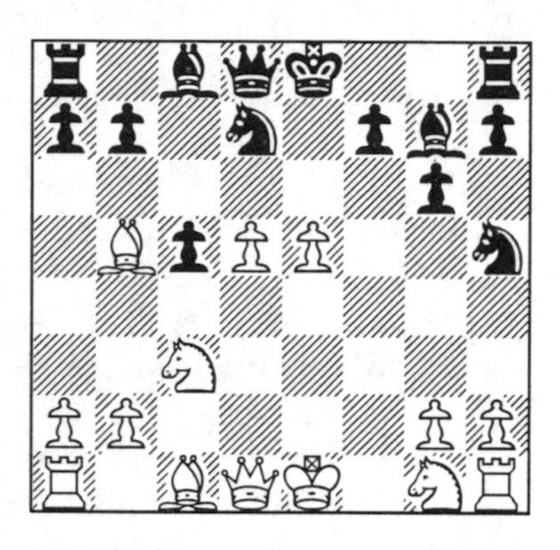

11 e6

White also has the quieter move 11 ♘f3!? at his disposal. Practical play has seen: 11...0-0 12 ♗g5 (12 g4? ♘xe5 13 gxh5 ♗g4 14 ♗e2 ♘xf3+ 15 ♗xf3 ♖e8+ 16 ♔f1 ♗h3+ 17 ♗g2 ♕f6+ 18 ♔g1 ♕h4–+) and:

a) 12...f6 13 ♗h4 ♘xe5 14 ♘xe5 ♕e7 15 0-0 ♕xe5 16 ♖e1 ♕d4+ 17 ♗f2 ♕xd1 18 ♖axd1± Gustavsson-Kountz, Dortmund 1989.

b) 12...♕a5 13 0-0 a6?! (Interesting is 13...♘xe5!?) 14 ♗xd7 ♗xd7 15 d6± Hauschild-Voigt, Dortmund 1992.

c) 12...♕b6 13 ♕e2 a6 (After 13...♘xe5?! 14 ♘xe5 ♗xe5 as in Grooten-Hendriks, Enschede 1992, White should have played simply 15 ♕xe5 f6 16 ♗xf6 ♘xf6 [16...♖xf6 17 0-0-0±] 17 0-0 ♗f5 18 d6 ♖ad8 19 g4±) 14 ♗a4 (Not so good is 14 ♗c4?! ♘xe5 15 ♘xe5 ♖e8 16 0-0 ♖xe5 17 ♕d2 ♕b4!∓, as in Cherepkov-Katishonok, Leningrad 1990, but quite playable is 14 ♗xd7!? ♗xd7 15 d6 c4 [15...f6!? 16 ♘d5 ♕b5] 16 ♕d2 ♗c6 17 0-0-0 ♗xf3 18 gxf3 ♗xe5 19 d7 with a strong initiative, Wells-Hodgson, British Ch., Southport 1983) 14...♕b4 15 0-0-0! b5 16 ♗c2 ♘b6 17 a3 ♕a5 18 ♘d2±, as in Petursson-Muller, San Bernardino 1989.

11 ... ♕h4+

Weaker is

11...fxe6? 12 dxe6 0-0

Or 12...♕h4+? 13 g3 ♗xc3+ 14 bxc3 ♕e4+ 15 ♕e2 ♕xh1 16 exd7+ ♔d8 17 ♗g5+ ♔c7 18 0-0-0 winning.

13 ♘f3!

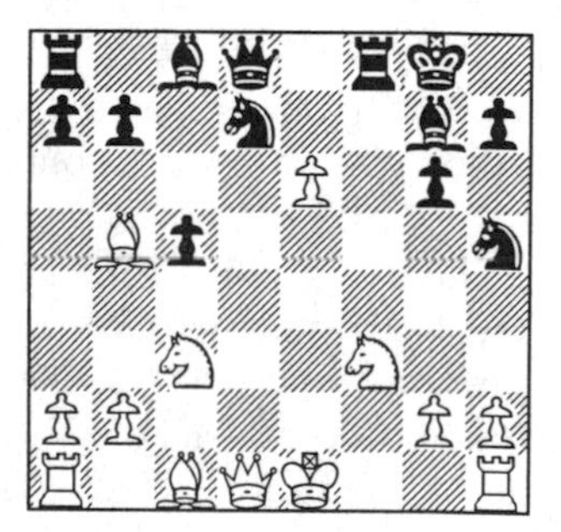

and now:

a) 13...♘df6 14 ♕xd8 ♖xd8 15 e7 ♖d6 16 ♘g5! ♗e6 17 0-0 a6 18 ♘xe6 axb5 19 ♘c7 ♖c8 20 ♘3xb5 is winning for White (Nei).

b) 13...♖xf3 14 ♕xf3 and now:

b1) 14...♗xc3+ 15 bxc3 ♘e5 16 ♕e4 ♕f6 17 e7! ♕xe7 18 0-0 ♗f5 19 ♕d5+ ♔g7 20

♗g5! ♕xg5 21 ♕xe5+± Kapengut.

b2) 14...♘e5?! 15 ♕d5 ♕h4+ 16 g3 ♕e7 17 ♗g5 ♗f6 (17...♕xe6 18 ♕d8+ ♗f8 19 0-0+-) 18 ♗xf6 ♕xf6 19 ♖f1 ♕xe6 20 ♕d8+ 1-0 Wessman-Melgosa, Tunja 1989.

c) 13...♗d4 and then:

c1) 14 ♕b3?! is very unclear, 14...♕e7 15 ♗e3 ♘e5 16 ♘xe5 ♗xe3 17 ♘d5 ♗f2+ (After the alternative 17...♕h4+? 18 g3 ♗f2+ 19 ♔e2 ♕e4+ 20 ♘e3 ♕xe5 21 e7+ ♗e6 22 exf8♕+ ♖xf8 23 ♕xe6+ White was better in Mestel-Hodgson, British Ch., Southport 1983) 18 ♔e2 ♕xe6 19 ♘c7 ♕xb3 20 axb3 ♗d4! 21 ♘xa8 ♗xe5 22 ♖xa7 ♗g4+ with enough compensation for the exchange – Martin.

c2) 14 exd7! ♗xd7 15 ♗g5 ♕e8+ (15...♕b6? 16 ♕b3+!+-) 16 ♗e2 ♘f4 17 ♗xf4 ♖xf4 18 ♘d5! ♖xf3 (the only move) 19 gxf3 ♕e5 20 ♘c3 and White's enormous material advantage assures him of victory, Simoncini-Caruso, corr. 1989.

12 g3

12 ♔d2!? is very complicated – 12...fxe6! 13 dxe6 and now:

a) 13...0-0? is bad for Black. 14 exd7 ♗xd7 15 ♗xd7 ♖ad8 (15...♖f2+ does not help: 16 ♘ge2 ♖d8 17 ♕a4! ♗xc3+ 18 ♔xc3 ♕f6+ 19 ♔c2 ♖xe2+ 20 ♔b1+-) 16 ♔c2 ♖f2+ 17 ♔b1 ♗xc3 18 ♕g4! ♗f6 19 ♘h3 ♖xd7 20 ♘xf2 1-0 Alexandrov-Wojtkiewicz, Wisla 1992.

b) 13...♗xc3+! 14 bxc3 (14 ♔xc3? ♕b4+ 15 ♔c2 ♕xb5 16 exd7+ ♗xd7 17 ♕e1+ ♔f7 hands the advantage to Black) 14...0-0 ***15 ♘f3!*** (15 exd7? ♗xd7 16 ♗xd7? ♖f2+ 17 ♘e2 ♖d8 18 ♔c2 ♕e4+ 19 ♔b3 ♖xe2 20 ♗g5 ♖xd7 is losing for White) 15...♕f2+ 16 ♕e2 ♕xe2+ 17 ♔xe2 ♖e8 18 ♔f2 ♖xe6 19 ♗c4±. Probably the play of both sides can be improved. It is worth noting that very few players of the white side choose this risky line.

12 ... ♘xg3
13 hxg3

Weaker are:

a) 13 ♘f3? ♗xc3+ 14 bxc3 ♕e4+ 15 ♔f2 ♘xh1+ 16 ♕xh1 fxe6 17 dxe6 0-0! 18 exd7 ♗xd7 19 ♗xd7, as in Littlewood-Hartoch, London 1984, and now 19...♖ad8! 20 ♗b5 c4 21 ♗e3 ♖d3 22 ♖e1 g5! 23 h3 h5! with a strong attack.

b) 13 exd7+?! ♗xd7 14 ♗xd7+ ♔xd7 15 ♕a4+ ♕xa4 16 ♘xa4 ♘xh1 17 ♘f3 ♖he8+ 18 ♔f1 ♗d4 19 ♔g2 ♖e2+ 20 ♔xh1 ♔d6 with a better ending for Black.

13 ... ♕xh1

Bad is 13...♕xg3+? 14 ♔d2 ♗xc3+ 15 bxc3 ♕g2+ 16 ♕e2 ♕xd5+ 17 ♔c2 ♕xe6 18 ♕xe6+ fxe6 19 ♗h6 with a decisive advantage for White, Fecht-Betker, corr. 1989.

14 ♗e3!

Another option for White is

14 exd7+ ♗xd7 and now:

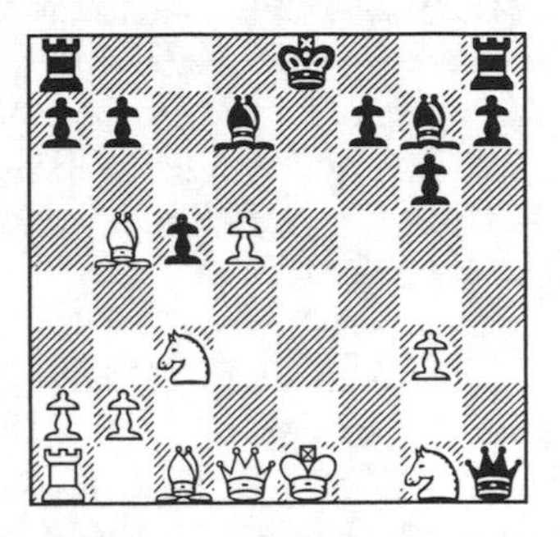

a) After 15 ♕e2+? Black has:

a1) 15...♔d8 16 ♗g5+! f6 17 0-0-0 ♖e8 18 ♕f1 fxg5 19 ♗xd7 ♔xd7 20 ♕b5+ was played in Savchenko-Sandler, Belgorod 1989, and here Savchenko gives the variation: 20...♔c7 (the only move) 21 d6+ ♔d8 22 ♘d5 ♕g2 23 ♘c7 ♕xb2+ as finally leading to equality. This analysis is innacurate, however, as 22...♕g2?! can be improved by 22...b6!?, 23 ♘c7? by the move 23 ♕xb7 and finally 23...♕xb2+? by the decisive 23...♖e4!–+.

a2) 15...♔f8! 16 ♗e3 ♖e8! 17 ♗xd7 (17 ♔d2? proposed by some commentators as good for White is refuted by ***16...♗h6! 18 ♘d1 ♕xd5+***-+) 17...♖xe3 18 ♕xe3 ♗d4 19 ♕f3 ♕xg1+ 20 ♕f1 ♕xg3+ 21 ♔d2 ♔g7 is clearly better for Black, Gil-Kuczynski, Sharjan 1985.

b) 15 ♗xd7+ ♔xd7 and then:

b1) After 16 ♕a4+ Black can play 16...♔d8 (16...♔c8?! 17 ♗e3 ♗xc3+ 18 bxc3 ♕xd5 19 ♖d1 ♕c6, Rabinovich-Cordy, European Junior Ch. 1993, 20 ♕c4!?±) 17 ♗g5+ f6 18 ♗e3 ♖e8 19 ♔d2 ♗h6 20 ♗f4 with complicated play, Helmers-Obers, Netherlands 1995.

b2) 16 ♕g4+ f5 (16...♔d8? gave White a powerful attack in the game Zaja-Kutuzovic, Croatia 1995: 17 ♗g5+ f6 18 0-0-0! ♖e8 19 ♘ge2 ♕h2 20 ♘f4! fxg5 21 ♘e6+ ♖xe6 22 dxe6+ 1-0) 17 ♕a4+ ♔c8 18 ♗e3 ♗xc3+ (After 18...♗h6?! White quickly developed a winning attack in the game Burgess-Anderson, London 1985: 19 ♗xc5 ♕g2 20 ♕c4 ♖e8+ 21 ♘ge2 ♕xg3+ 22 ♔d1 ♕g4 23 ♗d4+ ♔d7 24 d6 ♖ac8 25 ♕f7+ ♔xd6 and now 26 ♘b5++-) 19...bxc3 ♕xd5 20 ♖d1 ♕c6 and now:

b21) The endgame after 21 ♕xc6+ bxc6 22 ♗xc5 is equal. Sandler-Gobleja, USSR 1988, continued 22...♖e8+ 23 ♔f2 ♖b8 24 ♖d2 a6 25 ♘f3 ♖b5 26 ♗e3 ♖d5 27 ♖b2 ♖b5=.

b22) After 21 ♕c4 b6 (Or 21...♖e8 22 ♔f2 b5 23 ♕xc5 ♕xc5 24 ♗xc5 ♔c7 25 ♘f3 ♖ad8 26 ♗d4 which was slightly better for White, Comas-Gallego, Spain 1991) White had a certain initiative that was not converted into anything serious in the game Comas-Martin, Catalonia Team Ch. 1996: 22 ♕a6+ ♕b7 23 ♕a4 ♖d8 24 ♖xd8+ ♔xd8 25 ♗g5+ ♔c7 26 ♗f4+ ♔d8 27 ♔f2 ♕e4 28 ♕b3 ♔d7 29 ♕b5+ ♔e7 30 ♘f3 ♖e8

31 ♘e5=.

14 ... ♗xc3+!

Weaker is 14...0-0?! (Not 14...fxe6? which loses to 15 dxe6 0-0 16 exd7 ♗xd7 17 ♗xd7 ♖ad8 18 ♕b3+ ♔h8 19 0-0-0+-) 15 exd7 ♗xd7 16 ♗xd7 ♖ae8! 17 ♗xe8 ♖xe8 reaching a position much explored by English players in the mid-1980s:

a) White achieved only a small edge after 18 ♔d2 ♗xc3+ 19 bxc3 ♕xd5+ 20 ♔c2 ♕e4+ 21 ♕d3 ♕xe3 22 ♖f1!, Crouch-Martin, England 1985

b) Better is 18 ♕e2! ♗d4 (18...♗h6!? 19 ♔f1) when:

b1) 19 0-0-0 ♖xe3. This position was reached in the game Littlewood-Norwood, Commonwealth Ch. 1985. Now instead of 20 ♕c4?! a6 White could have played 20 ♕c2! with a clear advantage. For example: 20...♖xg3 21 ♘ge2 ♕h6+ 22 ♔b1 ♖g2 23 ♕a4!± (Konikowski).

b2) 19 ♔d2!? b5 20 ♖d1 b4 21 ♗xd4 ♖xe2+ 22 ♘gxe2 bxc3+ 23 ♗xc3 ♕xd5+ 24 ♔c1 also gave an advantage to White in Flear-Norwood, London 1984.

15 bxc3 a6

15...♕e4?!

does not promise Black an easy life:

16 ♕f3 ♕xf3 17 ♘xf3

Less convincing is 17 exd7+ ♗xd7 18 ♗xd7+ ♔xd7 19 ♘xf3, as in Kouatly-Schmittdiel, Augsburg 1989, because of 19...♔d6!? 20 c4 f6 and Black can hold the position.

17...fxe6 18 dxe6 0-0?!

More resilient is 18...a6 19 exd7+ ♗xd7 20 ♗xd7+ ♔xd7 21 ♗xc5. White has an extra pawn compared to a similar ending in Comas-Gallego. The game Urban-Ciemniak, Polish Ch. 1993, continued 21...♔c6 22 ♗e3 ♖ae8 23 ♔d2 ♖e4 24 ♘d4+ ♔d5 25 ♔d3 ♖c8 26 ♘c2 ♖ce8 27 ♖b1 with an advantage for White.

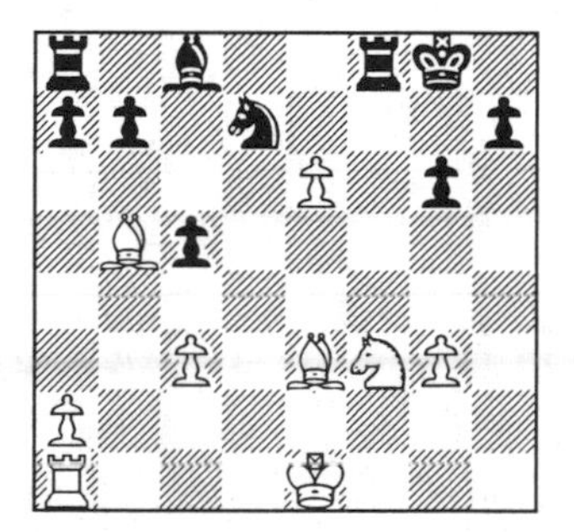

19 ♗h6!!

Only this fantastic move confirms White's superiority in this position. In the game Lautier-Ivanchuk, Monaco (rapid) 1995, White played 19 ♔e2?, and after 19...♘f6 20 e7 ♖f7 21 ♗xc5 ♗g4 22 ♖d1 ♘d5 23 ♖d3 ♘xe7 24 ♗c4 ♘c6 25 ♔f2 ♖e8 26 ♗xf7+ ♔xf7 27 ♘d4 ♘e5 Black gained an advantage. Was Ivanchuk bluffing or had he found an improvement for Black?

19...♖xf3

19...♖e8 changes nothing,

e.g. 20 0-0-0 ♘f6 (20...♖xe6 21 ♗c4 ♘b6 22 ♘g5!+-) 21 ♗xe8 ♗xe6 22 ♗a4 ♗xa2 23 ♘e5±.

20 ♖d1! ♖xc3

Or 20...♘f8 21 e7 ♗d7 22 exf8♕+ ♖axf8 23 ♗c4+ which is winning for White.

21 exd7 ♗xd7 22 ♖xd7 a6 23 ♗f1!

This winning move was suggested by Kalinin after his correspondence game against Konev (1991): 23 ♖g7+? ♔h8 24 ♖xb7 axb5 25 ♗g7+ ♔g8 26 ♗xc3 b4 27 ♗e5±.

23...♖f8 24 ♖g7+ ♔h8 25 ♖xb7

and White wins.

16 exd7+ ♗xd7

17 ♗xd7+ ♔xd7

18 ♕b3!

A fresh idea that was introduced in this game. White's plan – to keep the queens on and to play for the attack – is very strong. Before this game White had always gone into various forms of the endgame:

a) 18 ♕f3 ♕xf3 19 ♘xf3 (similar to Kouatly-Schmittdiel in the note to Black's 15th move) 19...♖he8 (19...♔d6!? deserves attention, e.g. 20 c4 f6 with the idea of meeting 21 a4 b5 22 ♘d2 with 22...♖ae8!) 20 ♔f2 when Black has tried:

a1) 20...♖e4 21 ♗xc5 ♖ae8 22 ♖e1 ♖xe1 23 ♘xe1 b6! 24 ♗xb6 ♔d6 25 ♘c2 ♔xd5, Thuesen-De Firmian, Farum 1993, and now White should have played 26 ♘b4+ ♔e4 27 a4 with at least equal chances.

a2) 20...♔d6?! is too slow. 21 c4 f6 was played in Illescas-Topalov, Alcobendas 1994, and now according to Illescas 22 a4! was strong, e.g. 22...b5 23 ♘d2±.

b) 18 ♕a4+ b5 and then:

b1) 19 ♕g4+ f5 20 ♕f3 ♕xf3 21 ♘xf3 ♖he8 22 ♔f2 ♖e4 23 ♘g5 ♖c4 24 ♘xh7 ♖h8 25 ♖h1 ♔c8 26 d6 with a complicated ending, as in Remlinger-Brownscombe, San Mateo 1994.

b2) 19 ♕f4 ♖he8 20 0-0-0 ♕e4 21 ♗xc5? (Perhaps 21 ♕xe4!?) 21...♕xf4+ 22 gxf4 ♖ac8 23 ♗d4 ♖e4 24 ♘f3 (Not 24 ♘h3? ♖xd4!-+) 24...♖xf4∓ Remlinger-Shabalov, Las Vegas 1993.

c) Also deserving attention is 18 ♕g4+ f5 19 ♕f3 (19 ♕g5 promises nothing after 19...♕e4 20 0-0-0 h6) 19...♕xf3 20 ♘xf3

18 ... b5

19 0-0-0

After 19 ♗xc5 ♖ac8 is not so good for Black due to 20 ♗f2

♖he8+ 21 ♔f1 ♖c4 (Stohl) and then 22 a4! A more promising alternative is 19...♕g2!?

19 ... ♖he8

It is not easy to defend against the threat of penetration by White's queen into the black camp:

a) 19...♖ac8?! 20 d6! [20 ♕a3!?] 20...c4 21 ♕c2 ♖he8 22 ♕f2 f5 23 ♘f3±, Sokolov.

b) 19...c4?! 20 ♕b4 ♖hc8 21 ♗g5±.

c) 19...♕g2 20 d6! (20 ♕a3!?) 20...c4 21 ♕c2 followed by 22 ♕f2 with a clear advantage.

d) 19...♖hc8?!

20 ♗xc5

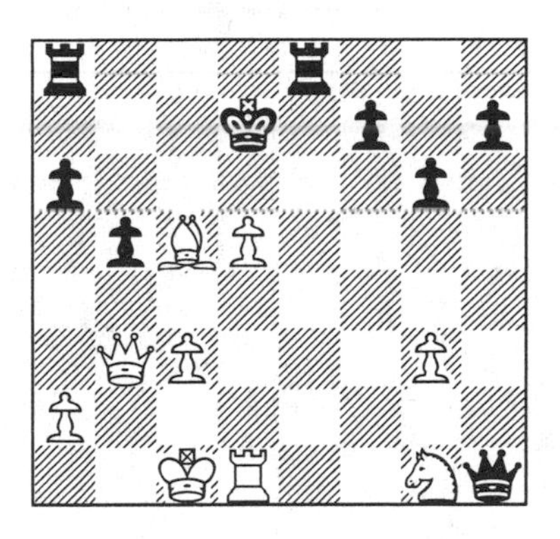

20 ... ♖ac8?!

A critical alternative try is 20...♕g2!? Black's previous move (19...♖e8) allows him to meet 20 d6 with 20...♖e6, while this queen move prevents the development of White's knight and covers the important c2-square. After 21 d6 ♖e6 White has:

a) The direct 22 ♘h3? did not work in the game Cuevas Rodriguez-Eriksson, Yerevan Women's Olympiad 1996: 22...♕xh3 23 ♕d5 ♖b8 24 ♗a7 ♕h6+ 25 ♔b1 ♕f8 with advantage to Black.

b) White should try *22 ♗b4!?* preparing 23 a4. At least in the case of 22...♕xg3 23 ♕d5 ♕e3+ 24 ♔b2 ♕e4 25 ♕c5 ♕c6 26 ♕f2! White's queen and knight find freedom and can organise a strong attack.

21 ♗d4 ♕g2

After 21...♖c4 White's knight enters the game with unpleasant consequences: 22 ♘e2 ♕f3 23 ♘f4 is clearly better for White. 21...♖e4, threatening 22...♖xd4, can be met by the quiet 22 ♔b1.

22 ♕a3

As a consequence of the move 20...♖ac8?! the a6-pawn is unprotected.

22 ... ♕xg3

After 22...♖a8 both 23 c4! and 23 ♕c5! are very strong.

23 ♕xa6 ♖xc3+

Faced with a bad position, Topalov tries a tactical trick. 23...♕g5+ does not help as 24 ♔c2 ♕g2+ 25 ♖d2 ♕f1 26 ♘e2+-.

24 ♔b2?!

24 ♔b1! ♖b3+ 25 ♔a1! would have won more quickly.

24 ... ♖cc8

Black could have given some more checks with 24...♕g2+ 25 ♔xc3 ♖c8+ 26 ♔d3 but the result would have been the same.

25	**♕xb5+**	**♔d6**
26	**♔a1**	**♕a3**
27	**♗b2**	**♕c5**
28	**♕a6+**	**♔d7**
29	**♕a4+**	**1-0**

Game 18
Yuneev-Kostometov
St Petersburg 1995

1 d4 ♘f6 2 c4 c5 3 d5 e6 4 ♘c3 exd5 5 cxd5 d6 6 e4 g6 7 f4 ♗g7 8 ♗b5+

8 ... ♘fd7

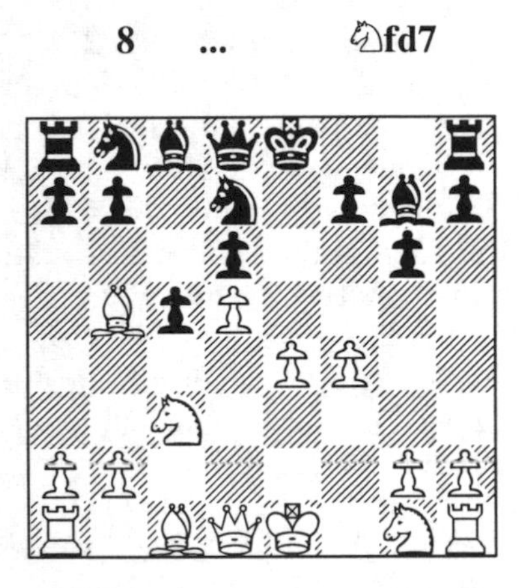

If the conclusions of the previous game are borne out by future practice, it follows that this is the only playable move after 8 ♗b5+. White can be happy, however, as the harmony of Black's development has been disrupted. When the knight comes back from d7 to the natural square f6, we get a kind of Four Pawns Attack with an extra tempo for White.

For the purposes of completing White's repertoire we will analyse only one good line, 9 a4, although 9 ♗d3, 9 ♗e2 and 9 ♘f3 are all not bad either.

9 a4 0-0

Black can also choose instead 9...♕h4+ or 9...♘a6. The move 9...a6 will transpose to other lines, e.g. 10 ♗e2 0-0 11 ♘f3 is examined later in the game and 10 ♗e2 ♕h4+ in line a below.

a) 9...♕h4+ 10 g3

Black probably has fewer problems after 10 ♔f1. White quickly obtained an advantage in the game Litinskaya-Fischdick, Baden Baden 1980: 10...0-0 11 ♘f3 ♕e7 12 ♔f2 ♘a6? 13 ♖e1 ♘b4 14 ♔g1 a6 15 ♗f1 ♖d8 16 ♗e3 ♕f8 17 ♗f2, but after 12...♗xc3! 13 bxc3 ♘f6 Black is okay.

Kapengut suggests that Black should try and prevent White from 'castling by hand' by 10...a6! 11 ♘f3 ♕d8 12 ♗d3 ♘f6 13 h3 ♘h5 14 ♔f2 c4! 15 ♗xc4 ♕b6+ 'with enough counterplay'. This needs further analysis – instead of 13 h3, 13 e5! looks strong.

After 10 g3 Black can try:

a1) 10...♕d8 11 ♘f3 0-0 12 0-0 a6 (12...♘f6?! 13 e5! dxe5 14 fxe5 ♘g4 15 ♕e2 a6 16 ♗c4 ♖e8 17 e6!± Finegold-Jaulin, Paris 1989) 13 ♗e2!? (13 ♗c4!? deserves attention, e.g. 13...♘b6 14 ♗e2 ♗g4 15 ♘g5! ♗xe2 16 ♕xe2 ♕e7 17 a5 ♘c8 18 ♗d2 ♘d7 19 ♖ae1± Olafsson-Psakhis, Moscow 1989)

13...♖e8 (13...♘f6?! 14 e5!) and now White has a pleasant choice between:

a11) 14 ♖e1 ♘f8 (White has more than enough play for the pawn after 14...♗xc3?! 15 bxc3 ♖xe4 16 c4 ♘f6 17 ♗b2, Arkhipov-Sax, Hungary 1984) 15 ♗f1 ♗g4 16 h3 ♗xf3 17 ♕xf3 ♘bd7 18 ♗d2 ♕c7 19 b3 with a small but stable White advantage, Kouatly-Tringov, France-Bulgaria 1985.

a12)14 ♔g2 ♘f8 15 e5! (15 h3!?) 15...♗g4?! 16 ♘g5! ♗xe2 17 ♕xe2 f6 18 ♘ge4 dxe5 19 f5!± Savchenko-Pigusov, Aalborg 1992.

a2) 10...♕e7

11 ♘f3 0-0

11...♗xc3+?! is very dangerous: 12 bxc3 ♕xe4+ 13 ♔f2 0-0 14 ♖e1 (Interesting is 14 ♘g5 ♕e7 15 ♗d3 c4 16 ♗xc4 ♘c5 17 ♖e1 ♕c7 18 ♗f1 and White is better, Platonov-Berelovich, Russia 1996) 14...♕f5 15 ♗f1! ♕f6 16 ♖a2 c4 17 ♗e3 ♘c5 18 ♗d4± Midoux-Caruso, Cannes 1995.

12 0-0 ♘a6

The move 12...a6 creates problems with the development of the queen's knight, e.g. 13 ♗e2 (Also good for White is 13 ♗d3 ♖e8 14 ♔g2 ♘f8, Sergienko-Parkanyi, Nagykanizsa 1993. Now instead of 15 h3 ♘bd7 16 ♗d2 ♖b8 17 ♖b1± White could opt for the attacking 15 f5!?) 13...♘f6 14 e5 ♘e8 15 ♖e1! (Less clear is 15 e6) 15...♗g4 16 e6 ♗xf3?! 17 ♗xf3 fxe6 18 dxe6 ♗xc3 19 bxc3 ♘c6 20 ♖b1 with a large White advantage, Levitt-Zamansky, Groningen 1990.

After 12...♘a6, White can choose to prepare e4-e5 or play it immediately:

a21) 13 e5!? dxe5 (Weaker is 13...♘b4?! 14 ♘e4! ♘b6 [14...dxe5 15 d6 ♕d8 16 fxe5 ♘c6 17 ♗g5± ♕b6 18 ♘f6+ ♔h8? 19 ♘d5+- Pecenka-Nun, corr. 1987] 15 ♘xd6 ♘6xd5 16 ♗d2 ♗g4 17 ♕b3 ♖ad8 18 ♗c4 ♘b6 19 ♗xb4 cxb4 20 ♗xf7+! ♖xf7 21 ♘g5 with a big advantage for White, Bagirov-Malaniuk, Baku 1983) 14 d6 ♕d8 (14...♕e6? 15 ♘g5 ♕f5 16 ♘d5+-) 15 ♘d5! e4 16 ♘g5 (16 ♘e5!?) 16...♗d4+ 17 ♗e3! ♗xe3+ 18 ♘xe3 ♘f6 19 f5 with the initiative (Kapengut).

a22) 13 ♖e1!

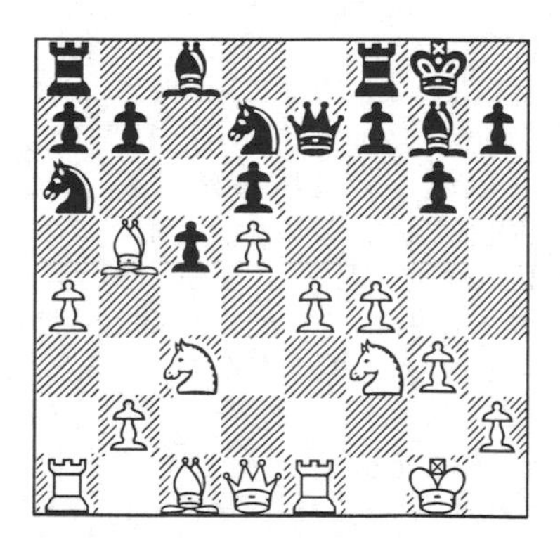

13...♘b4 14 e5!?

White could also keep a small advantage without major complications after the quiet 14

♗f1.

<u>14...a6 15 ♗f1 dxe5 16 d6 ♕e8 17 fxe5 b6?!</u>

It is better to continue with 17...♘xe5!? 18 ♘xe5 ♗xe5 19 ♘e4! ♕c6 (19...♗d4+? 20 ♕xd4+-) 20 ♗g2 ♔h8 21 ♗h6!, but White still has an initiative.

<u>18 e6!? fxe6 19 ♗c4</u>

Black is in a very dangerous position, as in Tal-Velimirovic, Moscow Interzonal 1982. Now, even after the best move 19...♔h8! 20 ♖xe6 ♕f7 21 ♗f4 ♗b7 22 ♘g5 ♕f5 23 ♖e7 White's threats are still stronger.

b) Black's attempt to immediately develop the queen's knight and attack White's bishop on b5 before it can retreat to f1 seems logical but fails tactically:

<u>9...♘a6 10 ♘f3 ♘b4?!</u>

Or 10...♘c7 11 0-0 ♘xb5? (White has a strong initiative similar to that in Kasparov-Nunn after 11...a6?! 12 ♗xd7 ♗xd7 13 f5! 0-0 14 ♗g5, Baumbach-Danner, corr. 1985. Better is 11...0-0 transposing to variation a) 12 ♘xb5! ♘b8 (Alternatively 12...♘b6? 13 a5+-; 12...♕b6? 13 ♘d2+-) 13 f5 (13 e5!?±) 13...a6 14 ♘c3 0-0 15 ♗g5 ♕b6?! 16 ♕d2± Trostianecky-Sliapkin, corr. 1988

<u>11 0-0 a6?!</u>

11...0-0 was necessary, transposing to the note to Black's 11th move.

<u>12 ♗xd7+!</u>

Black's knight on b4 is not well placed in this line and even 12 ♗e2 is not bad for White, but the text is more energetic.

<u>12...♗xd7 13 f5! 0-0</u>

Black does not have much joy after 13...gxf5 14 ♗g5 f6 15 ♗f4 ♕c7 16 ♘d2 0-0-0 17 ♘c4! or 13...c4 14 ♗g5 ♕b6+ 15 ♔h1 ♘d3 16 f6 ♗f8 17 a5! ♘f2+ 18 ♖xf2 ♕xf2 19 ♘a4 (Kasparov).

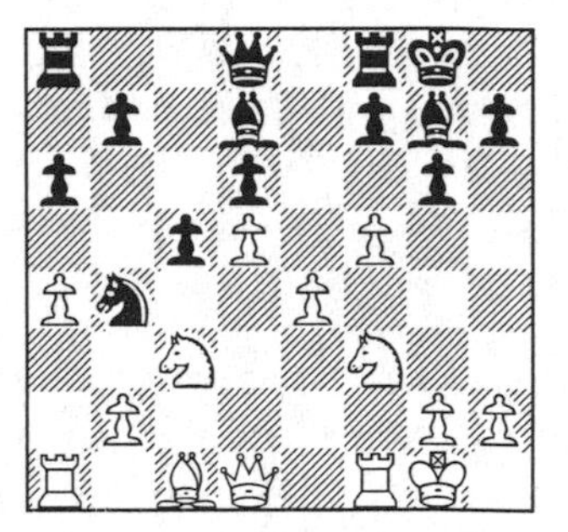

<u>14 ♗g5</u>

Kasparov-Nunn, Lucerne Olympiad 1982. Even after the best move 14...♗d4+! 15 ♔h1 f6 16 ♗h6 ♖e8 White has a dangerous initiative.

10 ♘f3 ♘a6

Alternatively:

a) White created a decisive attack after the suspicious looking 10...♖e8 11 0-0 ♗xc3?! 12 bxc3 ♖xe4 13 ♘g5 (13 ♗d3!? ♖e8 14 c4) 13...♖e7 14 f5 ♘e5 15 f6 ♖c7 16 ♕e1± b6? 17 ♘xh7! Vaisser-Chess Genius Aubervilliers (rapid) 1994.

b) The knight's return to f6 let White get a clear advantage after 10...♘f6?! 11 0-0 (11 e5!?) 11...♗g4 (The inclusion of the moves 11...a6 12 ♗e2 does not help Black, e.g. 12...♗g4 13 e5 ♗xf3 14 ♗xf3 dxe5 15 fxe5 ♘fd7 16 e6 ♘e5 17 ♗g4± Semkov-Popov, Bulgarian Ch. 1980) 12 ♖e1 ♘bd7 13 e5 dxe5 14 fxe5 ♘h5 15 ♗xd7! ♕xd7 16 h3 ♗xf3 17 ♕xf3, Vaisser-Schalkx, Ostend 1992.

c) 10...a6?! 11 ♗e2

and now:

c1) 11...f5 trying to justify 8...♘fd7 weakens the e6-square and can be met by 12 ♘g5!?, 12 exf5 or even 12 0-0.

c2) Black is far from equality after 11...♕c7 12 0-0 c4 and now:

c21) In Chekhov-Berelovich, Russia 1996, White played 13 ♗e3 with success: 13...♘c5 14 ♗xc4 ♘xe4 15 ♘xe4 ♕xc4 16 ♘xd6 ♕b4 17 ♘xc8 ♖xc8 18 f5±.

c22) More complicated but also good for White was 13 ♘d2 b5 14 axb5 ♘b6 15 ♔h1 ♘8d7 16 e5! dxe5 17 ♘de4 ♗b7 18 bxa6 ♖xa6 19 ♖xa6 ♗xa6 20 f5!± Li Zunian-Sax, Biel Interzonal 1985.

c3) 11...♖e8

12 0-0 ♘f8

12...♘f6 transposes into the main line of the Four Pawns Attack with an extra tempo for White. After 13 e5 dxe5 14 fxe5 ♘g4 15 ♗g5 f6 (15...♕b6 16 a5!±) 16 exf6 ♗xf6 17 ♕d2 ♗f5 18 h3 White is clearly better.

13 e5!? ♘bd7

No better is 13...♗g4 14 ♘g5! ♗xe2 15 ♕xe2 dxe5 16 f5 e4 17 ♘gxe4 with advantage to White.

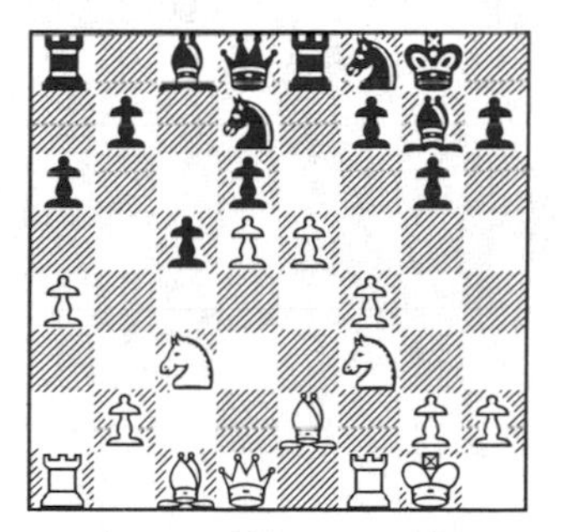

14 ♘g5! dxe5 15 f5

A typical attacking manoeuvre.

15...♘f6 16 g4! b5! 17 axb5 c4 18 ♗e3 h6 19 ♘ge4 ♘xe4 20 ♘xe4 ♗b7 21 ♗xc4 axb5 22 ♖xa8 ♕xa8 23 ♗b3

with a stable White advantage, Petursson-Perenyi, Saint John 1988;

11 0-0 ♘c7

After 11...♘b4?!, the position of Black's knight on b4 looks pleasant but is far from the main battle:

(see following diagram)

12 ♖e1! (Preparing e4-e5 and ♗f1 at the same time. 12 f5!? also deserves attention, e.g. 12...♘e5 13 ♘xe5 ♗xe5 14 ♗f4 ♗d4+ 15 ♔h1 a6 16 ♗d3± Pein-Ivanka, Budapest 1990)

12...a6 13 ♗f1. Now White quietly prepares e4-e5 by ♗c1-e3-f2-g3 and, if necessary ♗c4. Black practically has no counterplay and must await the execution of White's plan:

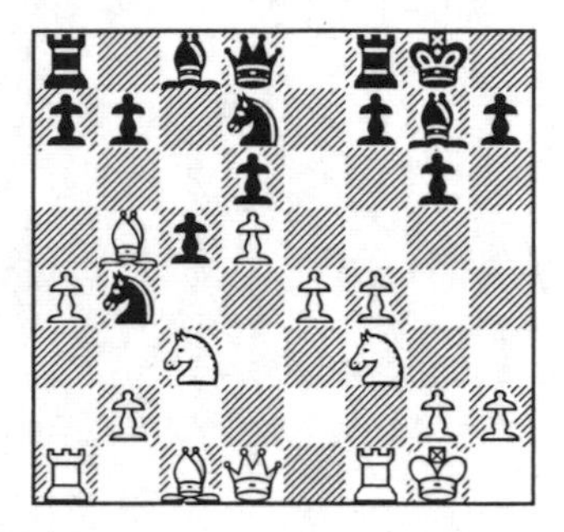

a) Here are convincing examples from recent practice after 13...♘f6?! 14 h3!:

a1) 14...h5 15 ♗e3 ♖e8 16 ♗f2 b6 17 ♗h4 ♕c7 18 ♗c4 ♘h7 19 e5 ♗f5 20 ♖c1 ♗h6 21 ♗g3 ♕d7 22 e6!± Matamoros-Hernandez, Capablanca Memorial 1996.

a2) 14...b6 15 ♗e3 ♗b7 16 ♕d2 ♕c7 17 ♗c4 ♘d7 18 ♗f2 ♖ae8 19 ♗g3 ♗d4+ 20 ♔h1 ♘f6 21 ♖ac1 ♘h5 22 ♗h2 ♗g7 23 e5± Dao-Kristensen, Amsterdam 1996.

b) 13...♖e8 14 h3! and now:

b1) Passive defence leads to an unpleasant position: 14...♖b8 15 ♗e3 ♘f6 (15...b5 16 axb5 axb5 17 ♘xb5 ♘f6 18 e5 dxe5 19 ♗xc5±) 16 ♗f2 ♘h5 17 g3 ♘f6 18 ♕d2 ♘d7 19 g4 b6 20 ♖ac1 ♗b7 21 ♗c4 ♗a8 22 ♖cd1 ♕c7 23 ♗g3± Tataev-Blodstein, Voskresensk 1993.

b2) Over-ambitious activity, however, was also quickly punished in the game Maximenko-Kotsur, Azov 1991: 14...♘f6 15 ♗c4 ♘d7 16 ♗e3 h6 17 ♗f2 g5?! 18 e5! dxe5 19 fxg5 hxg5 20 ♘e4 ♘b6 21 ♘fxg5! ♗f5 22 b3 with a large White edge.

b3) The game Komarov-S.Kovacevic, Massy Open 1993 saw interesting complications ending up in White's favour: 14...f5 15 e5! dxe5 16 d6 e4 17 ♘g5 ♖f8 18 ♘e6 ♕f6 19 ♘xg7! ♔xg7 20 ♗e3 b6 21 a5 b5 22 ♘d5 ♘xd5 23 ♕xd5 ♖a7 24 b4!±.

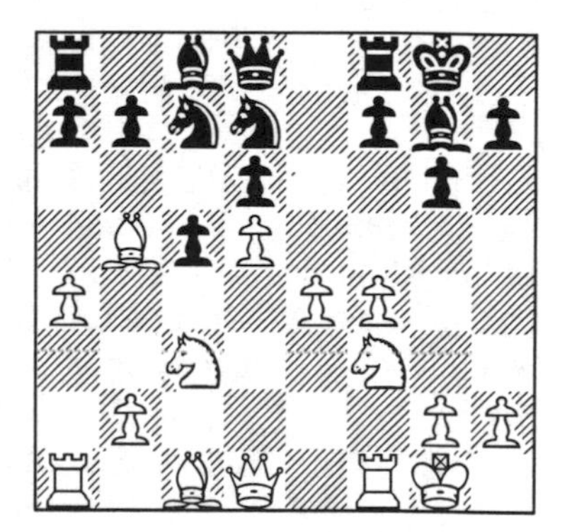

12 ♗c4

12 ♗xd7!? deserves attention e.g. 12...♗xd7 13 f5 gxf5 14 ♗g5 f6 15 ♗f4, as in Djukic-Mihajlovic, Budva 1996, while 12 ♗d3 is another promising move.

12 ... ♖e8?!

It is dangerous to leave the f7-pawn unprotected while the white rook is still on f1. Thanks to this factor, the central breakthrough e4-e5 becomes dangerous.

Instead:

a) After 12...a6 13 ♖e1 (13 e5 dxe5 14 d6 ♘e6 15 ♗xe6 fxe6 is not dangerous for Black) Black has a number of moves:

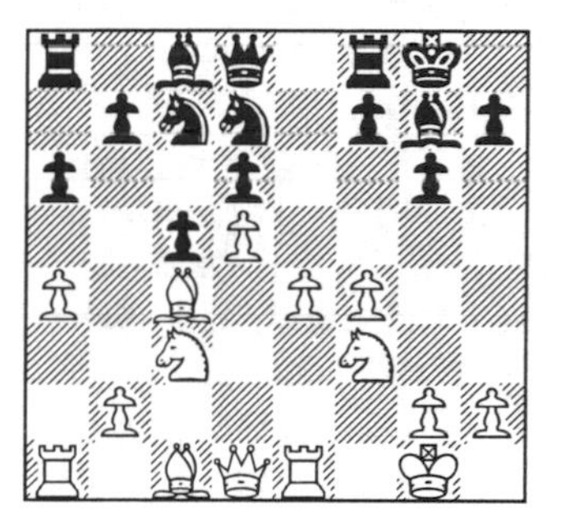

a1) After 13...b5?! 14 axb5 ♘b6 15 ♗f1 axb5 16 ♖xa8 ♘bxa8 17 ♘xb5 ♘xb5 18 ♗xb5 ♕b6 19 ♗c6 ♗b7 20 ♗xb7 ♕xb7 21 e5 ♘c7, Skembris-Bellon, Genova 1989, Black has insufficient compensation for the pawn.

a2) 13...♖b8 14 e5 (14 a5?! b5 15 axb6 ♘xb6 16 ♗f1=) 14...b5 is better than its bad reputation but still White can hope for some advantage after 15 axb5 (Black has a strong position after 15 e6?! bxc4 16 e7 ♕e8 17 f5 ♘f6) 15...♘b6, Silakov-Kristol, USSR 1972, and now instead of 16 e6? fxe6 17 dxe6 ♕e7 18 ♗f1 axb5∓ White should have played 16 exd6! (16 ♗f1?! gives nothing after 16...axb5 17 ♘xb5 ♘xb5 18 ♗xb5 dxe5 19 ♗c6 ♗b7) 16...♕xd6 (Or 16...♘xb5 17 ♗xb5 axb5 18 ♘xb5±; while 16...♘e8 17 ♗f1 axb5 18 ♘e5!⩲) 17 ♘e5! ♘xc4 (17...axb5? 18 ♘e4±) 18 ♘xc4.

a3) White won quickly after 13...♖e8 14 e5 dxe5? 15 d6 ♘e6 16 fxe5 ♘d4 17 ♗g5! Flear-Oei, Mondorf 1991. Critical for this line is the complicated position after 14...♘b6 15 ♗a2 ♗g4.

a4) 13...♘b6!? deserves attention and is similar to line b, e.g. 14 ♗a2 ♗g4 15 h3 ♗xf3 16 ♕xf3 as in Chachere-Blees, Krumbach 1991.

b) 12...♘b6 13 ♗a2 ♗g4 14 h3 ♗xf3 15 ♕xf3. White seized the initiative in Jelen-Skembris, Cannes 1995, after 15...♘d7?! 16 e5! dxe5 17 f5 ♘e8 18 ♘e4 c4 19 ♔h1 ♖c8 20 ♗g5 f6 21 ♗e3 a6 22 ♖ac1 b5 23 b3. More precise is 15...a6!? (Psakhis).

13 e5!?

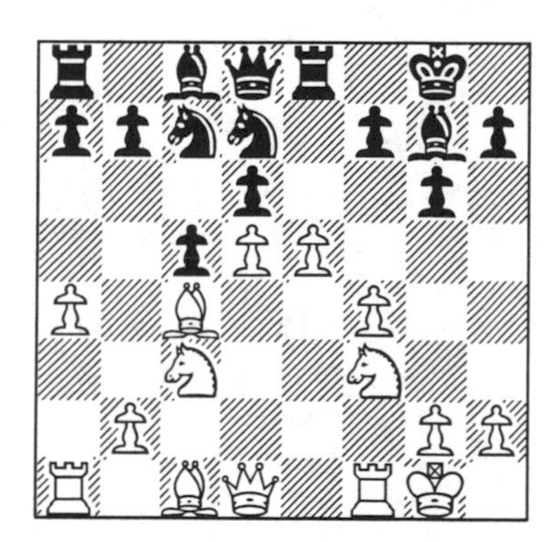

13 ... dxe5

Black also has problems after 13...♘b6 14 ♗a2 ♗g4 (Or 14...a5 15 ♘e4! dxe5 16 fxe5

♘bxd5 17 ♗g5 ♕d7 18 ♘d6±) 15 h3 ♗xf3 16 ♕xf3. For example: 16...♕d7 17 a5 ♘c8 18 ♘e4 dxe5 19 fxe5 ♗xe5 (19...♖xe5 20 ♘xc5) 20 ♗h6! ♕f5 (20...♗d4+ 21 ♔h1 f5 22 d6+ ♔h8 23 dxc7± ♖xe4?? 24 ♕xe4) 21 d6! ♗d4+ 22 ♔h1 ♖xe4 23 ♕xe4! ♕xe4 24 ♖xf7 winning.

14 ♘g5 e4?!

After 14...♘b6 15 ♗a2 e4 (15...h6 16 ♘xf7 ♔xf7 17 a5 ♘d7 18 fxe5+ ♔g8 19 e6±) 16 d6 ♘e6 17 a5 ♘d7 18 ♘cxe4 threatening 19 f5 White has a strong attack according to Se.Ivanov and Yuneev.

15 d6 ♘e6

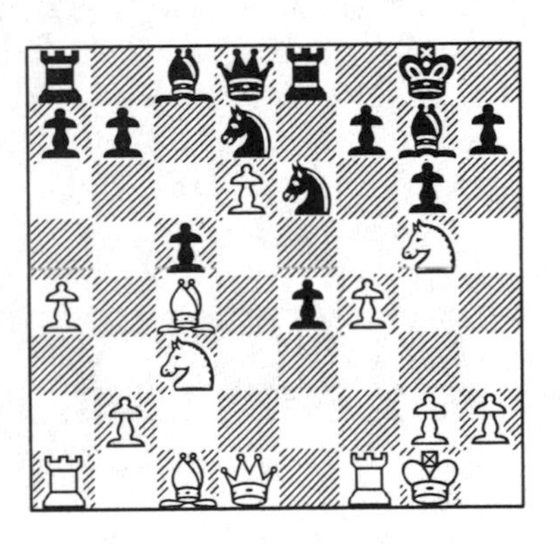

16 f5! ♗d4+

It is not easy for Black to find a defence now.

17 ♔h1 ♘xg5

18 fxg6 hxg6

I would be surprised if Black can survive after 18...♔g7 19 gxf7 ♖e5 20 ♘b5.

19 ♗xg5 ♕xg5

Or 19...♗f6 20 ♖xf6! ♘xf6 21 ♘d5 ♘g4 22 ♗xd8 ♘f2+ 23 ♔g1 ♘xd1 24 ♘f6+ ♔f8 25 ♗e7+ winning.

20 ♗xf7+ ♔g7

20...♔f8 loses more quickly after 21 ♗xe8+ ♔xe8 22 ♘xe4 ♕d5 (22...♕e5 23 ♕b3) 23 ♕g4 ♘f8 24 ♖ae1!

21 ♗xe8 ♘e5

22 ♘xe4 ♕h4

23 ♘xc5! ♗f5

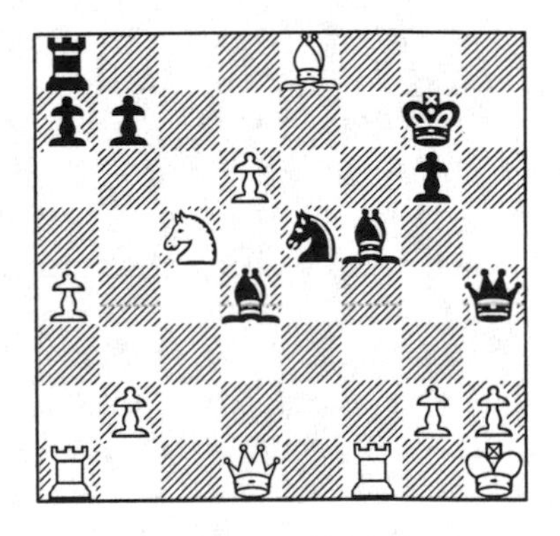

24 ♖xf5! ♖xe8

24...gxf5 25 ♕xd4+-.

25 d7 ♘xd7

26 g3 1-0

8 Mikenas Attack

1 d4 ♘f6 2 c4 c5 3 d5 e6 4 ♘c3 exd5 5 cxd5 d6 6 e4 g6 7 f4 ♗g7 8 e5

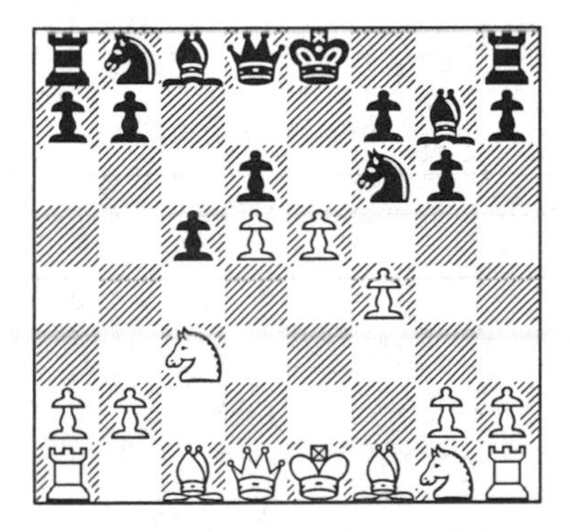

In this chapter we discuss the Mikenas Attack, in which White pushes e4-e5 without any of the preparation that we see in other variations of the Four Pawns Attack. This overly-aggressive system was popular at the end of the 1950s and the first half of the 1970s, but nowadays it has been practically abandoned in favour of the Taimanov variation and the main line of the Four Pawns Attack. As you will see below, many of the old theoretical that have been passed from book to book are either incorrect or incomplete. I believe that there are still many more improvements to be found in this system. The variations below are mostly given from Black's point of view.

Game 19
Meszaros-Stefanov
Satu Mare 1987

1 d4 ♘f6 2 c4 c5 3 d5 e6 4 ♘c3 exd5 5 cxd5 d6 6 e4 g6 7 f4 ♗g7 8 e5

8 ... ♘fd7

This is more solid than
8...dxe5?! 9 fxe5 ♘fd7 10 e6
which gives White a dangerous initiative. Let us look at the main line of this variation:

10...fxe6 11 dxe6 ♕e7! 12 ♘d5! ♕xe6+ 13 ♕e2! ♕xe2+ 14 ♗xe2 0-0

After 14...♗e5 15 ♘f3 ♘f6 16 ♗c4 ♘xd5 17 ♗xd5 ♗f6 18 0-0 ♘c6 19 ♗g5 White has a strong attack even without the queens on the board, Lputian-

Norwood, Lvov 1986.

15 ♘c7 ♘c6 16 ♘xa8 ♘b4

In this critical position instead of giving back a rook with 17 ♘f3?! ♘c2+ 18 ♔d1 ♘xa1 19 ♗c4+ ♔h8 20 ♖e1 a6! 21 ♗e6 ♘e5! with complications favourable to Black, Shereshevsky-Semeniuk, USSR 1974, White should have played 17 ♔d1. Certainly, Black has a strong initiative, but it is a moot point whether this is sufficient compensation for a whole rook. For example: after 17...♘e5 18 ♗d2 ♘bd3 (or 18...♖d8 19 a3 ♘bd3 20 ♗xd3 ♘xd3 21 ♔e2 ♗g4+ 22 ♘f3) 19 ♗xd3 ♘xd3 20 ♘f3 ♘f2+ 21 ♔e2 ♘xh1 22 ♖xh1 (Konikowski) Black does not have enough. Probably the best try for Black is 17...♘f6!? threatening 18...♘e4.

9 ♘b5

The alternatives are:

a) After 9 e6?! fxe6 10 dxe6 ♘b6! 11 ♘e4 (Not 11 f5? ♕h4+) 11...0-0 12 ♕xd6 ♕xd6 13 ♘xd6 ♗xe6 14 ♘xb7 ♘a4 Black has more than enough compensation for a pawn. The game Mileika-Elkon, Riga 1959, continued 15 ♘f3 ♘d7 16 ♗b5 ♘xb2 17 ♖b1 ♖ab8! with better chances for Black.

b) In the case of 9 exd6?! 0-0 10 ♘f3 ♘f6 11 ♗e2 ♘e8 12 0-0 ♘xd6 with equality we can see a difference compared to the similar line 8 ♘f3 0-0 9 ♗e2 ♖e8 10 e5 ♘fd7?! 11 exd6 (see page 9) - Black's knight comfortably uses the free square e8.

c) 9 ♘f3 0-0 10 ♗e2 dxe5 11 0-0 does not promise much:

c1) After 11...a6?! 12 a4 exf4 13 ♗xf4 ♘f6 14 h3 ♘bd7 15 d6 ♘h5 16 ♗h2 White had strong pressure in Kristiansen-Holm, Denmark 1977.

c2) However, better is 11...e4 12 ♘xe4 ♘f6 13 ♘c3, and now instead of 13...♗g4?! 14 h3 ♗xf3 15 ♗xf3 ♕b6 16 ♗e3± Nogueiras-Grünfeld, Zagreb Interzonal 1987, Black should have played 13...♘e8, transposing to the solid position of variation b minus one, practically insignificant tempo.

d) 9 ♘e4 is just a transposition of moves after 9...dxe5 10 ♘d6+.

9 ... dxe5

10 ♘d6+ ♔e7

The correct square for the king. After 10...♔f8?! 11 ♘f3! h6 12 ♗e2, both 12...f5 13 fxe5 ♘xe5 14 ♘xc8 ♕xc8 15 0-0, Gliksman-Kosansky, Yugoslavia 1972, and 12...♘a6 13 0-0 e4 14 ♘e5!? ♗xe5 15 fxe5 ♘xe5 16 ♘xe4 ♔g7 17 ♗f4, Bozinovic-Sindik, Makarska 1994, were in White's favour.

11 ♘xc8+

Other moves cannot be recommended:

a) 11 fxe5?! ♘xe5 12 ♘xc8+ ♕xc8 13 d6+ ♔f8 14 ♘f3 ♕e6 15 ♘xe5 ♗xe5 16 ♗e2 ♔g7 17 0-0 ♘c6 with a clear plus to Black, Kavalek-Trapl, Czechoslovakia 1963.

b) 11 ♘b5?! is too slow due to 11...♖e8! 12 d6+ ♔f8 and Black has completed his castling by hand with an active position. Now Black stands better after both:

b1) 13 ♗e2 ♘c6 14 ♘f3 ♘d4 15 0-0 ♘xe2+ 16 ♕xe2 exf4 17 ♕d1 ♖e4 18 ♘c7 ♖b8 19 ♕d5 ♘f6 20 ♕xc5 b6, Anikaev-Gorelov, Moscow 1981; and

b2) 13 ♘c7?! exf4+ 14 ♗e2 (After 14 ♘xe8?! ♕xe8+ 15 ♗e2 ♘e5 16 ♗xf4 ♘bc6, as in the game Smirnov-Kapengut, Minsk 1979, White had the additional problem of developing his kingside) 14...♘c6 15 ♘xe8 ♕xe8 16 ♘f3 ♘d4 17 ♘xd4 ♗xd4 18 ♗xf4 ♘e5, Taylor-Donnelly, corr. 1990, and here the natural 19 ♕d2 ♗f5 20 0-0-0 ♕a4! would have given Black a strong attack.

11 ... ♕xc8

12 ♘f3

12 d6+?! prevents Black from castling by hand but allows Black the c6-square for his knight and that factor seems more important here. After 12...♔f8 13 ♘f3 e4 (13...♘c6!? is not bad either) 14 ♘g5 (14 ♘e5 ♘c6!) 14...h6 White is practically forced to sacrifice a knight with 15 ♘xf7 (After 15 ♘xe4 ♕e8 16 ♕e2 ♘c6, Partos-Holm, Skopje Olympiad 1972, White's position is very disagreeable) 15...♔xf7 16 ♗c4+ ♔f8 17 f5 ♗d4!? (Black must be precise here, as demonstrated in the spectacular game Maffeo-Pastor, USA 1973: 17...g5?! 18 ♕d5 ♘e5? 19 f6! ♗xf6 20 0-0 ♔g7 21 ♖xf6! ♔xf6 22 ♗xg5+ with a very dangerous attack) 18 fxg6 ♔g7 19 ♗e6 ♕d8 20 ♕b3 ♕b6 21 ♕g3 ♘f6 and White's attack is over, Sulava-Namgilov, Budapest 1990.

12 ... ♖e8

As we shall see, the main line of this variation eventually leads to equality. One of Black's possible ways of playing for a win is to try 12...e4!? 13 ♘g5 ♘b6 (It is amazing how many authors simply repeat Rajkovic's old analysis without verification: 13...♖e8? 14 d6+ ♔f8 15 ♘xf7 ♘c6 16 ♘g5 h6 17 ♗c4 hxg5 18 fxg5±. In fact after 15 ♘xf7? Black can survive with 15...c4!, but 15 ♕d5! wins for White: 15...♔g8 16 ♕xf7+ ♔h8 17 ♗c4 and Black has no good defence against the threat 18 ♕g8+!) 14 d6+ (14 ♕b3?! ♕f5! 15 d6+ ♔f8 16 g4 ♕d7 is good for Black) 14...♔f8 15 a4! (Not 15 ♗c4? ♘xc4 16 ♕d5 ♘xd6 17 ♕xd6+ ♔g8 18 0-0 ♗d4+ 19 ♔h1 ♕f5 20 g4 ♕d7 21 ♘xe4 ♕c6 22 ♖e1 ♔g7 with a decisive advantage for Black, Kerr-Povah, London 1976) 15...h6 16 a5 hxg5 17 axb6 a6 18 ♕d5 ♕c6 19 ♗c4 ♕xd5 20 ♗xd5 ♘d7 21 ♗xb7 ♖b8 22 ♗c6 ♘xb6 with an unclear endgame, Kooiman-Povah, London 1976.

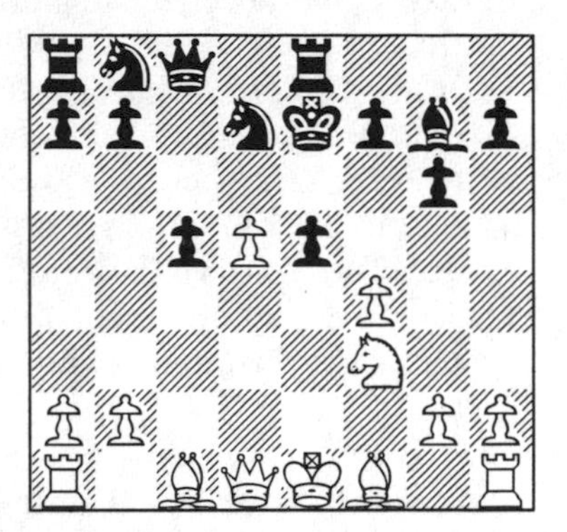

13 ♗c4

This is a critical moment for White. Besides the text move he can play 13 fxe5 or 13 ♗e2.

a) After

13 fxe5

Black can play a more or less drawing variation, 13...♘xe5, or take a risk trying to play for a win with 13...♔f8!?:

a1) 13...♘xe5 14 ♗b5 ♘bd7 15 ♘xe5

15 0-0 is just a transposition of moves after 15...♔f8 16 ♘xe5. However, in this line 15...a6? is a mistake due to 16 ♘xe5 ♗xe5 17 d6+! ♔f8 (Or 17...♗xd6 18 ♖e1+!) 18 ♕d5 ♗d4+ 19 ♔h1 ♘f6 20 ♗h6+ ♔g8 21 ♖xf6! ♗xf6 22 d7 and White wins.

After 15 ♘xe5 Black has a choice:

a11) After 15...♗xe5? 16 0-0 White stands better, as shown by the following practical examples:

a111) 16...♕c7 is met by 17 ♕g4! ♔d6?! 18 ♖xf7 ♗d4+ 19 ♔h1 ♘e5 20 ♖f6+ ♔xd5 21 ♕e2 c4, Shereshevsky-Kapengut, Minsk 1974. Now 22 ♗f4 would have decided the game.

a112) 16...♔f8 17 ♕f3 f5 18 g4 ♗d4+ (Or 18...a6 19 gxf5! axb5 20 fxg6+ with a strong attack) 19 ♔h1 ♘e5 20 ♕g2 ♖d8 21 gxf5 ♔g7 22 ♗g5 ♖d6 23 ♖ae1 with a clear advantage for White, Rajkovic-Planinc, Maidanpek 1976;

a113) 16...c4 17 d6+ ♔f8 18 ♗h6+! (Black managed to survive after 18 ♕d5 ♕c5+ 19 ♕xc5 ♘xc5 20 ♗xe8 ♔xe8 21 ♖e1 ♘d3 22 ♗f4 ♘xe1 23 ♖xe1 f6 24 ♗xe5 fxe5 25 ♖xe5+ ♔d7 26 ♖e7+ ♔xd6 27 ♖xb7 a5 in A. Petrosian-Kapengut, USSR 1975) 18...♔g8 19 ♕d5 ♕c5+ 20 ♕xc5 ♘xc5 21 ♗xe8 ♖xe8 and now not Kapengut's 22 ♖ae1?, spoiling White's advantage because of 22...♘d3!, but 22 ♖fe1!±, with the idea of 22...♘d3 23 ♗g5!

a12) 15...♔f8!

A necessity.

16 0-0 ♖xe5 17 ♗f4

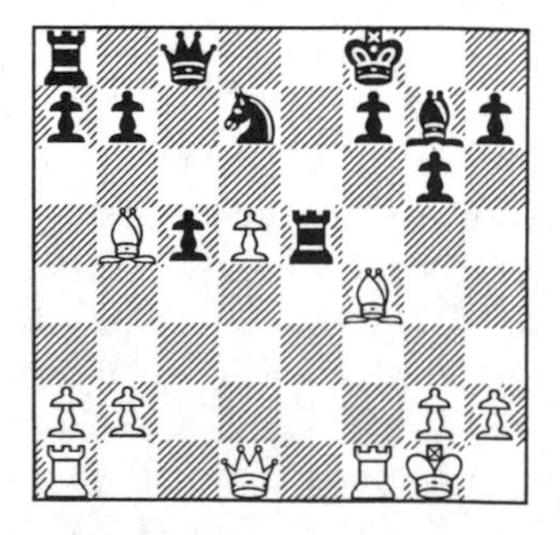

In this position Black had serious problems until Kapengut's impressive discovery 17...c4! was revealed in 1975:

a121) 17...♖e4?! 18 ♕f3 f5 19 ♖ae1 ♗d4+ 20 ♔h1 ♖xe1 (20...♘f6!?) 21 ♖xe1 ♘f6, Kagan-Artishevsky, Minsk 1975, and now White could have played 22 d6! ♘e4 23 d7! with a big advantage.

a122) 17...a6?! is met by 18 ♗xd7 ♕xd7 19 ♗xe5 ♗xe5 20 ♕f3 (This is stronger than 20 ♕b3?! ♔g7 21 ♖ae1 f6 22 ♔h1 b5 with equality, Shereshevsky-Savon, USSR 1975) 20...♔g7 21 d6! with a clear plus for White.

a123) 17...♖f5 18 ♗d6+ (Or 18 g4 ♗d4+ 19 ♔h1 ♖f6!) 18...♔g8 19 ♖xf5 gxf5 20 ♗xd7 (20 ♕f3!? deserves attention, trying to use the bishop pair) 20...♕xd7 21 ♗xc5 ♗xb2 22 ♖b1 ♗e5 23 ♕d2 f6 with equality, Kutin-Lobron, Yugoslavia 1980.

a124) 17...c4!

And now:

a1241) 18 ♗xe5?! ♘xe5 19 ♔h1 ♕c5 20 ♗a4 ♖d8 and Black's chances are better.

a1242) 18 ♗xd7?! ♕c5+ 19 ♔h1 ♖xd5 20 ♕g4 (20 ♗d2 ♕d6!; 20 ♕a4 b5!) 20...f5 21 ♕h3 (21 ♗e6? does not work due to 21...fxg4 22 ♗d6+ ♔e8 23 ♗xc5 ♖xc5 24 ♖ae1 ♖e5 25 ♖xe5 ♗xe5 26 ♖e1 ♖d8! with a clear advantage for Black, Kapengut) 21...♖xd7 22 ♕xh7 ♔f7 and Black keeps his extra pawn with the advantage, Yuferov-Kapengut, Minsk 1976.

a1243) 18 ♕d4!

The only move that allows to White to equalise.

18...♖f5

Also possible is 18...♖h5 19 ♕xc4 ♘b6 20 ♕b4+ ♔g8 21 ♖ac1 (21 d6? a5! 22 ♕b3 ♕c5+ 23 ♗e3 ♕xd6∓) 21...♕f8 22 ♕b3 ♖xd5 and the position is not far from equality, Astolfi-S. Kovacevic, Cannes 1989.

19 ♕xc4

Not 19 ♗h6? ♗xh6 20 ♗xd7 ♗g7! 21 ♕xg7+ ♔xg7 22 ♗xc8 ♖xf1+ 23 ♔xf1 ♖xc8 winning for Black, as in Legky-Shvedchikov, USSR 1978.

19...♘b6

Or 19...♕xc4 20 ♗xc4 ♗xb2 21 ♖ad1 ♘e5 22 ♗h6+ ♔e7 23 ♖xf5 gxf5 24 d6+ and a draw was agreed, Shakarov-Schmulenson, corr. 1976.

20 ♕xc8+ ♖xc8 21 ♗d6+ ♔g8 22 ♖xf5 gxf5 23 ♖d1 ♖d8 24 ♗c5 ♖xd5

with a drawn position in Yuneev-Korsunsky, Alma-Ata 1980.

a2) 13...♔f8!?

Here White has tried:

a21) 14 ♗b5?! a6 (14...c4!?) 15 ♗xd7 (Or 15 ♗a4 b5) 15...♘xd7 16 e6 fxe6 17 0-0 ♔g8 18 ♔h1 exd5 19 ♕xd5+ ♔h8 20 ♘g5 ♘e5 21 ♗e3 ♕c6 22 ♕xc6 ♘xc6 23 ♗xc5 ♔g8 with a better ending for Black, N. Garcia-Danailov, Alcobendas open 1994.

a22) 14 e6 fxe6 15 ♗e2

Black gained a substantial advantage in the game Vukovic-T. Petrosian, Bor 1980, after 15 d6?! ♔g8 16 ♗c4 ♘c6 17 0-0 ♘b6 18 ♗b3 ♘d4 19 ♘g5 ♕c6 20 ♕g4 ♘xb3 21 axb3 ♕xd6 22 ♗f4 ♕d7. However, 15 dxe6!? deserves attention.

15...exd5 16 0-0

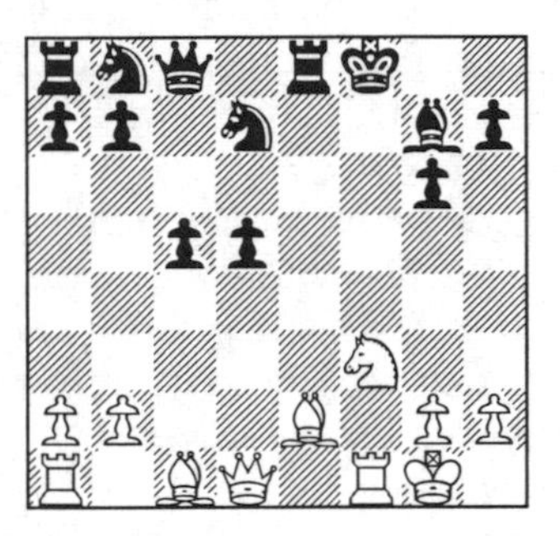

The game Sobek-Hardicsay, Ostrava 1979, saw 16...♘f6? 17 ♘g5 ♕c6 (Not 17...♔g8? 18 ♖xf6! ♗xf6 19 ♕xd5+ ♔h8 20 ♘f7+ ♔g7 21 ♗h6+ ♔g8 22 ♘d6+ ♕e6 23 ♗c4 winning or 17...♔e7? 18 ♗b5 ♘c6 19 ♗e3 d4 20 ♕b3 with a strong attack) and now instead of 18 a4 c4 19 ♘xh7+ ♔g8 20 ♘xf6+ ♗xf6 21 ♖xf6 ♕xf6 22 ♕xd5+ ♕f7 23 ♕xf7+ ♔xf7 24 ♗xc4+ ♔g7 25 b4 ♘c6 26 ♗b2+ ♔h6 with equality, as occurred in the game, Hardicsay gives the variation 18 ♗b5!? ♕xb5 19 ♘xh7+ ♔g8 (19...♔e7? 20 ♗g5 ♘bd7 21 ♕xd5+-) 20 ♘xf6+ ♗xf6 21 ♕xd5+ ♔g7 22 ♗g5 ♘d7 23 ♖xf6 ♘xf6 24 ♗xf6+ ♔xf6 25 ♖f1+ ♔g7 26 ♕f7+ with a perpetual check. However, the last of these lines can be improved on move 21 by ***21 ♖xf6 ♔g7 22 ♖d6!*** and Black is in trouble. For example: 22...♕e2? 23 ♕xe2! ♖xe2 24 ♖d8 ♔f7 25 ♗g5+-; 22...d4? 23 ♕d2! ♖h8 24 ♕g5 ♕e8 25 ♕f6+ ♔h7 26 ♖e6+-; and 22...♕b4 23 ♗g5±.

So, can we conclude that 13...♔f8 has been refuted? No! In the position of the last diagram Black can play ***16...♔g8!*** 17 ♕xd5+ ♔h8 and it is not evident how White can prove compensation for the pawn. For instance, 18 ♘g5 ♘e5 19 ♗b5 ♘bc6 20 ♕xc5 h6 21 ♘e4 ♘f3+ and 18 ♗b5 ♘c6 19 ♗f4 ♘b6 20 ♕xc5 ♘d4! are clearly better for Black. So it seems that White's last chance in this line rests with 15 dxe6!?

b) 13 ♗e2!?

This is better than its reputation. After

13...♔f8 14 0-0 e4

14...c4!? is also interesting.

15 ♘g5 h6?! 16 f5! hxg5 17 fxg6

The game F. Mainson-Podzielny, Groningen 1974, now continued 17...♘f6 18 ♗xg5 ♕d8 19 ♕b3 ♘bd7 20 ♗b5 ♖e5 21 ♕g3 ♖xg5 22 ♕xg5 ♘b6 23 ♖f5 e3 24 ♖af1 ♘bxd5 25 ♗c4 e2 26 ♗xe2 ♕d6 27 ♗c4±. However, Larsen's improvement here:

17...♘e5

has been quoted by every

author as practically a refutation of this line. The reality is not as simple.

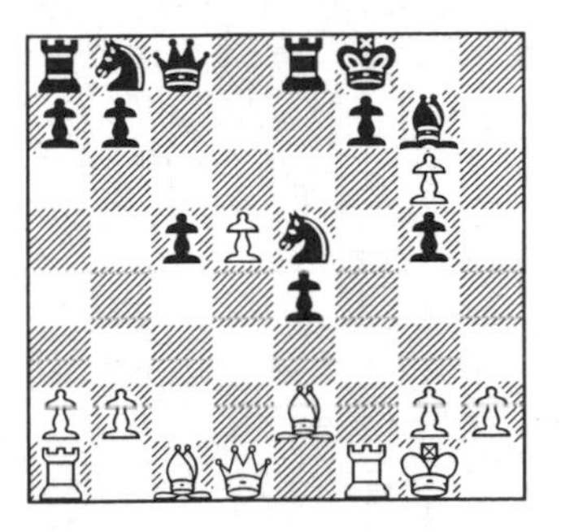

After ***18 gxf7*** White has good compensation for a piece. Black has three ways of meeting the threat to his rook, but only one of these is playable:

b1) 18...♘xf7? 19 ♗h5 ♖e7 20 ♗xg5 ♖d7 21 ♕g4 ♘a6 22 ♗f6+-.

b2) 18...♖d8? 19 ♗xg5 ♖d6 20 ♕a4! c4 (Black's alternatives are unattractive: 20...♖g6 21 ♗h5! ♕d7 22 ♕xe4! ♖xg5 23 ♕h7 ♘a6 24 ♕g8+ ♔e7 25 d6+!+-; 20...♘xf7 is met by 21 ♕xe4 ♕e8 22 ♕xe8+ ♔xe8 23 ♗h5 winning; and 20...♘bd7 21 ♕xe4 ♖g6 22 ♕h4 ♖xg5 [Not 22...♘xf7? 23 ♗h5 ♘de5 24 ♗xg6 ♘xg6 25 ♕h7 ♘ge5 26 d6+-] 23 ♕xg5 ♕d8±) 21 ♕a3 ♕d7 (21...♕c7 22 ♕h3!) 22 ♗h5 ♘a6 (Or 22...♘d3 23 ♗f4! ♘xf4 24 ♖xf4 ♕e7 25 ♖xe4+-) 23 ♕e3! ♖xd5 24 ♕xe4 and Black has no defence against 25 ♕h7, e.g. 24...♕e6 25 ♕h7 ♘f3+ 26 ♖xf3 ♗d4+ 27 ♗e3! and White wins.

b3) The only move is 18...♖e7. Now White has several interesting possibilities:

b31) 19 ♗g5 ♖xf7 20 ♕c2! with compensation. For example: 20...♘bd7 21 ♕xe4 ♔g8 (21...♕c7 22 ♕h7!) 22 ♗h5 ♖xf1+ 23 ♖xf1 ♕c7 24 ♗e7! and White is at least equal.

b32) 19 ♗h5 c4! 20 d6 (20 ♗xg5 ♕c5+ 21 ♔h1 ♘bd7! results in an unclear position) 20...♕c5+ 21 ♗e3! (An idea of Destrebecq's) 21...♕xe3+ 22 ♔h1 ♖d7?! (Black is also suffering after 22...♕c5?! 23 b4! ♕b6 24 dxe7+ ♔xe7 25 f8♕+! ♗xf8 26 ♕d5±. It is therefore better to play 22...♘bc6! 23 ♕d5 ♕d4!) 23 ♕d5 ♘bc6 24 ♕e6 ♘e7 25 dxe7+ ♖xe7 26 ♕f5 ♕d4 27 ♖ad1 ♕xb2 28 ♖f2 ♕xf2 (28...♕c3? 29 ♕h7 ♘xf7 30 ♖af1+-) 29 ♕xf2 ♘xf7 (29...♘d3 30 ♕f5 e3 31 ♕h7 ♖xf7 32 ♗xf7 e2 33 ♖e1!±) 30 ♕c5 ♖ae8 31 ♖f1 ♔g8 32 ♕xc4 ♖f8 33 g3 with advantage to White. These long variations can probably be improved but they illustrate the strength of the pawn on f7 perfectly.

Returning to move 15. Instead of 15...h6?! a better choice is 15...♗d4+ 16 ♔h1 ♘f6 (16...h6?! allows a strong attack, as in the game F. Meinsohn-Wittmann, Imperia 1973: 17 f5! hxg5 [17...gxf5!?] 18 fxg6 f6 19 ♗xg5 ♔g7 20 ♗g4! ♕c7 [20...fxg5 21 ♖f7+ ♔xg6

22 ♕f1 ♗f6 23 ♗h5+! ♔xh5 24 ♕f5 mating] 21 ♕b3 ♕b6 22 ♗h6+! and White soon won) 17 f5! ♔g7 18 fxg6 hxg6 19 ♕b3 ♘bd7 20 d6 ♖f8 21 ♗f4 b5!? with complicated play, Destrebecq-Michalski, corr. 1984.

13 ... ♔f8

Another option is 13...♘b6!? 14 ♗b5 (After 14 d6+?! ♔f8 15 ♗b5 ♘c6 16 0-0 ♔g8 17 fxe5 ♗xe5 18 ♘xe5 ♖xe5 19 ♗f4 ♖d5 White has insufficient play for a pawn) 14...♖d8 15 0-0 ♖xd5 16 ♕e1 ♔f8 17 fxe5 ♘c6 (If 17...c4?! 18 ♘g5! with a dangerous attack) 18 ♗xc6 ♕xc6 19 ♕h4 ♔g8 20 ♘g5 h5 21 ♘xf7 ♖f8 22 ♘h6+! (22 ♗h6?, Mikenas-Suetin, Yerevan 1962, could have been punished by ***22...♖xf7!*** 23 ♖xf7 ♗xh6) 22...♔h7 23 ♘f7 and Black has nothing better than 23...♔g8 with a repetition.

14 0-0 e4

After 14...♘b6 15 ♗b5 ♖d8 16 d6!? (Instead 16 fxe5 transposes to the game Mikenas-Suetin) 16...a6 (16...exf4 17 ♗xf4 ♘c6 18 ♗e3±, Boleslavsky) 17 ♗e2 (17 fxe5 axb5 18 ♘g5 deserves further analysis) 17...e4 (Nunn) 18 ♘g5 ♗d4+ 19 ♔h1 the position is very unclear. Now 19...f5?! can be met by 20 ♕b3 c4 21 ♕h3 h5 (21...♕d7 22 ♗e3) 22 ♗e3! ♘c6 23 ♗xh5! ♖xd6 24 ♗xg6!±.

15 ♘g5

Black was able to fend off White's attack in the game Malkotsi-Dzjordzjesku, corr. 1971, after 15 ♘e5 ♘b6 16 ♗b5 ♘8d7 (16...♗xe5!?) 17 ♘xd7+ ♘xd7 18 f5 ♗d4+ 19 ♔h1 a6 20 fxg6 hxg6 21 ♕g4 ♘e5 22 ♕h4 axb5 23 ♗g5 ♘f3! 24 gxf3 e3∓.

15 ... ♘b6

In the case of 15...h6? White should not play 16 ♘xf7? ♗d4+ 17 ♔h1 ♔xf7 18 f5 ♘f6! 19 fxg6+ ♔g7 20 ♖xf6 ♗xf6 21 ♕h5 e3 winning, Gigerl-Grünfeld, Groningen 1974, but, as proposed by Yuneev, 16 f5! hxg5 17 fxg6 ♘e5 18 d6!±.

16 ♗b5 ♖d8

16...♗d4+ 17 ♔h1 h6?! 18 f5! proved too dangerous for Black in Yuneev-Varlamov, Leningrad 1982. That game continued 18...hxg5 19 fxg6 f6 20 ♗xg5 ♔g7 21 ♖xf6! ♗xf6? (21...♖h8!) 22 ♕h5 ♗xg5 23 ♖f1! ♖h8 24 ♖f7+ ♔g8 25 ♖h7 and White won.

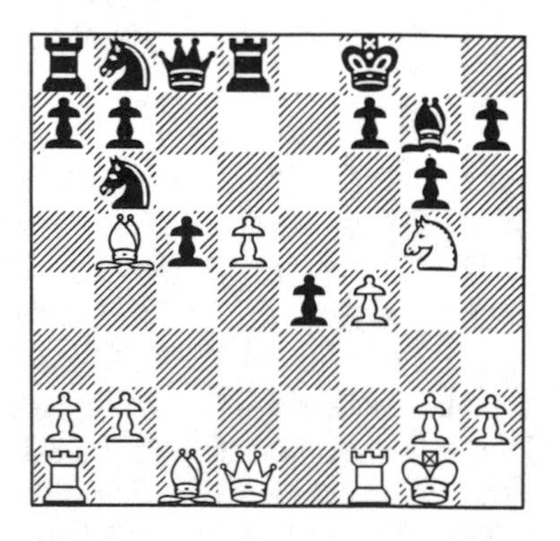

17 ♘xh7+?!

It was better to play 17 d6!? transposing to the note with 14...♘b6 above.

17	**...**	**♔g8**
18	**♘g5**	**c4!**
19	**♕e1**	

As so often in this system, White sacrifices a piece.

19	**...**	**♕c5+**
20	**♗e3**	**♕xb5**
21	**f5!**	**♖xd5**
22	**fxg6**	

Perhaps 22 ♕h4!? gxf5.

22	**...**	**♖xg5?**

And as so often, Black defends badly against this attack. Here he underestimates the extremely dangerous pawn on f7. It was necessary to play 22...fxg6 23 ♕h4 (Neither 23 ♘e6 nor 23 ♘xe4 is of any help to White) 23...♖xg5 24 ♗xg5 ♘bd7, when White's attack disappears but Black retains his material advantage.

23	**gxf7+**	**♔f8**
24	**a4!**	**♕a5**

If 24...♕e5 25 ♕b4+.

25	**♕h4**	**♖f5?**

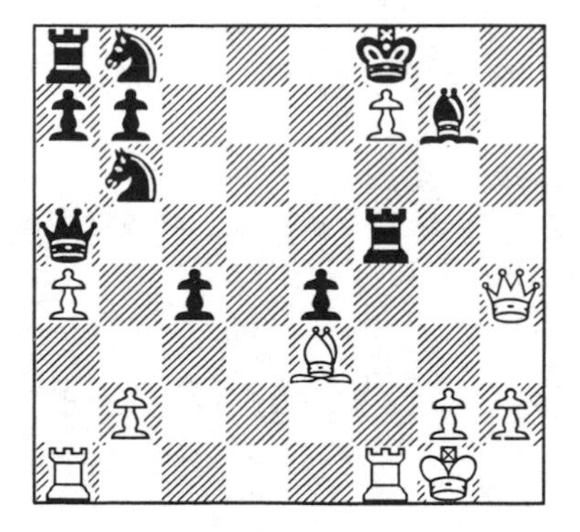

A losing move. 25...♖d5 26 ♕h7 (The amazing 26 ♕h8+?! ♗xh8 27 ♗h6+ ♔e7 28 f8♕+ ♔d7 is inferior; Black's chances look better) 26...♘bd7 27 ♕g8+ ♔e7 28 ♕xg7 ♖f8 would have kept Black in the game.

26	**♕h7**	

Less convincing is 26 ♖xf5?! ♕xf5 27 ♖f1 ♕xf1+ 28 ♔xf1±.

26	**...**	**♖xf1+**

If 26...♖xf7 27 ♖xf7+ ♔xf7 28 ♖f1+ mating.

27	**♖xf1**	**♘8d7**
28	**♕g8+**	**♔e7**
29	**♕xg7**	**♖f8**
30	**♖d1?**	

White could have won with 30 ♗g5+! ♔d6 31 ♕h6+! ♔c7 32 ♗e7. Now it is Black's turn to take command.

30	**...**	**♕h5!**
31	**♕d4**	**♔xf7!**
32	**♕d6**	**♔g8**
33	**a5**	**♖f6**
34	**♕d2**	**c3!**
35	**bxc3**	**♘c4**
36	**♕xd7**	**♘xe3**
37	**♖e1**	**♕c5**
38	**♔h1**	**♕xc3**
39	**♖b1**	**♕e5**
40	**♕c8+**	**♖f8**
41	**♕xb7**	**♘g4**
42	**♕b3+**	**♖f7**
43	**g3**	**e3**
44	**♕b8+**	**♕xb8**
45	**♖xb8+**	**♔g7**
46	**♖e8**	**♖f2**
47	**♖e4**	**e2**
48	**♖xg4+**	**♔f6**
	0–1	

Index of Variations